ONE WEEK LOAN

Robert S. Stering

Associate Professor of Criminal Justice
Mount Ida College
Newton, Massachusetts

State Coordinator for Patrol Procedures
Municipal Police Training Committee of Massachusetts

American Society for
Law Enforcement
Training

JONES AND BARTLETT PUBLISHERS
Sudbury, Massachusetts
BOSTON   TORONTO   LONDON   SINGAPORE

D1382475

World Headquarters

Jones and Bartlett Publishers
40 Tall Pine Drive
Sudbury, MA 01776
978-443-5000
info@jbpub.com
www.jbpub.com

Jones and Bartlett Publishers
Canada
2406 Nikanna Road
Mississauga, ON L5C 2W6
Canada

Jones and Bartlett Publishers
International
Barb House, Barb Mews
London W6 7PA
United Kingdom

Production Credits

Publisher, Public Safety: Kimberly Brophy
Acquisitions Editor: Chambers Moore
V.P., Production and Design: Anne Spencer
Associate Production Editor: Jenny L. McIsaac
Marketing Manager: Alisha Weisman
V.P., Manufacturing and Inventory Control: Therese Bräuer
Cover Design: Kristin E. Ohlin
Interior Design: Anne Spencer
Senior Photo Researcher: Kimberly Potvin
Composition: Interactive Composition Corporation
Printing and Binding: Courier Company
Cover Printing: Courier Company
Cover and interior image (siren): © Comstock Images/Alamy Images
Cover image (officers): © Jim McGuire/Index Stock Imagery

Library of Congress Cataloging-in-Publication Data

Stering, Robert.
  Police officer's handbook : an introductory guide / Robert Stering.
      p. cm.
  Includes bibliographical references and index.
  ISBN 0-7637-4789-0 (pbk.)
  1. Police patrol—United States—Handbooks, manuals, etc. 2. Police—United States—Handbooks, manuals, etc. I. Title.
  HV8080.P2S74 2005
    363.2'3'0973—dc22

2004020273

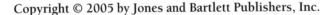

Printed in the United States of America
08 07 06 05 04   10 9 8 7 6 5 4 3 2 1

Dedication

With heartfelt gratitude, this book is dedicated to my wife Pat, my two sons, Dan and Russ, and my future daughter-in-law, Paula. The support and encouragement they showed and provided was a driving force and an incentive to make this happen.

It is also dedicated to those who have provided comments, ideas, and subliminal pushes. These people deserve special thanks as well: John, Judy, Carol, Gene, Len, my brother Ron and his family, the Welchs, the Savis, the Bodines, Mom, Dad, Mel, and Mrs. D.

You all know who you are, and I graciously thank you from within.

CONTENTS

Part I - The Basics

Part II - Putting It Together

This text was developed to provide a hands-on tool for law enforcement training. It offers practical exercises coupled with essential law enforcement information. Students are encouraged to read the text and then use the resources presented and their own reasoning to come up with viable conclusions or workable solutions to the scenarios presented.

Due to the wide range of laws, policies, techniques, and procedures used by law enforcement agencies across the country, as well as internationally, this text presents information and scenarios that are not jurisdiction specific.

The course instructor materials contain additional scenarios as well as reasonable solutions to all of the exercises and problems presented in the text. Some instructors may want to enhance the practical aspects of the exercises by using training props to add a touch of realism. However, instructors should obtain any necessary agency, school, or institution approvals prior to using certain props. The use of some props, such as fake narcotics and weapons, may be restricted, and, if used, they should be clearly identified as being fake.

Each chapter in Part I has a number of different features:

- Knowledge Objectives—This feature lists the *cognitive objectives* of the chapter and identifies what the students are expected to learn.
- Skills Objectives—This feature identifies the *psychomotor objectives*. It identifies the physical skills needed to accomplish the goals.
- Your Assignment—This feature provides a *scenario* that students resolve by the end of the chapter.
- In-Service Training—This feature provides *helpful information* to the student.
- From the Experts—This feature is a *voice of experience,* words of wisdom from experts in the field.
- Caution—This feature offers *officer safety tips.*
- Key Terms—Key terms are highlighted in the text and *defined* at the end of the chapter.
- Your Assignment–Results—This feature offers the *solution* to the scenario at the beginning of the chapter. In many cases, there may not be a "right" answer, but the solution given will be a practical and responsible approach for dealing with the issue that was presented. These solutions are always open to classroom discussion and may vary based on the local or state laws that prevail in the jurisdiction in which the course is taught.
- Your Next Assignment—This is *another scenario* that will provoke questions or discussion.
- Call for Service—This feature offers *additional scenarios* for students to ponder.

Part II presents specialized topics accompanied by scenarios. Chapter 18 consists entirely of scenarios.

■ Acknowledgments

I would like to express my gratitude to Officer Derek Mayer of the Broomfield, Colorado, Police Department, who, during the development of this project, reviewed the manuscript. His comments and suggestions were extremely helpful.

I would also like to thank all others who assisted me with the writing of this book, unbeknownst to them. During my career as a police officer, a professor, and a State Coordinator, many people have crossed my path and presented opportunities to make this book a reality through their contributions both physically and mentally.

Specifically, my tenure with the Waltham Police Department, the Municipal Police Training Committee, and the friends and colleagues I am privileged to have known were important in making this happen.

The Basics

■ Introduction

Who should read this book?

- College students interested in law enforcement
- Police officers
- Private security personnel
- Police recruits
- Civilian academy members
- Police-sponsored youth groups (Explorers, Boy Scouts, high school peer groups)
- High school programs
- Anyone interested in law enforcement

The purpose of this course is to explore what police work is like in a controlled classroom environment. You will take a close look at the role of police officers as we know it today. You will not just read about what police officers do; you will put yourself in the role of the police officer, examining some of the day-to-day incidents that officers face on the street. You will be presented with an overview of a law-enforcement-related subject area. You will then place yourself in the shoes of the police officer who has been called upon to respond to a particular incident. Your instructor will provide classroom exercises and situations.

This book is written on a national platform. The questions, answers, and situations will be understandable and functionally sound for readers across the United States.

After reading the text, you will have an the understanding of the situations, problems, and conflicts that police officers face daily. The expected result of this course is for you to gain practical knowledge and walk away with a sense of understanding and accomplishment. You will learn how to understand and resolve a variety of conflicts.

You will also learn to exercise good judgment and to make sound decisions. You will learn the amount of force deemed appropriate to resolve a dangerous situation. You will learn about the proper demeanor and tactics—verbal, physical, assertive, or passive—to use to resolve an incident. You will also learn that *assertive* does not always translate into being physical or strong. Discretion plays an important role in solving community problems.

This is a hands-on course. Role-playing is used to facilitate learning and to enable you to apply information from life experiences, the media, and common sense to a given situation. *Note that there will be no physical confrontations when conducting the role-playing situations. All enactments and situations will be presented at a walk-through pace.*

After you successfully complete a simulated call for service, you will come closer to understanding what really transpires in the field. The projected outcome of the course is to come as close to real life as possible, while eliminating any exposure to injury or unnecessary risks.

This is the type of learning environment where errors in judgment will take place. There is a tremendous value in failing and trying again. Every day, police officers make mistakes on the job. The idea that police officers are perfect and immune from wrongdoing is not realistic; mistakes should be acknowledged and then corrected. This course will allow mistakes to be made without the actual risk of malfeasance, incurred liability, serious injury, or even death.

This course is not just about police officers and their use of physical tactics. It also shows you the basic tools that the police use. It highlights that police officers must be able to speak with, reason with, and listen to people. You will explore this in various scenarios. The primary intention of this book is to familiarize you with the communication skills that police officers need to manage a wide range of situations. Physical tactics and tools, though readily available, are secondary to the primary response of communication.

After completing this course, you will have a better understanding of whether you have what it takes to meet the challenges of police work. You will gain an understanding of the curriculum that police recruits are required to complete and the knowledge, skills, abilities, and values that are taught in an academy classroom. The course provides you with the opportunity to see if police work is a career choice that you may wish to pursue.

The Police: Who Are They and What Do They Do?

Knowledge Objectives

- Identify the various duties performed by the police.
- Define the powers that police have.
- Know where police powers originate.
- Discuss the different types of patrols.
- Discuss the different modes of response used in patrol deployment.

Skills Objectives

None

You work in the patrol division and have been assigned to a new platoon and shift with a new supervisor. Your new supervisor speaks to you and tells you that he has heard good things about you. He states that he is aware of your initiatives and would like to utilize them to everyone's benefit.

In order to do so, he is offering you your choice of foot, cruiser, bicycle, or motorcycle patrol in order for you to expand on your ideas.

- What are your ideas?
- Which method of patrol do you choose and why?

■ Introduction

In this chapter, you will learn what police officers do and how they accomplish these tasks. The chapter also will look at how policing has changed over time and how these changes have resulted from the use of different patrol methods. You also will learn where the powers of the police come from. Finally, you will learn the benefits of different patrol methods.

■ Policing

Today the function of police is the same as it was in the past; however, the nature of the incidents that the police deal with has changed. The primary responsibility of the police is "to protect and to serve," a message often advertised on police cruiser door panels, police literature, and, of course, television.

Police officers are peacekeepers, upholders of the law, and mediators. They maintain the public peace. When an officer responds to a call, the officer, as the phrase goes, "puts on several hats." Depending on the particular type of call, an officer may have to put on one of several "hats." An officer may have to be a mediator, a counselor, a negotiator, a consoler, a lawyer, a social worker, or a tactical expert in self-defense and weapons or take on some other role to address the issues and concerns presented by a particular call. All of these roles fall under the police umbrella of "to protect and to serve."

Unfortunately, officers do not have the time to prepare for each call, and thus must face each situation as it occurs. Police officers only discover what they are facing once they are in the process of responding to a call. Then, the right decisions have to be made in a split second. Officers do not have days, weeks, or months to look over case files, case briefs, or prior histories, as other professionals do.

The police respond to an ever-growing number of calls. The types of **calls for service**, also known as **CFS**, change on a daily basis. Changes in the types of calls are brought on because crime is a product of the environment. For example, when a new drug hits the streets, the police have to respond with new techniques and investigative measures to meet the new challenge. If the legislature creates new laws, the police have to uphold them and gain the knowledge they need to do so through new training programs.

Nothing has changed our way of life more than the events of September 11, 2001. These events created myriad "new" items to look out for. The terms *suspicious persons, suspicious packages,* and *unusual letters or mail* all have new meanings. Prior to September 11, the police were accused of, and indeed found guilty of, conducting **racial profiling**.

Racial profiling is the singling out of particular people based on their race, appearance, ethnicity, and so on. Racial profiling was challenged in the courts, and the police were given new directions, as well as restrictions, on how they could stop and question suspects. Race or ethnic background was no longer to be the "determination" of a suspect.

In the wake of September 11, this changed. I observed this when I had to fly out of state on September 15, 2001. This was the first day that the airports were open after the tragic events. It was obvious that people in the airport terminal, men and women alike of all races and ethnic backgrounds, were checking out and closely watching the other passengers in the gate areas who were going to be riding on the same plane. Everyone got an up and down glance. Thus, the concept of racial profiling has in some cases been set aside. These cases are specific to incidents that affect homeland security, where suspicion of terrorism plays a part. There is still significant monitoring of police in regard to criminal law violations, such as drugs, motor vehicle stops, and field interviews when dealing with our diverse population.

The events of September 11 have added significantly to the workloads of law enforcement agencies around the world at the local, national, and international levels. This of course does not even touch how police *procedures* have changed in response to the tragic events that turned our world upside down. Our world has changed forever. Our peace and tranquility and the safe haven of the soil of the United States have been stolen from us, our children, and generations to follow. We will never feel as safe again as we did before the events in New York City, Washington, D.C., and a field in Pennsylvania.

■ Powers of Police

The police get their powers from the U.S. Constitution, of which the Bill of Rights plays a large part. Powers also are derived from the laws and ordinances of the state and municipality in which a police officer works. Police powers change as laws are changed and updated by state and federal legislatures or struck down or changed by the courts (**FIGURE 1-1**). Mandates from lawmaking bodies or the courts can expand or restrict the powers that the police presently enjoy. Two examples of change mandated by the courts are *Miranda* [*Miranda v. Arizona*, 384 U.S. 436 (1966)] and *Tennessee versus Garner* [*Tennessee v. Garner*, 471 U.S. 1 (1985)]:

- *Miranda* provides that an accused person must be read his or her rights prior to being questioned: "You have the right to remain silent, anything you say can be used against you . . ."

FIGURE 1-1
The United States Supreme Court.

- *Tennessee versus Garner* limits the use of deadly force on fleeing felons. In this case, a 15-year-old boy (Garner) in Memphis, Tennessee, was fleeing an unoccupied home that he had broken into, from which he had stolen a ring worth $10.00. As Garner was running away, he was shot by a police officer. This was legal according to Tennessee statutes in place at that time and was also proper operating procedure. The case ruling stated that the only time that the police can use force on a fleeing felon is when there is reasonable belief that the fleeing felon may kill or cause serious bodily harm to others or to a police officer if allowed to get away.

As the laws change, police officers must be brought up to date on new law enforcement procedures. Police officers can be kept up to date through training offered by state or municipal training academies, law updates provided for by legislative bodies or the U.S. or District Attorney, and other methods of instruction or distribution that are unique to each jurisdiction. The legislative process will be discussed in depth in the other criminal justice, government, or political science courses that you will take.

Police officers receive training in a variety of different ways. The following are some of the most common ways that police officers receive information and training:

- **Formalized training:** Classes that have been specifically designed to deal with the issue that is being changed. For example, if a state has changed the machine used to test for alcohol for Driving Under the Influence (DUI) cases, then the operators of those machines will require formal training in their use. Or, if a new statute or law requires certain responses or reporting, then a class must be specifically designed for that purpose.

- **In-service training:** An annual training session that all police officers are required to attend, or at least strongly encouraged to attend. In-service training sessions may examine legal updates in criminal law, motor vehicle law, or constitutional law. The training also may include firearms training or recertification for police batons, chemical sprays, defensive tactics, CPR, first responder, or other certification need.

- **Roll call:** A briefing prior to the start of a shift where supervisors take attendance, inspect uniforms and equipment, inform the oncoming shift of any outstanding incidents that may have occurred, inform officers of suspects to be looking out for, relate any law or procedural changes, and so on. This is an informal briefing, but does constitute training in the sense that the officers have been initially advised of some change or inception of some policy or statute and this will advise them until such time as a more formal type of training can be initiated. An example would be if on Tuesday afternoon the U.S. Supreme Court handed down a ruling that takes effect immediately, there may not be sufficient time to publish a bulletin or set up a training class. This roll call briefing will provide sufficient information until such time as it is possible to elaborate.

- **Roll call training:** Training conducted by the department and led by department training personnel that deals with procedural issues or agency-specific issues. Such training is usually done at roll call, which is a shift briefing prior to the beginning of a daily tour of duty.

- **Specialized training:** Training needed to meet certification requirements, such as for fingerprinting, crime scene processing, evidence collection, accident investigation, photography, and so on.

- **Written directives:** A directive or order that is initiated by the department to convey a specific goal, order, or mandate or to provide information. The following are different types of written directives:
  - **General order:** These are the most authoritative directives and are permanent. They usually mandate a procedural or policy change. They can amend or supersede a previous order.

- **Special order:** Orders that are created to reach a specific outcome and that temporarily change a current policy. These orders usually expire once their objectives have been met. (Example: "Due to the recent blizzard, all personnel will be denied vacation or time off.")
- **Personnel order:** Orders used for personnel changes, such as reassignments, promotions, suspensions, and so on.
- **Memorandum (or memo):** An informal "note" to all or selected personnel that serves as an informational reminder. They are used provide information on policy infractions, available equipment, out-of-service cruisers, and so on.
- **Bulletin:** Usually refers to specific issues such as training school announcements, step-by-step procedures, safety tips, or other reminders.

■ Types of Patrol

Many patrol officers consider patrol to be the backbone of the police function. This is largely true, because a large portion of the calls and services provided by police are generated by patrol. Patrol calls originate from calls for service from citizens and/or other agencies or from the officers themselves based on the observations they make while on patrol. Patrol calls can be in response to calls concerning domestic violence situations, missing persons, or motor vehicle accidents or from an officer's motor vehicle stop, whereby the officer initiates the contact. Patrol responses are aided or hindered by the equipment and vehicles that the officer has to work with, or, as we shall call them, the "tools of the trade."

Foot Patrol

Foot patrol is the walking beat, whereby the officer is actually on the street. Foot patrol is one of the most valuable tools that police have. The ability of officers on foot patrol to interact with citizens and members of the community is tremendously beneficial to the community and to the police department (**FIGURE 1-2**).

FIGURE 1-2
A police officer walking her beat.

An officer routinely assigned to foot patrol in the same area, or **beat**, becomes part of that neighborhood. The community looks to this officer to solve their problems and address their needs as presented. In most cases, because of their relationships with and in the community, officers on foot patrol have been very effective in resolving neighborhood problems.

Bicycle Patrol

Bicycle patrol is used mostly in urban areas where exposure is important for the police in the community. The increase in the use of bicycles came as a result of grant money and the "community policing" concept that swept the nation in the 1990s (**FIGURE 1-3**). The idea was to get officers out into the neighborhoods to be seen and to speak with residents and neighborhood businesspeople in order to address their needs and concerns. The goal was for the police to create proactive partnerships to improve the **quality of life** in these neighborhoods.

Bicycle patrol does have its limitations. Like the motorcycle, the amount of equipment that can be carried and the number of occupants that can be accommodated are limited. But probably the most significant issue is response time. Granted, in some cases, such as during rush hour traffic, an officer on a bicycle can respond faster than a motor patrol, but this is the exception rather than the rule. Advantages of bicycle patrol include the capability for a quiet response and the ability or residents to easily approach officers.

FIGURE 1-3
The use of bicycle patrol grew in popularity as a result of community policing concepts.

FIGURE 1-4
Motorcycle patrol.

Motorcycle Patrol

Officers on motorcycle patrol have more maneuverability and can go places that a four-wheel-drive vehicle cannot (i.e., narrow alleys and paths, walkways, etc.). Motorcycle patrol offers quick response time, but its use is limited due to equipment storage issues, the number of passengers, and the weather (**FIGURE 1-4**).

Cruiser or Patrol Vehicle

Patrol vehicles can be sedans, sport utility vehicles, pick-up trucks, vans, or wagons. Vans and wagons are specialized vehicles reserved for a specific use. Patrol vehicles afford the officer the most efficient method of response with regard to safety, coverage ability, and response time. Four-wheel-drive patrol vehicles are large enough to contain a portable office and a computer terminal as well as storage for equipment and specialized weapons and can carry two or more officers, if needed. Patrol vehicles also can transport additional officers, suspects, victims, or other persons (**FIGURE 1-5**).

FIGURE 1-5
Police officers patrolling in cruisers, the traditional method of patrol.

FIGURE 1-6
A mounted police patrol.

Mounted Patrol

Horses go way back in law enforcement. Consider all of the Western movies and their portrayals of sheriffs and marshals, galloping across the countryside on horseback. Horses are adaptable for all types of terrain, including mountains, woods, and parks, and are a tremendous asset for public relations and for crowd control. The main drawback of mounted patrol is the maintenance and housing of the horses. It has been said that it costs more to house a horse for a year than it costs to maintain a cruiser (**FIGURE 1-6**).

Aircraft and Watercraft

These specialized modes of transportation and patrol are unique to the jurisdiction in which they are used. Aircraft and watercraft are expensive, but effective. In cases of motor vehicle pursuits, or "chases," aircraft are a tremendous asset. They allow the responding officers to maintain safe distances and speeds while the suspect vehicle is being observed from the air. This can reduce the danger to innocent bystanders. If the suspect feels that he is no longer being pursued, he may slow down, reducing the risk to others as well as to himself or herself.

Watercraft also has its advantages, as long as the jurisdiction has water to patrol, such as lakes or an ocean (**FIGURE 1-7**). In some cases, these jurisdictions overlap with environmental police, municipal police, and federal agencies. The type of waterway and the expected

FIGURE 1-7
Police patrol the waterways.

encounters determine the types of watercraft that are needed. If the jurisdiction is a lake with recreational facilities, a small motorboat may be adequate. However, in cases where there is a main waterway, river, or the ocean and drug encounters may be an issue, then more sophisticated boats and watercraft may be needed and utilized. In some communities with limited bodies of water, such as a pond or a small lake, the boats may be maintained and utilized by other emergency services.

Chapter Wrap-Up

In-Service Training

To keep up to date with changes to laws and procedures, police officers receive instruction through formalized training, in-service training, roll call, or from professional magazines and newsletters. Other ways that officers become aware of changes are through departmental directives such as general orders, personnel orders, special orders, memos, and bulletins.

From the Experts

When assigned to cruiser duty in the hot summer months, do not isolate yourself from the community by driving around with the windows rolled up and the air conditioning blasting. This can irritate citizens because it gives the appearance that you are content in your world (the cruiser) and do not care about theirs. With the windows rolled up you cannot hear what is going on outside. Roll down the windows a bit, you will still be cooled, but you will be in touch with what's going on outside the cruiser. It also will give the appearance that you are concerned with your surroundings.

Caution

Prior to the beginning of a shift, always check your cruiser, bike, motorcycle, and so on for the proper equipment and to make sure that all is in working condition. If you are required to carry an oxygen bottle in your cruiser, make sure you have a full or adequately full cylinder. It would be a shame to arrive at the scene and be unable to offer oxygen to a victim in need because you "assumed" the tank was full.

Key Terms

beat: An area a police officer is assigned to patrol whether on foot or in some other mode of transportation. This is his primary area of responsibility, where he is usually required to remain during his shift, unless otherwise assigned.

bulletin: Specific issues such as a training school announcement, or a step-by-step procedure for some police function, safety tips, and reminders.

CFS: The calls that an officer responds to in the course of his tour of duty. These calls may be citizen, victim, witness, etc., generated.

formalized training: Training classes that have been designed specifically to deal with the issue that is being changed. (Example: If a state has changed the machine used for alcohol testing of Driving Under the Influence cases, then the operators of those machines need to be trained.

general order: The most authoritative directives and are permanent; usually mandate a procedure or policy change, and can also amend or may supersede a previous order.

in-service training: An annual training session that all police officers are required to attend. These sessions can include legal updates in Criminal Law, Motor Vehicle Law, and Constitutional Law. This annual training may also include Firearms qualifications, re-certification for police batons, chemical sprays, defensive tactics, CPR, First Responder, etc.

memorandum (or Memo): An informal note to all or selected personnel as an informational reminder. These are used to inform personnel of policy infractions, available equipment, out of service cruisers, etc.

personnel order: Specifically used for personnel changes in the department, such as a reassignment, promotion, suspension, etc.

quality of life: Concerns in a neighborhood that may not necessarily be a crime, such as kids hanging around, kids skateboarding, shops or businesses operating loudly during late night or early morning, dumpsters being emptied in the early morning, etc.

racial profiling: Any police-initiated action that relies on the race, ethnicity, or national origin of the individual under suspicion, rather than the behavior of that individual or intelligence that leads to a specific individual coming under suspicion.

roll call: A briefing prior to the start of a shift where supervisors: take attendance, inspect uniforms and equipment, inform the on-coming shift of any outstanding incidents that may have occurred, inform the shift of suspects to be looking out for, or relate any law or procedural changes, etc.

roll call training: Training conducted by the department and most likely instructed by department training personnel that deal with issues that are procedural within the department, or to discuss specific issues that deal with that agency. This is usually done at roll call, which is a shift briefing prior to the beginning of a tour of duty.

specialized training: Training where specific certifications may be obtained, such as fingerprinting, crime scene processing, evidence collection, accident investigation, photography, etc.

special order: Orders that are recreated to reach a specific outcome and may temporarily affect a change in a current policy. These orders are usually expired once their objectives are met. (Example: "Due to the recent blizzard, all personnel will be denied vacation or time off.")

written directives: A directive or an order that is initiated by the department to convey a specific goal, order, mandate. Can be informational.

Your Assignment—Results

Your decision would be based on the community in which you work and the issues that need to be addressed. Base your answer on your community. Identify what you would like the police department to do or implement and determine what method of patrol would best accomplish this goal.

Your Next Assignment

You are assigned to patrol a mixed-income neighborhood. The kids in the neighborhood are usually well behaved, but on occasion they gather in large groups and make noise, disturbing the neighbors. Some people are afraid to go out at night, although their fears appear to be unjustified. You speak with the residents and you speak with the kids. The kids state that there is no place for them to go. While in the neighborhood, you see that the local playground, which has a jungle gym and baseball and basketball facilities, has a "No Trespassing after Dark" sign posted. As a police officer trying to resolve this problem, what might you do to improve the quality of life for everyone involved? Make sure your solution goes beyond removing the posted "No Trespassing" sign.

You are assigned to a call where an individual is loitering around a closed business. It is a summer night, lightly raining, and the time is 1:30 A.M. The business is a barbershop and is located on the outskirts of a business section that borders a residential area. You approach the scene and observe a small-framed white male sitting on the curb outside the shop. He does not appear to have any weapons or tools on him; he is just sitting there rocking back and forth. You approach the man and speak with him; it appears that he may be emotionally disturbed. You are in a one-person cruiser, which is equipped with a security barrier between the front seat and the back seat (also known as a cage). The subject states that he knows where he is and knows what time it is, and that he is just waiting for a haircut in the morning when the shop opens. He is able to tell you his name and that he is living at a half-way rehabilitation house about two miles away in the residential neighborhood.

1. Would you transport him to his home using the cruiser? If so, where would you place him in the cruiser and why?

2. Would you transport him to the hospital to be checked for exposure and have his emotional stability evaluated? Why or why not?

3. Would you transport him to the police station and have the halfway house pick him up? Why or why not?

4. Would you have the station contact the halfway house and have them come to the barbershop to pick him up? Would you wait for them or leave? Why or why not?

5. Because the man has done nothing wrong, does not appear to be armed, and seems coherent enough to make decisions, would you just leave him and go on your way? Why or why not?

What Types of Calls Do the Police Respond to?

Knowledge Objectives

- Describe each of the following types of calls for service: alarm calls, assault, assault and battery, assault and battery with a dangerous weapon, breaking and entering, conflict resolution, crisis intervention, disturbance, disorderly conduct, domestic violence, driving under the influence, drug investigations, hazardous materials, larceny, medical response, motor vehicle accident, motor vehicle stop, motor vehicle theft, quality of life, robbery (armed and unarmed), suspicious persons, unknown problem.
- Define the terms *assault*, *battery*, *felony*, and *misdemeanor*.

Skills Objectives

None

You have been assigned to respond to a single-car motor vehicle accident. (Only one car is involved and the vehicle either ran off the road or struck a fixed object such as a tree, wall, etc.) When you arrive, there are no injuries, and the only person around is the driver (operator) of the vehicle. The vehicle apparently struck the curb, blew two tires, and then came to stop on the sidewalk. You approach the vehicle to speak with the driver. You ask the driver if he is all right and if he has any injuries, he says that he is "fine, very fine." When he turns to face you, you smell a strong odor of alcohol. You also observe an open bottle of vodka with the contents spilling out onto his lap. You observe that the driver is still in the driver's seat and that the keys are in the ignition:

- Would you assume that the driver is drunk and arrest him?
- Would you tell the driver to walk home and have his car towed because no other vehicles or property were damaged?

■ Introduction

In this chapter, you will learn about the different types of calls that police officers respond to. You will see that there are many different types of calls for service and that many do not result from the commission of a crime. You will learn that the police have some discretion with regard to some of the events that they investigate whereas for others their actions are mandated. You will also learn what felonies and misdemeanors are. These terms indicate the severity of an offense, which affects how the crime is punished.

■ Police Calls

Police respond to many different types of calls. No two calls are ever exactly alike, although many are similar. There is always something that makes a particular call unique. Keep in mind that the type of call, such as a motor vehicle stop, may occur more than once per shift but the specifics of the stop (e.g., running a red light, driving under the influence, license violation, etc.) are unique to each call. The situation and contact are what make the call unique.

Types of Calls

Alarm Calls

Alarm calls can range from responses to home burglar alarms and business alarms to medical alert alarms. Many burglar alarms, whether residential or business related, are set off by accident, having been set off by an employee or a resident who forgot to secure the alarm or to turn it off when entering.

Assault, Assault and Battery, Assault and Battery with a Dangerous Weapon

In most states, **assault** by itself is a verbal assault and does not constitute an unlawful touching, or a **battery**. An assault and battery occurs when there is an unlawful touching. These calls can be enhanced when an object or weapon is used in the battery. The weapon or object can be anything capable of inflicting injury.

Breaking and Entering (Housebreaks, Business Breaks, Burglary, etc.)

These calls arise from an unlawful entry by some known or unknown person. The entry can be into a house, apartment, shed, business, condominium, or other structure. The intent also can differ. For example, the perpetrator may have an intent to steal, commit sexual assault, kidnap, seek refuge, and so on.

Conflict Resolution/Crisis Intervention

These calls result from the need to resolve a conflict or crisis. The conflicts may be squabbles and arguments between a parent and child or a boyfriend and girlfriend or individuals in need of counseling or just someone to talk to. Calls in response to persons contemplating suicide are included in this category.

Disturbance/Disorderly Conduct

When the public's peace or tranquility is disturbed, disturbance calls or disorderly conduct calls often result. An example of a disturbance call would be if the police were called to respond to a group of kids hanging around and making noise. Disorderly conduct calls are similar and usually involve issues of indecency or morality, such as loud swearing in a public place, public sex acts, or some sort of public inconvenience.

Domestic Violence

These calls are a result of some sort of domestic disturbance and may include an unlawful touching. In some states, domestic violence laws cover married people, roommates, brothers and sisters, boyfriends and girlfriends, or anyone in a significant dating relationship. The laws vary from state to state, and depending on each state's law, the police officers have different mandates. For example, in some states, if one person *says* that he or she was struck by the other person, the officer *must* make an arrest.

Driving Under the Influence of Alcohol/Drugs

These calls are initiated by an officer's observations while on patrol, as a result of a single- or multi-vehicle accident, or from observations or complaints from citizens. Specifically, driving-under-the-influence calls are usually observed either by an officer who sees erratic behavior, such as swerving, crossing the center line, etc., or they are found at the scene of an accident, or have been reported by other motorists who may have observed them or had a close encounter with them (e.g., had to swerve to avoid being hit).

Drug Investigations

These calls can range from a simple call of a subject smoking a marijuana cigarette to drug sales to long-term investigations utilizing undercover officers.

Hazardous Materials

Calls in response to incidents where hazardous materials may be present creates a whole new list of obstacles that the police need to deal with. These calls can be in response to someone draining oil from their car or lawnmower down a drain or to a motor vehicle accident where fuel and or oil has been spilled. Other more sophisticated types of hazardous material, or "HazMat," calls involve tankers or trucks carrying dangerous chemicals and suspicious packages received in the mail.

Larceny (Theft, Stealing, Shoplifting, etc.)

Larceny is the unlawful taking of something. In some states, the law further requires that the object or item be carried away or transported. Larceny also can be committed by fraud, by false pretenses, by mail, over the Internet, and so on. In some states, the level of the crime is based on the value of the object taken. Hence, the terms *larceny over* a certain amount, *larceny under* a certain amount, *grand larceny,* and so on.

Medical Responses (Medical Assists and Check the Welfare)

Medical response calls can be initiated or generated by anyone. They can be in response to calls to help an elderly or handicapped person into bed, to assist the fire department or ambulance service in times of need, or to help someone who has slipped on ice or off a curb or sidewalk. *Check the welfare* calls can result when a neighbor does not see another neighbor for a long period of time, when mail or newspapers build up outside an house unexpectedly, or when someone hears calls or cries for help.

Motor Vehicle Accident

These are calls to respond to the scene of an accident. In most cases, there is a causal factor for the accident, and someone could or should receive a traffic citation or ticket. Someone did something wrong to cause the accident.

Motor Vehicle Stops

Motor vehicle stops, any instance when an officer deals with a citizen who is in a motor vehicle, are the most common type of call an officer assigned to routine patrol will encounter. These calls, although the most common, can also be the most dangerous. Officers in most cases do not know who the offender is.

Motor Vehicle Theft

This is a call in response to a report that a motor vehicle has been stolen.

Quality of Life Issues

These are calls in response to incidents that may or may not be crimes. However, in the wake of community policing, these are responses to events that have been determined to affect the quality of life in a neighborhood. In some cases, the incident may violate local ordinances or bylaws. Examples of quality of life issues include people placing their trash containers at the curb days before trash pick up, rubbish trucks picking up dumpsters in the early morning hours, kids that just hang around and prevent people from passing along the sidewalk, kids skateboarding where they shouldn't, and so on.

Robbery (Armed and Unarmed)

Robbery is when a perpetrator takes money or other property either at gunpoint or at knifepoint or by some threat of force against the victim. One of the common elements in every robbery is that the victim has been threatened.

Suspicious Persons, Prowler, etc.

These calls are usually initiated by a citizen's call or by an officer's observations. These calls are prompted when a person does or says something that arouses the suspicion of the observer.

Unknown Problem

This is a common type of call. The officer must sort out and deal with the issue that confronts him or her upon arrival.

Other

There are many different types of crimes, and crimes vary from state to state. Some state laws include old common law violations that are still on the books as crimes. Whether they are enforced or prosecuted depends on the nature of the crime and the discretion of the prosecutorial element. For the purposes of this course, the crimes just presented are the ones that we will examine more closely. It would be impossible to cover all crimes in all jurisdictions.

Misdemeanors and Felonies

Crimes usually fall under one of two major categories: misdemeanors or felonies. The severity of the act is the determining factor within each jurisdiction as to which crimes are felonies and which are misdemeanors.

Misdemeanors

A **misdemeanor** is a crime that is punishable by imprisonment in a local or county jail, not in a prison run by state or federal authorities. A misdemeanor may be distinguished by the value of the property stolen. In some cases, a person can only be arrested for a misdemeanor without a warrant if the crime is committed in the presence of a police officer.

Felony

A **felony** is a more serious crime that is punishable in the state or federal prison system. These crimes usually involve a physical injury or of a serious nature. Most crimes against another person are felonies, such as rape, murder, sexual assault, assault and battery, assault and battery with a dangerous weapon, kidnapping, and so on. Crimes that are committed against high-value property, such as art theft, jewelry theft, auto theft, arson, and so on, are also considered to be felonies.

Chapter Wrap-Up

In-Service Training

When calls are received at the dispatch center, it is important to remember that the people calling the center do not necessarily understand what the elements of the crime are and what the incident actually may be. The call that you are responding to may be entirely different from what was assigned or dispatched to you. For example, say that you are dispatched to a call for a break-in in progress (i.e., a break-in is occurring as the caller reports it). You arrive and observe an individual standing near an open window on the front porch of the residence. As you approach, the "suspect" announces that he is the owner of the residence and that he has been locked out. He is able to produce proper identification to verify this.

From the Experts

Use the time it takes to respond to a call to think about what you are going to do when you get there. If you have a partner, you can discuss your individual roles. If you have had the same partner for a period of time, the roles that you perform may already be arranged. *Always* be prepared and ready to modify your procedures, strategies, and tactics if the situation turns out to be different than you originally thought based on your initial dispatch information.

Caution

To lessen volatile reactions and responses from the people you are dealing with, be professional. You should treat and speak to people in a manner that is conducive to your position. Arriving at the scene and screaming or talking in a demeaning manner can provoke an unneeded response from those you are trying to deal with. Treat them as you wish to be treated.

Key Terms

assault: In most states, assault by itself is a verbal assault and does not constitute an unlawful touching, or a battery. An assault and battery occurs when there is an unlawful touching. These calls can be enhanced when an object or weapon is used in the battery. The weapon or object can be anything capable of inflicting injury.

battery: An unlawful touching. These calls can be enhanced when an object or weapon is used in the battery. The weapon or object can be anything capable of inflicting injury.

felony: Serious crimes that are punishable in the state or federal prison system. These crimes usually involve a physical injury or of a serious nature. Most crimes against another person are felonies, such as rape, murder, sexual assault, assault and battery, assault and battery with a dangerous weapon, kidnapping, and so on. Crimes that are committed against high-value property, such as art theft, jewelry theft, auto theft, and arson, are also considered to be felonies.

misdemeanor: A crime that is punishable by imprisonment in a local or county jail, not in a prison run by state or federal authorities. A misdemeanor may be distinguished by the value of the property stolen. In some cases, a person can only be arrested for a misdemeanor without a warrant if the crime is committed in the presence of a police officer.

Your Assignment—Results

This driving under the influence incident has a number of factors that you should consider. The fact that you smell alcohol does not necessarily mean that the driver has been drinking. It could be from the spilled contents of the bottle on his lap. He may have gone to the store, bought the bottle, and it broke from the force of the accident.

Because he is not injured, you should ask him to step out of the car and observe his actions, his steadiness on his feet, and whether his eyes are glassy and blood-shot. Is his speech impaired? You could give him a field sobriety test, or give him a gaze test to observe the movements of his eyes and his ability to visually track a moving object.

Whether you would just let him go home or arrest him has to be based on additional observations.

Your Next Assignment

It is 2:00 A.M., and the dispatcher tells you to respond to the bank, specifically the ATM machine. A motorist who was driving by the bank called from her cell phone and stated that there was a female kicking, punching, and pounding on the bank's ATM machine. As you arrive, you observe a woman at the ATM machine who is slapping the ATM keyboard panel. When she sees you approaching, she stops pounding the keyboard and stands there. You speak with her and she states that she has lost her ATM card in the machine and desperately needs it back because she is leaving town in the morning.

1. Would you tell her to move along and contact the bank in the morning? Why or why not?
2. Once you realize that this is not a police matter, would you just go on your way? Why or why not?
3. Would you arrest her for possibly damaging the bank property because you observed her striking the machine? Why or why not?
4. Would you tell her that because she no longer has any business with the bank and the card is gone that she should leave or she will be arrested for trespassing? Why or why not?

Call for Service

You are on patrol in a residential neighborhood. You parked your cruiser and are walking through the neighborhood to familiarize yourself with the residents and to make yourself available to them. This is part of a community policing program called "Park and Walk." It is 11:30 A.M. on a Tuesday afternoon in September. As you turn the corner on Elm Street, you observe a youth who is around 16 years of age. He is about a half block ahead of you, standing on the sidewalk, looking in the direction of a house.

As you approach, the youth sees you, turns, and begins to walk away at a quick pace. His pace is creating a greater distance between you. You yell to him to stop for a second. He turns and looks at you and then begins to run away.

Based on the information provided, write out a detailed description of what you would do. Think about what you believe your options are, what the youth has done, and what action you should take in this instance. Be sure to explain fully all the actions that you have taken or reasons for not taking any action.

CHAPTER

3

Equipment and Technology: How It Affects Patrol

Knowledge Objectives

- Describe how computers have affected police work.
- Discuss whether the affect of computers on policing has been positive or negative.
- Identify the equipment used by police officers.
- Discuss if the police are regulated by the policies and procedures of the equipment they use.

Skills Objectives

None

It is 1:00 P.M., and you have responded to a call for a possible breaking and entering into a residence. The resident has come home and found the front door open and the house ransacked. The resident has not checked the house to see if the intruder is still there.

- What equipment or tools should you have with you and why?
- What questions might you ask the resident before entering the house?

■ Introduction

In this the chapter, you will learn how computers have affected policing and influenced the ability of the police to suppress, investigate, and detect crime. You will also see how computers have helped with administration and opened new doors for law enforcement. You will learn about the various pieces of equipment utilized by police officers and how they are used in the field. You will also learn that every agency has its own equipment requirements.

■ Equipment Used in Policing

The equipment, or the "tools of the trade," used by police officers changes every day; new innovations offer better ways to do things. Computers have made it easier for law enforcement to apprehend criminals, maintain records, and perform checks and balances, as the need to do so increases. But computers have also generated new types of crime.

A variety of computer crimes can be committed over the Internet, including fraud, larceny, the possession of child pornography, and identity theft. However, with computer crimes, the police often have trouble determining the proper jurisdiction. When determining the proper jurisdiction, the police ask the following questions, some of which may not have answers:

- Who owns the Internet?
- Where did the crime begin?
- Where did the crime end?
- Where did the crime committed over the Internet travel while it was being committed?
- Do we prosecute based on where the victim lives?
- Do we prosecute based on where the suspect lives?
- If the crime crosses state lines, do we turn it over to the federal authorities?
- What if the crime crosses international borders?
- What equipment do we confiscate for evidence?
- If the crime was committed on a networked computer, do we take the server and all the terminals?

Some of these questions are still awaiting clarification through the courts. Until then, prosecutors are hard pressed in certain conditions to press charges and prosecute.

Computers and the Internet have made it easier for the police to research case law, transmit information from one agency to another, and locate information that may be important to a particular case or event. Computers have also provided new tools for administrative support. Police departments now place department manuals on the department's computer network for easy access and reference. Computers can relay memos, orders, and bulletins to all members of the department with a push of a button through an e-mail system. Records and reports can be stored electronically, eliminating the vast piles of paperwork and cases of papers and files that have always been a storage problem.

Many police cruisers now have laptops or Mobile Data Terminals, or MDTs, that are linked by a wireless network to the department computer system, state computer systems, and so on. Many cruisers also have video cameras. These enhance the likelihood of convictions of crimes that are recorded during police responses.

Law enforcement also uses other types of high-tech equipment (e.g., infrared cameras, binoculars, wired microphones, other audio and visual aids, etc.), but they are mostly used in investigative or covert operations, and are not usually associated with patrol.

Degrees of Force

All police equipment that is used for a protective or defensive purpose is governed by parameters set forth in departmental policies and statutes. The different levels of force are referred to as the *degrees of force* or the *use of force*. These degrees of force are generic and are explained in the following list. Keep in mind that every department can write policy to define its own levels of force as long as they are in compliance with state, federal, and court decisions. The following lists the different levels of force:

- **Nondeadly force.** The use of force that is not likely to or intended to cause serious physical harm or death. Such force includes the use of approved defensive/physical tactics, approved chemical substances, canines, and the authorized baton.

- **Presence/appearance.** The image that an officer portrays just by his or her mere presence can, in many cases, affect the outcome of a situation. The officer's appearance should be an expression of the officer's power. The officer should be neat and well groomed. The officer should also be aware of his or her body language. The officer should always maintain the highest level of professionalism.

- **Verbal communication.** Effective verbal communication can in many instances decrease or reduce an anxious, aggressive, or violent situation by calming or quelling a subject's behavior. The appropriate use of verbal persuasion can, on occasion, prevent or minimize the need for any escalation to physical force.

- **Initial (light) physical tactics.** The application of light physical contact or tactics is only appropriate when the subject's physical resistance is minor in nature and not hazardous or dangerous. If the behavior can be easily controlled, this method should be used. Light physical tactics include guiding a cooperative subject into a handcuffing position, out of a vehicle, or into another room.

- **Chemical substances.** Chemical sprays or substances should not be used if the suspect's resistance is minor and not dangerous or if any light physical tactics would achieve the same result. Chemical substances may be used in self-defense or in the defense of another person. They may also be used to restrain a person who is physically resisting arrest or to discourage someone who is engaged in violent conduct. Chemical substances may be used with the subject who resists the police officer's initial physical contact or who shows signs of immediate physical resistance. They can be used when a physical confrontation would be necessary in self-defense or in defense of another. Chemical substances may not be appropriate if the use could affect innocent bystanders, particularly children. If outdoors, the officer should always know which way the wind is blowing so the chemicals do not hinder the officer's abilities as well.

- **Defensive physical tactics.** These tactics include the use of appropriate and adequate physical strength or hand control to overcome any light (passive) or heavy (defensive) resistance that is not intended as an act of overt aggression toward an officer after a subject has refused to comply with verbal instructions to submit.

- **Baton.** The baton (also called a *nightstick* or a *billy club*) may be used by an officer for self-defense or in defense of another. It can be used to subdue a person who physically resists arrest or to stop a person(s) engaged in violent conduct. The use of the baton may also be considered when lesser methods of force have failed or would obviously not work.

- **Canine.** The use of a trained canine is a use of force. K-9 officers may only use trained canines when it is reasonable and necessary to achieve a lawful objective.
- **Deadly force.** This level of force is likely to result in the death of or serious physical injury to another person. The discharge of a firearm toward a person is an example of the use of deadly force. An officer may use deadly force in self-defense or in the defense of another person.

Other terms that play a part in the proper use of force include the following:
- **Philosophy of less-lethal force.** The level of force that meets the objectives with *less potential* for causing death or serious physical injury than the use of deadly force. Examples include the use of beanbag projectiles, rubber pellets, wooden plugs, and so on.
- **Minimum amount of force.** The least amount of force that is proper, reasonable, and necessary to achieve a lawful objective.
- **Reasonable belief.** Would an ordinary and prudent person act or think in a similar way under similar circumstances? What would an average person do or think?
- **Reasonableness.** Is an action within reason? Is it justified or suitable to the confrontation?
- **Serious bodily injury.** A physical injury that creates a greater risk of death, can cause serious permanent disfigurement, or can result in long-term loss or impairment of any body part or organ.

Weapons and Other Equipment

Many types of weapons are available to the police for use in specific instances. Weapons include handguns, shotguns, less-lethal ammunition (bean bags, rubber pellets, etc.), patrol rifles, and sniper rifles for tactical and SWAT operations. For our purposes, we will deal specifically with the normal patrol function and not those circumstances that may warrant additional firepower or equipment.

Service Weapons

Service weapons may be revolvers or semiautomatic handguns (**FIGURE 3-1**). The officer is authorized to use the service weapon while on duty. In most cases, a police department selects a particular service weapon based on extensive research and testing. Many departments assign officers a particular handgun, and the officers are required to use specific ammunition. These mandates ensure that the officer is qualified and trained on a specific

FIGURE 3-1
Service weapons may be revolvers or semiautomatic handguns.

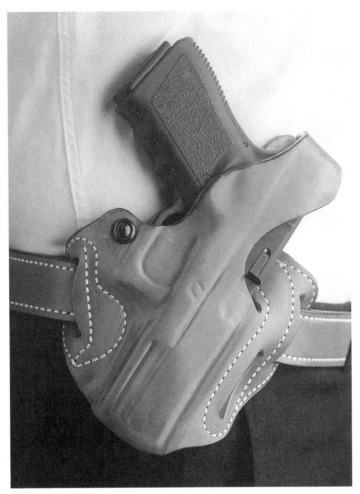

FIGURE 3-2
Safety holsters have several safety features, which enable a police officer to retain the weapon during a struggle.

weapon. Such training reduces a department's liability and offers protection against lawsuits if an officer uses his or her weapon in the line of duty.

Safety Holster

The safety holster is designed to assist the officer in maintaining his or her handgun in a struggle while ensuring handgun retention. Safety features include well-placed latches and snaps and retentive steel strips and plates for specific weapons. These holsters enable the officer to maintain his or her weapon in the case of a struggle with a suspect who is trying to grab or take the officer's weapon (**FIGURE 3-2**).

Baton

A baton is a device used to apply force and can be used as an extension of the officer's arm. The baton can be used to strike, block, or prod or to provide leverage. There are many different types of batons: straight batons of various lengths, expandable batons that expand on a snap or flick of the wrist, and shaped batons with handles (**FIGURE 3-3**). Officers are trained in the use of the specific type of baton that is authorized by their department.

Handcuffs

Handcuffs are restraining devices. Under normal circumstances, they are applied to a suspect's wrists. Note that officers also carry a key to unlock the handcuffs. There are several types of handcuffs. The most common type is the chained cuff, which connects two wrist

FIGURE 3-3
Police batons, also referred to as *nightsticks* or *billy clubs*, come in a variety of sizes and shapes. Each style has a specific purpose.

bracelets by means of a short chain of three to four links. The second most common type is the hinged cuff, in which the bracelets are connected by a solid hinge instead of a chain. This type of cuff does not allow any movement beyond the hinges of the cuff.

Other variations have larger bracelets and longer chains. These are used to secure the legs of a suspect to prevent kicking or running. Other types include chains that are looped through a metal loop secured around the suspect's waist by a leather belt. These are specifically designed to keep the hands at the waist, and do not allow the suspect to raise his or her hands above that level. The bracelets are secured by short chains and attached directly to the metal loop of the belt (**FIGURE 3-4**).

Portable Radios

Most departments are in constant wireless communication with all officers, and each officer is either assigned a specific radio or given one at the beginning of a shift. These radios have long-distance capabilities; at a minimum, they cover the entire jurisdictional area. However, in some parts of the country there are "dead spots" where signals cannot be received or transmitted. Some jurisdictions have radios powerful enough to reach surrounding jurisdictions and may have inter-jurisdictional capabilities, enabling them to communicate with other departments or agencies. Some agencies use of cellular phones or pagers and message units with walkie-talkie capabilities instead of portable radios.

Wireless signals are usually transmitted through a series of antennas placed throughout the jurisdiction. The signal is returned to the dispatch site by means of a "main" antenna, also called a "repeater" (**FIGURE 3-5**).

Flashlight

You may think that only night patrol officers or other units assigned to the evening or early morning shifts need flashlights. Quite the contrary; all officers need flashlights, whether assigned to days or nights. A day patrol officer can be called upon to enter a darkened cellar or shed, which may be as dark as midnight in the afternoon. Flashlights need to be

FIGURE 3-4
Handcuffs may have chains or hinges.

FIGURE 3-5
Portable radios enable two-way communication between the officer and the department. They usually have a range that is adequate to reach anywhere within the boundaries of the jurisdiction.

reliable. Most flashlights come equipped with rechargeable batteries and their own wall-mounted recharge units. Flashlights may require anywhere from one to five batteries. A flashlight can be as small as a penlight or as large as a long-handled unit (**FIGURE 3-6**).

FIGURE 3-6
A reliable flashlight is a must whether the police officer is assigned to the day or night shift.

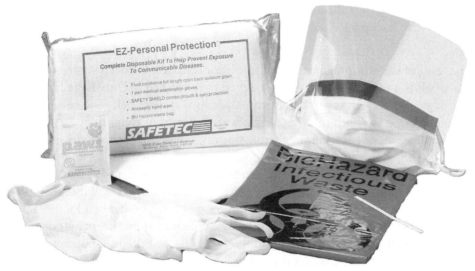

FIGURE 3-7
Protective gear such as rubber gloves, protective suits, and masks are essential pieces of equipment.

Rubber Gloves and Masks

Today, some enemies are far more dangerous than most individual suspects. Such enemies include bacteria and viruses. Fatal or dangerous bacteria and viruses can be transmitted by blood. Officers must be prepared to respond to any circumstance; they may have to place their hands in an open wound to shut off the blood supply from a severed main blood vessel. Rubber gloves can protect officers from becoming infected with blood-borne diseases. Masks may protect officers from inhaling disease-causing bacteria or viruses (**FIGURE 3-7**).

Chemical Sprays

Several types of chemical sprays are available. The most commonly used spray is called *OC spray,* which is also known as pepper spray. The "OC" stands for *oleoresin capsicum*. In most cases, OC spray is made from natural peppers, such as cayenne peppers (**FIGURE 3-8**). Usually, this spray will render a suspect incapacitated, by stinging the suspect's eyes and taking his or her breath away. The effects last for about 20 minutes and can be washed away with plain water.

FIGURE 3-8
Pepper spray.

Patrol Duty Bag

The patrol duty bag is a duffle bag or briefcase that officers use as a portable office and to hold equipment. This bag is prepared by the officer for his or her own use. A typical duty bag may hold:

- Extra rubber gloves
- Spare flashlight batteries
- Extra plastic handcuffs (or wire wraps)
- Paper, pens, and other office supplies
- Police reports and forms
- A reflective traffic vest or safety belt
- A raincoat and rain hat
- Traffic citation and ticket forms
- Personal items

These bags are used by officers assigned to cruisers and four-wheel-drive vehicles; abbreviated bags or pouches may be put together for bicycle, motorcycle, or other methods of patrol. Unfortunately, walking officers usually do not have the means to carry extra equipment. They do not carry backpacks.

Duty Belts

Now that we have all of the equipment we need to carry on patrol, we need someplace to keep it. The duty belt is a piece of equipment designed to do just that. Duty belts can be worn in several ways. A duty belt is a good sturdy "Garrison" type of belt. The belt should be of sufficient quality and strength to carry a significant amount of weight, for example, that resulting from the gun, holster, baton, chemical spray, handcuffs, rubber gloves, flashlight, radio, and, of course, the appropriate holders and cases for each.

Most duty belt systems consist of two belts. One is a smaller belt that you would normally wear; this should be a good, wide belt. The outer, or actual duty belt, which has all of the equipment, is worn over the pants belt, but not looped through the belt loops of the pants. These two belts are kept together in several ways. One way is by "keeper straps." These are narrow straps that are wrapped around the two belts and then snapped closed. These straps help to distribute the load on the duty belt to the pants belt. Velcro also can be used to secure the belts. In this case, the inner pants belt has a felt strip on the outside of the belt and the inside of the duty belt has the matching mate surface. Securing the Velcro surfaces together connects the two belts. This system keeps the belts from shifting and helps to evenly distribute the weight of the duty belt.

Some departments use shoulder straps or a "Sam Brown" belt that attaches to the belt in the front and then back diagonally across the shoulder. Some belts are made of what is referred to as "webbing" or "tactical materials." They are secured by a clip and buckle as opposed to a normal belt buckle. These types of clips are usually seen on backpacks, luggage, and so on.

Ballistic Vests and Armor

Ballistic vests and armor are sometimes referred to as *bullet-resistant vests, bulletproof vests, body armor,* and other terms. However, none of these are guaranteed to be bulletproof. Ballistic vests and armor are designed to stop bullets. They are rated based on the caliber of weapon they will stop and on how well they protect against sharp objects, such as knives and picks.

Ballistic shields are sometimes used in tactical situations. They come in a variety of different designs and capabilities. They are usually made of some type of metal or bullet-resistant material.

Stun Devices

Some departments utilize "Tazer" devices that apply a electric shock to a subject, immobilizing the person for a period of time. Not all states and departments utilize these. They are illegal in some states and jurisdictions.

Chapter Wrap-Up

In-Service Training

Some officers carry large wire wraps or wire ties. These are approximately 12 inches in length and can be used as an extra set of handcuffs. Officers can carry these either inside their hat, curved around the inside headband, or they may secure them in a pouch on their belt or carry them in their patrol duty bags.

From the Experts

Always make sure that your equipment is in perfect working order. Clean and maintain your service weapon prior to each shift and before you go on the street. Don't ever assume that it is fine, you need to be positive that it is working properly. The same goes for flashlights; make sure the batteries are charged or that extras are available.

Caution

Complacency is your worst enemy. Never assume that everything is routine. Even though your flashlight was charged last night and you didn't use it, make sure to check that it is working properly tonight as well. The same goes for all your equipment.

Key Terms

deadly force: A level of force that is likely to result in the death of/or serious physical injury to another person. The discharge of a firearm toward a person is an example of the use of deadly force. An officer may use deadly force in self-defense or in the defense of another.

minimum amount of force: The least amount of force that is proper, reasonable, and necessary to achieve a lawful objective.

nondeadly force: The use of force that is not likely to or intended to cause serious physical harm or death. Such force includes the use of approved defensive/physical tactics, approved chemical substances, canines, and the authorized baton.

philosophy of less-lethal force: The level of force that meets the objectives with *less potential* for causing death or serious physical injury than the use of deadly force. Examples include the use of beanbag projectiles, rubber pellets, and wooden plugs.

reasonable belief: Would an ordinary and prudent person act or think in a similar way under similar circumstances? What would an average person do or think?

reasonableness: Is an action within reason? Is it justified or suitable to the confrontation?

serious bodily injury: A physical injury that creates a greater risk of death, can cause serious permanent disfigurement, or can result in long-term loss or impairment of any body part or organ.

Your Assignment—Results

Before entering the house to search for any suspects, you should first determine who reported the incident, who else has access to the house, and whether anyone else is at home or could be at home. For example, this could be a case of an estranged partner (boyfriend, husband, wife, etc.) who has come back to the home.

Whatever equipment you are authorized to carry, such as your service weapon, baton, chemical spray, and handcuffs should be carried. Most important, especially if you are assigned to the day shift, you should carry a flashlight. You may not need to carry a large multicell unit, but at least carry a mini-light. Even though it is daytime, and most areas of the house may be lit or the lights can be turned on, you may still need to illuminate an attic, a cellar storage bin, a crawl space under the house, or other darkened areas. You should also make sure that the outside of the house has been secured and covered by backup units and have a partner or another officer search the house with you.

Your Next Assignment

You respond to a call for a fight in a bar. As you approach the scene, you observe that two men are fighting. As you enter the bar, the two men stop, one of them puts his hands up and states that he is done. Your partner goes over to speak with that subject. The second subject gives you a scowling look; it is obvious that he is highly intoxicated. He stands up from his bent over position, glares at you with angered eyes, and asks you in an agitated way, "Who do you think you are?" He moves toward you with clenched fists.

Using the information in this chapter, answer the following questions:

1. What equipment would you have ready before entering the bar? Why?
2. Would you have had any weapons "out" before entering, that is, in your hands, if any? Why or why not?
3. As he approaches you, what piece of equipment would you use? Why?
4. Say that the man attacks you, and you fight off his advances and subdue him. Write a report of what transpired, what you saw, and what action you took. Justify the use of any equipment that you may have used to restrain the suspect.

Call for Service

You are assigned to a call for a suspicious person looking into windows. Such a person is also referred to as a *Peeping Tom* or a *prowler*. You park your cruiser and begin to walk in the area where the suspect has been seen. As you approach a house, you observe a man walking toward the street from a back yard. He is wearing a white T-shirt and jeans, which matches the description given by the caller. The man appears to be highly intoxicated and very unsteady on his feet. As he presents himself at the front of the house, he sees you and begins to charge you. He is closing the distance between you and him; his arms are flailing and he doesn't appear to have a weapon.

- What action will you take?
- Would you use any of your equipment? If so, what would you use?
- What actions would you take after the incident?
- Write a detailed report of what transpired. Justify your actions.

What Do Communities Expect from Police Officers?

Knowledge Objectives

- Describe the different styles of policing: legalistic, watchman, and service.
- Recognize that communities expect a professional response.
- Discuss whether police officers should act ethically.
- Determine whether police officers are able to accept gifts and/or gratuities.

Skills Objectives

None

You are on patrol and have been assigned to respond to a local restaurant for an unknown problem. As you arrive, you are met at the front door by the restaurant's owner. He tells you that a customer forgot her pocketbook at the restaurant last night. The owner has called her, but she cannot pick it up until after the restaurant's closing time. He told her he would have the pocketbook brought to the police station and that she could then pick it up at her convenience. The owner is unable to drop it off at the station because he is the only one working, so he cannot leave. He had called the station, and the desk sergeant said that he would send someone down to pick it up.

You take the pocketbook and return to your cruiser. As you are getting ready to leave, the owner yells at you to stop. As he approaches, he hands you a coffee and a brown paper bag with some pastries inside. He thanks you for your help, smiles, and walks away.

- Do you take the coffee and the pastries?
- If yes, why? If not, why not?
- If not, what do you do with it?

■ Introduction

In this chapter, you will learn about the different styles of policing as defined by James Q. Wilson. Wilson explains that how police do policing is based on the make-up of the community. This chapter also examines what a community expects from its police officers with regard to professionalism, ethics, and responses to their needs.

■ Community Expectations

The community expects and demands that police responses and actions be professional, responsive to the community's needs, responsive to community's suggestions, and ethical. The public wants the police to be fair and just in the exercise of their powers and to use their discretion in a manner that satisfies the needs of the community.

The police serve several different types of communities. Communities vary based on a number of factors, including urban versus suburban; high income versus low income; the age of the citizenry, the size of the community with regard to population; and jurisdictional responsibilities.

Based on his study of eight communities (six in New York, one in Illinois, and one in California), James Q. Wilson in *Varieties of Police Behavior: The Management of Law and Order in Eight Communities*, developed categories for the different styles of policing based on the type of community serviced:

- **Legalistic style.** The **legalistic style** of policing is evidenced when the police department is required to enforce the laws the same way for everyone. This style requires standardized enforcement. Communities of any make-up can adopt this concept, and those that prefer the legalistic style of policing do not want the police to use any discretion when applying the law. Citizens in such communities view any police discretion or preferential treatment of some citizens as a product or sign of unethical police practice.

- **Watchman style.** This style of policing is found mostly in large communities, where large populations create numerous calls for service and the police will deal with them in the order of severity. With the **watchman style** of policing, the police maintain order and keep things in line with the status quo. Police will respond to and be on the lookout for "serious" crimes and may not even pay attention to calls for service that relate to minor offenses. The police are less likely to be concerned with misdemeanors, traffic violations, and other minor violations of the law. With this style of policing, the police will attempt to resolve as much as possible informally and will not refer cases to the next level or social services, such as juvenile services or family services, unless a serious crime has been committed.

- **Service style.** The **service style** of policing is most common in middle- and upper-class communities. As the name implies, the main priority of this type of policing is *service*. In these communities, the police will make arrests and use the courts only when necessary. Their focus is on keeping their community safe from outsiders who enter or pass through its protected boundaries. They treat the citizens with respect and act as responsibly and closely as they can with the community to protect the interests of its residents. These departments are generally well financed and are given the equipment and enforcement tools they need or request. These departments usually have the latest advances in police technology and are never in danger of losing resources or manpower because of budgetary restraints.

Now that you have learned about the different styles of policing, let's focus on what citizens expect of their officers.

Community Expectations

Citizens sometimes think that they pay police officers' salaries. Some will even say this to an officer when an officer responds and the citizen is unhappy with the outcome. Although citizens' tax dollars do in fact pay police officers' salaries, the actual amount that a single citizen pays toward the total cost of an officer's salary is insignificant. However, regardless of that fact, the police are there to "protect and to serve" the community.

The citizenry expects a professional-looking officer who is well dressed and who presents himself or herself in a professional manner. They expect the officer to be educated and knowledgeable in the laws they enforce and specifically in the ordinances or bylaws of their community.

Responding to the Community's Needs

It is extremely important for the police department to determine what is most important to the community. If a community has a large elderly population that is vocal in its complaints about kids skateboarding in the downtown shopping area, the police have to respond to the community's needs. The solution is to either move the kids to an area where they can skateboard in safety and away from the complaining public or to hold a town meeting or other public session to try to resolve the problem.

Issues such as the one just described is where community policing originated. With community policing, the police reach out into the community to see what issues the community is most concerned with and then works with the community to resolve them. For example, common community issues include high crime rates, kids hanging around, speeding cars, loud music from bars, or other quality of life issues.

Be Responsive to Suggestions

The department's ability to respond to suggestions from the community should always be an open channel. A successful department is receptive to the community and will consider valid points. Although rare, some police administrators may be reluctant to listen to the community, because they view the department as "theirs," and "they know best," and thus do not need or want the community's input. This may be reflective of the type of local government and the powers given to the chief of police. If the municipality has what is referred to as "strong chief," the chief may have the authority to make all of the relevant decisions of the department, regardless of what the city leaders say. In some cases, the "weak chief" has all of the powers, but needs the approval of the city leaders. A police chief's authority is usually determined by a combination of state law or city or town ordinances or bylaws and by employee contract. A successful police department listens to the community.

Ethical Conduct

The public does not want a corrupt police department or for the police to make up their own rules as they go along. Police ethics play a large part in police work. Ethics fall under many categories, such as corruption, failure to act, gifts, and gratuities.

Corruption has plagued many police departments across the United States and in other countries as well. Some examples of police corruption include:

- Officers turning their backs to crime.
- The acceptance of bribes.
- Providing information that may jeopardize an investigation to subjects or suspects of the investigation.
- Participation in the commission of a crime.
- Making false complaints or initiating court actions.
- Failure to testify accurately.
- Falsification of police reports or affidavits for search or arrest warrants.

Unfortunately, one corrupt police officer reflects on *all* police officers across the country. In general, the public views the police as being corrupt and protective of one another. The public believes that police officers have a secret oath and an obligation to be faithful to their brothers and sisters behind the badge—they call this the "Blue Line."

However, police officers take pride in their profession and value their integrity and respect from their profession. They do not want to betray the profession, the community, and, most important, the trust of their family. The bad cop is the *exception,* not the rule. The reluctance not to turn in the fellow corrupt officer is vanishing. The number of corrupt cops is minute compared with the large number of officers who are out there everyday doing their job the way it should be done and with the integrity and honor of the badge they wear.

Misfeasance and *malfeasance* are terms that describe when a police officers fails to act or is negligent to his duty. Police are required by law to do certain things at certain times, depending on the law being enforced. Any failure to act in accordance with the law would fall into this category. For example, if a police officer is on patrol and observes an elderly person fall and split her head open, and the officer does nothing about it because the officer doesn't want to get dirty, then this is a failure to act. Similarly, the officer would be negligent if he observed a motor vehicle accident and did not respond. Another example would be if a dispatcher requests that a unit close to a location check on an intoxicated person and the officer either doesn't respond that he is close by, gives a false location, or just drives in the opposite direction.

Gifts and Gratuities

This area is a tough area to address, because it is a matter of opinion whether the acceptance of gifts or gratuities is unethical. A **gift** is something given out of gratitude, such as a cup of coffee in a residence while on a call or a box of homemade cookies brought to the police station from a grateful citizen. These are items offered purely out of thankfulness, with no intent of redeeming any favors as a result. A **gratuity** is something of value given to an officer that may be interpreted as requiring a favor in return. Gratuities may affect on the officer's judgment. The intent of the "gift" will determine whether it is ethical or unethical to accept. Does the gift benefit the entire department or a particular unit, such as D.A.R.E., or another departmental entity? Or, does the gift benefit only the officer it is presented to? Note that gifts and gratuities should not be confused with courtesy (FIGURE 4-1). An offer of a glass of water or a cup of coffee in the home of a citizen to whom you have responded to is not inappropriate. State ethics laws determine whether certain

FIGURE 4-1
Police officers are obligated to be ethical and should not be persuaded
by gifts and gratuities.

gifts and gratuities are ethical and/or legal. Most ethics commissions set monetary limits
on what a public official can take and not report; in most cases the value cannot exceed
$50. These laws usually cover all public officials, not just the police. Examples of gifts or
gratuities include the following:

- A police officer orders coffee at a restaurant and the waiter or waitress gives the
  officer a free or discounted cup.
- The officer always goes to a restaurant where he or she is given a significant discount or free meal.
- A business gives discounts to police officers.

With all of these examples, the issue is whether the merchant expects some sort of
favoritism because of the gift. Perhaps a merchant hopes that the police may overlook customers who illegally park in front of the business. Or, in the case of a restaurant or a bar
with a liquor license, maybe the police will ignore the fact that the bar stays open past closing time if it offers officers coffee or a meal discount.

Some restaurants, especially fast-food restaurants, have a cash register key that automatically rings up the item(s) at a specified discounted rate. Although this may seem to be
of small significance, it is still unethical and police officers should not accept any discounts designed specifically for them by virtue of the position they hold as law enforcement officers. Such situations are to be avoided when possible, as it is ethically wrong to
accept privileged treatment and additionally, can be very embarrassing and humiliating.
Officers should either leave the correct amount on the counter or table (not discounted),
or just not frequent those establishments again.

If a merchant offers a discount to police officers *and* other city or municipal employees,
is the merchant specifically targeting the police officer for favoritism? Or is the merchant

looking to tap into the large pool of consumers in the community to enhance his or her business? Some police chiefs do not allow officers to patronize businesses that give police discounts. However, merchants state that it is their business and that they can offer discounts to whomever they please.

In law enforcement there are many opportunities for police officers to make poor decisions. A large percentage of police officers choose wisely. The few that do not have to live with themselves and the decisions they make. If an individual decides to be corrupt or unethical and is willing to face the consequences of his or her actions, than that is his or her choice. The thought of having to face one's family, children, relatives, and friends in the wake of a dismissal or arrest as a result of inappropriate actions should be enough of a deterrent.

Most people behave in an ethical way and do not even think of behaving unethically. Every day, people, and not just police officers, face ethical decisions. The choice of which path to take is your decision, and your decision alone. You should contemplate what is or what may be at the end of the chosen path and be willing to face the rewards or consequences of that decision.

Chapter Wrap-Up

In-Service Training

Do not abuse your position; don't fall prey to the temptations that are presented. Be proud of your uniform, be proud of your badge, and, most importantly, be proud of yourself and your personal values.

From the Experts

When you respond to a call, you will have a specific level of intensity based on what the dispatcher tells you the call involves. Be prepared to either escalate or deescalate the call based on what you find when you arrive.

Caution

Always be aware of the traffic around you when you make a motor vehicle stop or exit the vehicle for any reason. People will be drawn to the cruiser and to you like a moth to a flame and may not be paying close attention to their actions.

Key Terms

gifts: Something given out of gratitude, such as a cup of coffee in a residence while on a call or a box of homemade cookies brought to the police station from a grateful citizen. These are items expressed purely out of thankfulness, with no intent of redeeming any favors as a result of it.

gratuities: Something of value given to an officer that may be interpreted as requiring a favor in return. They may affect the officer's judgment.

legalistic style: When the police department is required to enforce the laws the same way for everyone. This style of policing requires standardized enforcement.

service style: Most common in middle- and upper-class communities. The main priority of this type of policing is *service*. Police will make arrests and use the courts only when necessary. Their focus is on keeping their community safe from outsiders who enter or pass through its protected boundaries.

watchman style: Found mostly in large communities. With this style of policing, the police maintain order and keep things in line with the status quo. Police will respond to and be on the lookout for "serious" crimes and may not even pay attention to calls for service that relate to minor offenses.

Your Assignment—Results

With regard to the opening assignment, the coffee and pastry are most likely an innocent gesture of thanks from the businessman. Some gifts are intended to "indebt" the officers in their favor. An example of this would be a restaurant that always gives free food to officers. If an officer always accepts the free food, he may be hesitant to issue parking violations to customers outside of the establishment. The greater the value of the gift or token of appreciation, the less likely the officer will be to address concerns against the owner. (These circumstances are the exception and not the rule.) Most police officers will not compromise their values for any amount of money or gifts. In this case, if you accept the coffee so as to not offend the owner, just get out of the cruiser and go inside and leave a few dollars on the counter as a "tip," making sure that the "tip" covers the cost of the items. Or, you can refuse the items or return them to the owner; you can always say that you just had breakfast and can't eat anymore, that you are on a diet and can't have a pastry, or that you do not drink coffee. Always offer a "thank you anyway." In this case, however, we can believe that there were no ulterior motives from the owner. It was a harmless, gracious gesture.

Your Next Assignment

You are planning on attending a sporting event that has been listed as sold out. However, the local ticket agency has a few tickets at a steep price. The agency places a service fee on top of the ticket price that is equal to the cost of the ticket. If you need two tickets, you will be paying the cost of four, plus taxes and an agency fee as well. These fees are all legal. You want these tickets badly as a gift to your father as a birthday present.

You call the ticket agency and explain "who" you are. You state that you are John Smith from the Anywhere Police Department and that you would like to get some tickets, but that you are not sure that you can afford them, hoping to get a break on the fees. The ticket agent tells you to stop by and pick up the two tickets; the cost will be only the face value and the small agency fee.

You reply that you will stop by and pick them up while you are working and thank him. You pick up the tickets for the price mentioned by the agent.

1. Is it right to identify yourself as a police officer when calling to inquire about the tickets?

2. Was it necessary to mention that you may not be able to afford the tickets, knowing well in advance what the tickets would cost?

3. Because you did not solicit the discount, did you do anything wrong in accepting the reduced price?

Call for Service

You and your partner have been working together for two years. You and your partner are assigned to investigate a call of breaking glass being heard in the downtown area. As you approach the downtown area, you are drawn to the sound of an alarm ringing.

You follow the sound and observe that the alarm is coming from the jewelry store. You see that the front glass door is smashed, and you cannot determine if anyone has entered the premises. You and your partner use the proper techniques to search the building and find no one inside. The owner arrives and is outside waiting with the backup units.

You go inside with the owner and check for any missing items. The owner determines that nothing has been taken. Everything looks untouched, but he will have to do an inventory to see if there is any missing jewelry. You inform him to notify the station when he completes the inventory to inform you of the findings so you can complete your report.

Based on what you see, it appears as if the broken door could be a result of vandalism or someone from a local bar leaning against or falling into it, causing the door to break and the alarm to go off.

You return back to your cruiser and notify the dispatcher that you are clear from the call and begin patrolling your area. After a few minutes, your partner shows you a watch that he saw and liked when he was checking out the cellar. As you look over, you observe a brand new watch on his wrist.

- Will you say anything? Why or why not?
- Will you tell him he has to return it to the store before the owner finds out? Why or why not?
- If you do ask him return it, will you take any further action? Why or why not?
- Will you say nothing and inform your shift supervisor? Why or why not?
- Will you just let it go and assume that the owner will list it as missing and the blame will be on the suspect? Why or why not?
- If you have a different solution, explain.

Reference

Wilson, James Q. 1968. *Varieties of Police Behavior: The Management of Law and Order in Eight Communities*. Cambridge, MA: Harvard University Press.

Preliminary Reports

Knowledge Objectives

- Describe what a preliminary report is.
- Identify what information should be included in a preliminary report.
- Determine who is responsible for gathering information for a preliminary report.
- Identify what happens to the preliminary report after it is written.

Skills Objectives

- Demonstrate the ability to ask proper questions.
- Demonstrate the ability to take efficient notes.
- Demonstrate the ability to write an accurate account of an event.
- Use correct grammar and punctuation in a preliminary report.
- Ensure that the events in a preliminary report are in proper sequence.

You are at the scene of a two-vehicle accident. You have determined that there are no injuries. The accident was a minor collision; however, the amount of damage requires that a police report be completed.

- What information, if any, will you gather about the drivers and passengers?
- What information would you gather about the vehicles involved?
- What other information might you acquire?

■ Introduction

In this chapter, you will learn about the first step of the reporting process—preparing the preliminary report. You will identify what information is required in the preliminary report and where it comes from. The chapter also discusses contraband, the signature of a crime, and staged crimes.

■ Police Reports

The reporting process begins with the preliminary report. The preliminary report is the first written record of an event once the police are called to a location or make an observation that initiates the law enforcement function. Police reports have three main parts: the preliminary report, the follow-up, and the conclusion. The follow-up and conclusion are covered in the following chapters. This chapter focuses on the preliminary report. Note that in most cases, the parts of the report are written at the same time, as one single report. This is because most police incidents often conclude in the same action and location as when they are first acted upon by the responding officer(s). Also note that an officer's first responsibility upon arriving at a scene is to establish the welfare and medical needs of any and all persons present and summon the appropriate help, if needed (FIGURE 5-1).

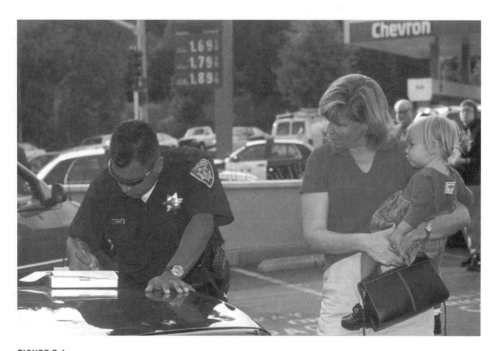

FIGURE 5-1
The primary responding police officer is responsible for acquiring the information necessary for a complete and thorough investigation.

A **preliminary report** is the first report that is written upon receiving a call for, or observing an incident that initiates the law enforcement function. The first officer on the scene is initially responsible for gathering all pertinent information and will be the reporting officer until such time as another officer who may be assigned the call. An example would be at the scene of a serious motor vehicle accident, the first officer on the scene will have to determine injuries, summon additional emergency services as needed, and gather information. The department may have a specialized accident investigator, and his arrival may be delayed. Upon his arrival he will become the investigating officer, and any information that was collected, as well as what steps the initial officer had taken, will be passed on to the investigating officer. The first officer will most likely submit a supplemental report to the incident detailing his actions.

However, some jurisdictions do not require that every call for service have a written report. The following example describes scenarios where an officer may or may not need to write a report.

Say that an officer receives a call from the dispatcher informing him that neighbors are complaining about a barking dog. Upon arriving at the scene, several different scenarios are possible: (1) The officer may not see or hear a barking dog. (2) The officer may locate the barking dog, notify the resident, and have the dog taken into the residence. (3) Or the officer may find a barking dog and not be able to locate the owners.

- With regard to the first scenario, where the officer is unable to locate the barking dog, the officer would most likely notify the dispatch center that he was "unable to locate" the dog or that there was "nothing in the area." That would be the end of the officer's response and obligation. The result of the call, that no dog was found, would be noted in the comments section of the dispatcher's record.

- With regard to the second and third scenarios, the officer would most likely write a police report of the incident. The report would need to be a documented incident in case there are ongoing problems or the dog becomes a habitual or constant object of neighbor complaints. The report would then serve to inform the Animal Control Unit of the problem or serve as evidence if the incident leads to a court case.

Incident reports will contain certain specific information, which is commonplace and generic for most police departments. This information is: date, time, and location of the call (or assignment); name and address of the person making the call; and an incident or offense number. This is a unique number that follows the case in all subsequent reports and documentation. This number is usually sequential starting with the first call received on January first and commencing with the last call on December 31st. List any identifying descriptors (hair, eyes, height, weight, etc.) of the suspect if there is one, date of birth, phone numbers, vehicle identification (make, model, registration number, color).

Reports should include the elements in a logical order. Some reports are what is called a "force choice" report, where the officer just fills in pointed questions on a form, such as hair color, where the options include: red; blonde, brown, black, etc. Other reports will have a heading where the officer will fill-in the basic elements, such as name date, time, etc. These reports are called narrative reports where the officer writes the events out. This narrative portion is the telling of the story that is read by other officers, prosecutors, defense attorneys, and judges, and could be the subject of higher courts through appeals. Sentence structure, grammar, and punctuation are crucial. It is very important that the officer gets the elements of his report clear and concise so he can organize these to prepare a complete and accurate report. To achieve this, it is important for officers to take good notes. The notes should be short and concise and to the point, but also complete enough for him to recall the event when he is preparing the report itself.

Now that we have an idea of when a report should be written, the next thing we need to determine is what elements need to be in the preliminary report. Preliminary reports have a number of standard elements that must be included: who, what, where, when, why, and how.

Who

The *who* of the preliminary report may seem simple enough, but a lot of information needs to be gathered about the who involved. First of all, the officer needs to record all of the names, addresses, dates of birth, and phone numbers or other contact information, which may include workplace information, for all **witnesses, victims,** and **suspects.**

- A **witness** is an individual who, by virtue of his or her presence or awareness of a situation, is looked upon for any information that will lead to the rightful facts in determining the events of an incident.
- A **subject** is an individual who is part of an investigation.
- A **suspect** is an individual who is believed to be responsible for the commission of a crime and is the primary focus of the investigation.
- A **victim** is an individual who has been hurt either physically, mentally, or emotionally as a result of the action of another.

If the suspect is not at the scene and is not known to the police officer, a full description of the person being sought is needed. This description may include the suspect's height, weight, age, eye color, hair color, scars, tattoos, physical deformities, clothing, and a description of the vehicle that the suspect may have used to flee. Vehicle information should include the vehicle's make, model, color, year, license plate or registration number, and any significant or observable damage or peculiarities of the vehicle (e.g., loud muffler, primer-painted right fender, smashed front-left headlight, etc.).

Why is it important to record what type of clothing the suspect was wearing? You should get a description of the suspect's clothing for several reasons. First, let's say that the suspect was involved in a physical assault. During the assault, some of the victim's body fluids may have landed on the suspect's clothes, linking the suspect to the scene.

If a suspect is apprehended at a later time or date, the suspect may have thrown away or changed his clothes from what he was wearing at the time of the arrest or offense. In this case, the police may want to apply for a search warrant to search the suspect's house or car to try and locate the clothes. This would allow the officers to search the house or vehicle, and, during the course of searching in locations where the clothes may be hidden, whatever contraband the officer observes in plain view can be seized.

What

When writing the preliminary report, you need to identify what has happened. What has occurred? What are the circumstances or the reason for the call? What action did the officer take after making an observation of some occurrence? The responding officer or the officer who will be conducting the investigation needs to find out exactly what has happened. Several officers may arrive at the scene, and the officer responsible for writing the report may not be the first to arrive. For example, if a call goes out for a traffic enforcement or accident investigation unit to respond to the scene of an accident, other units may respond and arrive prior to the investigating unit.

It is up to the preliminary reporting officer to ascertain what has transpired. The reporting officer needs to find out what information the officers who arrived at the scene earlier may have. What did the other officers observe? The preliminary reporting officer may obtain this information either through verbal interactions with the other officers or by having them provide their observations in a supplemental report. In the case of a supplemental report, the actual preliminary reporting officer will include the statements and observations of the other officers in the preliminary report and attach any supplemental reports.

During this phase of preliminary reporting, the officer, by virtue of establishing what has happened, will determine if a crime has in fact occurred. If a crime has not occurred, then the officer must either resolve the issue, if it is within his powers and ability, or determine if it is a matter that falls under some other jurisdiction, such as in a civil or social service area of responsibility. The officer is obligated to provide what information he can to the citizen who called the police as well to any agencies the officer refers the matter to.

If a crime has occurred, then the judicial process begins. Based on information from the victim and any witnesses, the officer will make some initial decisions based on his or her training and experience. Interviews with the victim and the witnesses will begin to bring the facts of the incident to light. If the officer is not sure whether a crime has occurred, the officer can call a supervisor or discuss the matter with other officers on the scene.

Where

The *where* is not as cut and dried as it sounds. An incident may not have occurred where the citizen/victim/witness contact was made. For example, say that an officer is summoned to a phone booth in the downtown area to meet with a battered wife (victim of domestic violence or abuse). The battering incident most likely did not occur in the phone booth. The victim may have fled the scene (her home) and run to a local phone booth or to a friend or neighbor's house.

The location where the contact is made in your jurisdiction does not always mean that the offense occurred in your department's boundaries. It may have occurred in a neighboring city or town. The same holds true for a hit and run or other type of motor vehicle or traffic incident. The incident may have occurred on a state highway or interstate, where a state agency may have jurisdiction. The off ramp the subject took to summon help might just happen to be in your city. Any location with a shared jurisdiction will have a protocol as to which overlapping agency has control of the area. For example, a downtown train station in your city may be under the jurisdiction of the Transit Authority. In such cases, the responding officer should protect and secure the scene and summon any emergency services needed (ambulance, fire, utility company, etc.) until the responsible agency arrives.

Sometimes the location determine the actions that can, or cannot, be taken. In some jurisdictions, a group of kids hanging around a shopping center, which is private property, are not breaking any laws. The proprietor of the business may want them to leave for the sake of the patrons who do not want to walk through a group of kids. Unless there is a "No Trespassing" or "No Loitering" sign present, the officers may not have any recourse other than to ask the kids to move along. In most cases, the kids will move along. Again depending on local laws, if the owner or person who has control of the property, such as manager or clerk, asks the kids to move along in the presence of the officer, informing them they are trespassing, and they don't move, then they may be subject to arrest for trespassing. If in fact a sign has been erected and the kids show up and hang around, they are again subject to arrest for the violation.

When

The *when* is the time that an incident actually occurred. The time of the incident determines whether an immediate response is needed. In most police reporting functions there is a time that is recorded as the incident time—this is when the police received the call and placed the incident into the formal police process. This may not necessarily be the time the event occurred. Estimates of the actual time should be as accurate as possible, but this may not always be the case. If a resident reports a house break-in, and the break-in occurred while they were at work from 8–4:00 P.M., there is an 8-hour window where the crime may have taken place. Unless neighbors or other elements can narrow the span, the time of the crime will reflect this time span.

Let's take a look at a rape incident.

If the rape occurred just moments prior to the victim summoning police assistance, then the identification and apprehension of the suspect are paramount. Is the perpetrator known to the victim? Was the perpetrator a stranger? These answers will assist in locating the suspect. If the suspect is known to the victim, where does the suspect live or hang around? If the suspect is unknown to the victim, what was the suspect's description? Did the suspect leave on foot or in a vehicle? This information would be broadcast in an *All Points Bulletin,* or APB, to the units in the jurisdiction of the incident as well as the surrounding areas.

Another reason why the time is important is with regard to the charges that may be made once the suspect is apprehended. Did the incident occur in the daytime or at night? Some state laws define crimes by the time of day (e.g., breaking and entering). The definition of daytime and nighttime may depend on sunrise and sunset. If a break-in occurred between one hour after sunset and one hour before sunrise, then the break occurred at night. It may be the difference between a felony and a misdemeanor if the break-in occurred in the daytime.

In cases where a suspect or victim is either 14, 15, 16, 17, or 18 years of age, depending upon the state definition, the offense may involve a juvenile. Offenses or crimes involving juveniles will have a different response and prosecution depending upon the age of the affected party.

Finally, when the crime occurred may affect the *statute of limitations*. The statute of limitations is the time specified by law for a crime to have been committed and to have the police apprehend the suspect and bring them before the court. The length of the statute of limitations depends on the nature of the crime. In most states, murder has no statute of limitations, whereas rape may have a 20-year limit on prosecution. This means that if someone comes into the police station and reports that they were raped or sexually assaulted 30 years ago, the statute of limitations in that state determines whether the police have any powers or authority to do anything about it.

Why

Why did the offense or crime occur? Was it provoked? Was it in retribution or retaliation? Was the offense part of an ongoing incident, such as long-running dispute between neighbors? These are some of the questions that should be asked in determining the motive for a crime.

If a wife is found murdered, and the husband is the likely suspect, was it because he was cheating? Was she cheating? Was she was spending too much money? Or was he an abuser or drinker with rages and fits of anger? There may be a past history of prior incidents, which can add to the motive and provide the reason for the attack.

Any issues that may be causal factors are important to identifying the motive and reasons for the occurrence. Statements from people not even at the scene of the crime can be very important. Returning to the murdered wife, the wife may have confided to her sister or mother about the abusive relationship with her husband and may have indicated or told others about the physical abuse or that she was fearful for her life.

The charges for many crimes are based on the suspect's intent when committing the crime. For example, did the husband who killed his wife intend to kill her? Or did he just push her, and he pushed her so hard that she fell and hit her head and died as a result of the injury? The fact that he pushed her shows that he had intention to hurt her, but not necessarily to kill her. This could mean the difference between a murder (first and second degree) and a manslaughter charge (voluntary or involuntary), depending on state law. Clearly, it is important to determine intent and motive.

How

How did the offense occur? Did the assailant strike the victim with a weapon? If so, what was the weapon? Was the strike a downward motion to the left, indicating a right-handed blow? Is the weapon still at the scene or did the assailant take it with him or her? These are all part of the *how* of the crime.

In cases where there is an illegal or unlawful entry into a residence or a business, how the assailant got in and what he or she used to get in are important. These can help to identify the *Modus Operandi,* or MO. This is what makes a crime unique to a individual. The MO can be used to link a suspect with other, similar crimes.

An example would be if a woman discovers a housebreak at her residence that occurred while she was away at work. Upon checking for missing items, the woman determines only that her child's video game unit and games are missing. This may indicate that the perpetrator is a juvenile who wants the video games and who may in fact be a friend of the victim's child. (How does the perpetrator know what games the victim had, where they were kept, etc.?). The fact that only video games, and no other valuables, such as jewelry, televisions, or stereos, were taken can mean that the thief was only interested in the games and may have not had adequate transportation to carry away any large items. This information can be used to link this crime with similar crimes in the area.

Other crimes have what is called a signature. A **signature** is a specific unique act that can link an individual to other crimes. Many serial killers and rapists have signatures. With regard to a thief, the thief's signature may be that he always sits down and has a glass of water in the kitchen. Or, in the case of a serial killer, maybe he always strangles the victim with a red scarf tied in a specific knot. These are examples of signatures.

Another aspect of the crime that investigators examine is the crime's staging. **Staging** is when the suspect tries to make the crime scene appear as if something else occurred or make it so the evidence will lead the investigators away from him or her. The following is an example of staging.

A woman is murdered and the body is discovered by her husband. The murdered woman also appears to have been sexually assaulted. The crime scene appears as if there was a break-in and robbery during which the suspect unexpectedly encountered the victim. Further investigation reveals that even though the house was ransacked, some items were left undisturbed, such as photos of the children on tables, family heirlooms, and so on. Also, the woman's panties were found down below her knees, which is not conducive for a sexual assault. In a true sexual assault, the panties would have been removed completely or torn off. In addition, the woman was found lying on her back in a fairly comfortable-looking position, not as if she had been struck on the head or stabbed and then fallen. All of this indicates that there was some "care" in the damage and staging of the house and the victim. Subsequently, the husband in this case was charged with his wife's murder.

These are all important factors in the how of the crime.

If we take all the elements that we have discussed and utilize them, the officer will have begun the investigation on the right foot by writing an excellent preliminary report.

Once a preliminary report has been written and is approved, it is submitted to the department and depending upon the nature of the incident, the report is either filed as a record of an event, or it is the beginning of an ongoing process.

Chapter Wrap-Up

When initiating contact and gathering information for your report, make sure that you get all of the information you need. Take a few seconds to make sure that you have all of the needed information; it can be embarrassing to return to a residence or to call people at a later date or time to retrieve important information that should be included in the report but that you forgot to obtain.

■ **From the Experts**

Your reports must reflect accurate information. Write what you know; do not include your personal feelings or emotions. Report what transpired. From the fictional television show, the point was very well made with a quote from Sergeant Joe Friday of the television series *Dragnet:* "Just the facts, only the facts."

■ **Caution**

When writing a report or traffic citation in your cruiser, always write at eye level, using the steering wheel for support. Do not write on your lap. By writing at eye level, you can observe what is going on around you rather than looking down and shutting out your environment.

■ **Key Terms**

preliminary report: The first report that is written upon receiving a call for or observing an incident that initiates the law enforcement function.

signature: A specific, unique act that can link an individual to other crimes. Many serial killers and rapists have signatures.

staging: When a suspect tries to make the crime scene appear as if something else has occurred or to make it so the evidence will lead the investigators away from the suspect.

subject: An individual who is a part of an investigation.

suspect: An individual who is believed to be responsible for the commission of a crime and is the primary focus of the investigation.

victim: An individual who has been hurt either physically, mentally, or emotionally as a result of the action of another.

witness: An individual who, by virtue of their presence or awareness of a situation, is looked to for any information that will lead to the rightful facts in determining the events of an incident.

■ **Your Assignment—Results**

In the opening scenario, you were asked what information you would gather regarding a two-vehicle accident. You should gather the following information:

Operator(s) (*passenger information as well)

- Name*
- Address*
- Date of birth*
- Driver's license number

- Driver's license state
- Phone numbers*
- Name of insurance company
- Statement of what happened

Vehicle information:
- Make of vehicle
- Model of vehicle
- License plate number
- Color of vehicle
- Year of vehicle
- Owner of vehicle (may be different from who was operating it)
- Damage to vehicle

Other information:
- Injuries, if any
- Statements and personal information, (e.g., name, address, etc.) from witnesses
- Diagram of the scene with the details drawn in
- Written statement of what you determined has occurred based on statements, diagrams, and the position of the vehicles involved

Your Next Assignment

You are responding to a call for a medical assist. You arrive at the residence and are greeted at the door by an elderly gentleman. He states that his wife has fallen out of bed and he needs help getting her back into bed.

When you get to the bedroom, you see an elderly woman on the floor. You determine that she is coherent and able to answer questions. You ask her if she is injured or if anything hurts her. She states that she is fine; however, you notice some bruising around her eye and cheek and some black and blue marks on her arms. You ask her how she hurt her face and her arms. She looks at her husband and says that they must be from the fall. She then states that she falls often. You help her get into bed and leave.

You will need some information to complete your police report. Answer the following questions and determine what additional information you may need and what else should be written into the report.

1. Which pieces of information should you gather from the husband?
2. Which pieces of information should you gather from the wife?
3. What information needs to be included in your report?
4. In the narrative or the summary, would you mention the bruises? If not, why not?
5. In the narrative or the summary, would you request a follow up from social services? Why or why not?
6. Would you inquire while at the scene as to who the family doctor is? Why or why not?

Call for Service

The following exercise is a report-writing challenge. With information provided, create your own version of what happened, writing an orderly and organized narrative of the incident.

A crime may or may not have been committed. If a crime has been committed, then have your witness and victims say so.

You are assigned to a call of a loud disturbance. The neighbor who called the disturbance in states that the husband and wife who live next door have been yelling at each other all day. When you arrive at the scene, you are met in the street by the neighbor, Mrs. Donna Masters. The family she is referring to is the Martins, John and Stephanie. You approach the residence and knock on the door. You hear some soft whispering, but no yelling or screaming. Mrs. Martin answers the door after a few minutes and appears to be upset, shaking and crying. She allows you to enter. The Martins have two children living at home: Timothy, age 11, and Cynthia, age 9.

In addition to the background provided, use the following information in creating your narrative:

Mrs. Donna Masters
145 Stewart Street
Any city, Any state
Phone: (321) 555-1441
Date of birth: February 17, 1955

Mr. John Martin
147 Stewart Street
Any city, Any state
Phone: (321) 555-1683
Date of birth: December 21, 1951

Mrs. Stephanie Martin
147 Stewart Street
Any city, Any state
Phone: (321) 555-1683
Date of birth: September 28, 1956

Follow-Up

Knowledge Objectives

- Describe what is considered "follow-up" information.
- Describe the two follow-up reports utilized in two different circumstances.

Skills Objectives

- Demonstrate the ability to seek additional information.
- Demonstrate the ability to ask proper questions.
- Demonstrate the ability to take efficient notes.
- Write an accurate supplementary account of an event.
- Use correct grammar and punctuation in a follow-up report.
- Ensure that the events in a follow-up report are in proper sequence.

In the previous chapter, we looked at a call for a medical assist regarding an elderly couple. It is now the next day, and you are the **TRIAD officer.** A TRIAD officer is an officer who is responsible for dealing with the welfare of the senior citizens in a community. Depending on the size of the department and the resources available, a department may or may not have a dedicated officer for these duties. You have just been forwarded a copy of the report regarding the elderly couple. You read the responding officer's information concerning the injuries and the comments the officer wrote regarding the looks that the wife gave her husband before answering the officer's questions.

- As the TRIAD officer, what would you do regarding this report?
- Would you contact any other agencies? If so, which agencies would you contact?

Introduction

This chapter examines the follow-up portion of the police report. We will see how information is retrieved from and added to the original report. Two examples of follow-up reports are provided. The first concerns a relatively simple case, and the second involves a more complicated case that includes a large amount of information. After reading the two cases, you will have a good idea of the follow-up information that is part of the police reporting process.

The Follow-Up Report

The last chapter discussed the preliminary report. Now, we examine the next part of the reporting process, the follow-up report. Follow-up reports are also referred to as *supplemental reports*. These are reports that are added to the case file when there is an ongoing investigation or when additional information has been identified.

In most cases, a call for service is completed during the initial investigation, and only a preliminary report needs to be written. However, follow-up is required when the incident cannot be resolved during the initial response, either because of the officer's work load; the unavailability of a victim, witnesses, or other figures; or the nature of the call.

Let's take a look at two examples of follow-up. The first example involves a minor incident that requires a very simple follow-up. The second example involves a major crime occurrence, where there is what seems to be endless follow-up.

Case 1

You have received a call that the residents at 123 Main Street leave their dog chained up outside during the day. The dog barks constantly, and the neighbors have finally decided to call the police. This is the first call to this address that your department has received regarding the dog issue. You arrive on the scene and observe that the dog is in good shape and well cared for. The dog has plenty of water, adequate shelter, and has plenty of room for exercise in the fenced-in yard.

You speak with the neighbor who called in about the problem, and as you do, several other neighbors come out and say that they, too, have a problem with the barking dog. You record all of their names and information for future reference in case it is needed and then approach the house. After knocking on the door several times, it is apparent that no one is home. A neighbor informs you that the owners of the dog are working and will return this evening. Because it is Friday, you are pretty sure you will find them at home the next day, Saturday, during your shift.

You return to your cruiser and inform the station dispatcher that you have cleared the call, that the dog is barking, that you will leave a note for the owners to call the station, and that you will return the next day to speak with them. (Depending on the jurisdiction and agency authority, this call may be referred to a municipal or county animal control unit if it does not fall under the control of the police department.)

Your preliminary report, which you submit prior to the end of your current shift (a normal requirement and expectation for most calls at most departments), states everything that occurred at the call. The preliminary report includes the following information: the neighbors' information; the time of day; the date; the condition of the dog; and the most important fact, that you heard the dog barking. You also note that you were unable to contact the owners, that you will do so on your next shift, and that you left a note for the owners to call the department so that they will know that you intend to return the next day.

The next day you arrive and observe that the dog is outside, but not barking. The owner is outside doing yard work. You speak with the owner and inform him of the problem. You tell him that you did in fact hear the dog barking and can understand why the neighbors called the police. You then inform the owner of his options, which are to either secure the dog inside, make arrangements with a dog sitter, or board the dog in a kennel while he is away at work. You also inform him that failure to correct the problem could result in a criminal complaint being issued for causing a disturbance in the neighborhood.

This completes the call. Until you get another call about the dog, you are finished with this incident. You may of course want to drive by the house every now and then and listen to hear if the dog is still barking.

The follow-up report contains the same reference or incident number as the original call. In most jurisdictions, all calls receive an incident number or some sort of reference number that is used to identify the call. Usually, the number is computer generated and signifies the order in which the call was arrived. For example, incident number 2004000001 was the first call received by the department in the year 2004; incident number 2004000002 was the second call received. The follow-up report contains the conversation the officer had with the dog's owner, the solutions offered, and the response of the owner. For example, the follow-up would include the owner's statement, "Okay, we will take care of it." You also may include in the report that you will occasionally drive by to check on the situation. You may either call the neighbor who complained and inform her of the results of the call or actually visit her. This would depend on whether the neighbor wants the owner to know who called or not. In most cases, a phone call, rather than a personal visit, is preferred.

Case 2

You have received a call to respond to the scene of housebreak in which jewelry and cash were taken. The burglary occurred while the occupants were away for the weekend. They just returned home and discovered the break-in. You are just arriving at the residence. It is Sunday evening around 7:30 P.M.

As you arrive, the owners of the house meet you in the front yard. They inform you that they arrived home about 5 minutes before they called the station. The husband states that when he got home, he entered the house and found the rear door kicked in. He then went upstairs and saw that his dresser drawers were on the floor and noticed that his small safe was missing. He then went outside and called the police. The husband also states that nobody but him has been in the house since they arrived home. His wife was busy with the kids and has not entered the house.

As the responding officer, you would most likely call for backup assistance. When backup arrives, you search the house from top to bottom to make sure that the suspect is not in the house.

After making sure that no one is inside who shouldn't be there, you clear the additional units. In some cases, the backup officers many write a supplemental report explaining what they did on the scene or the primary officer will note in his report that he was assisted by Unit #XXX on the call to search the premises.

At this point, depending on department policy, you may call the station for detectives to be sent to the residence to process the scene for fingerprints and other evidence. In some cases, the responding officer is capable of doing the printing and processing. (Processing may include photographing the scene as well as creating any sketches, if needed.)

You have checked the house and have identified where the thief entered. This is also called the *point of entry*. In this case, the point of entry is the back door. Field notes should include how the door was compromised; that is, whether it was smashed in, the lock broken, the lock picked, or the window on the door broken, and so on. If no obvious point of exit is found, it can be assumed that the suspect left the same way he came in—through the back door. The door will be checked for tool marks to determine if the thief pried it open with a crowbar, a screwdriver, or some other implement.

You and the owner then walk through the house to determine what has been moved, touched, or taken by the suspect. If anything looks as if it has been touched, it should be dusted for fingerprints or packaged for the purpose of processing it for prints back at the station.

After all of the items that have been touched have been printed and any items that have been taken or stolen have been identified and recorded, the next step is to do a neighborhood check to see if anyone has seen or heard anything over the weekend that was unusual or out of place.

In this case, all of the neighbors have been canvassed or asked except one family who is not at home. A note should be left for this family telling them to call the station. The note should include the reference number assigned to the case.

After checking with all of the neighbors and searching the house (inside and out) for evidence, you can now clear the call and write your preliminary report of the incident.

This preliminary report should have the following information:

- Names, addresses, phone numbers, and so on of all victims and neighbors
- When the house was vacant
- When the occupants returned
- What the point of entry was
- What the point of exit was
- How entry was made (smashed, pried, etc.)
- What was taken (full description and values)
- The type of house or dwelling (apartment building, condo, wood frame, etc.)
- If it can be determined, when the break-in may have occurred (this can be from witnesses who may have checked the house, relatives who entered to water plants, etc.)
- Any evidence recovered from the scene for processing (sometimes the thief will leave the tool used to open the door, etc.)
- Any other information that was gathered
- A narrative summary

In some agencies, preliminary reports may be "forced choice" reports, where all the options are on the form and the officer just has to check off the appropriate responses.

This would conclude the preliminary report for this call.

Over the next few days, additional information may be gathered. Fingerprints found at the scene may match a set in the "system," some of the stolen jewelry may turn up at the pawn shop, the owner may call or drop off a list of additional items also discovered missing that he did not identify initially, and so on. This information would be included in the follow-up report.

Note: In some states or jurisdictions, pawnshops may be required to provide a list of all transactions monthly to the police department and require proper identification on all exchanges. Proper identification may be a photocopy of a driver's license or an identification card. This information can lead police to a suspect. However, if there is no proof that the suspect actually entered the house and took the items, then the police may not be able to charge the suspect with the housebreak. However, the suspect could be charged with "receiving stolen property."

You can see the difference in the amount of information that can be generated after the preliminary investigation. After the initial response, anything that may lead you to the suspect will be included in the follow-up. The follow-up may include information such as the suspect's previous arrest records, fingerprint match information, identification information from witnesses, and information from the pawnshop owner. And, if you have a suspect who can be linked with other crimes, the suspect's signature information will also be included in the follow-up. All of this supplemental information is needed to prosecute the crime. The conclusion of the report and prosecution will be discussed in Chapter 7.

Chapter Wrap-Up

In-Service Training

All officers should carry a small notebook to take field notes in. A small spiral-bound or flip-type pad of paper that will fit in your pants or shirt pocket is best. Always make sure you have two working pens with you as well.

From the Experts

When writing a follow-up report, the who, what, where, why, when, and how are just as important as they were for the preliminary report.

Caution

You should never carry paperwork, writing pads, clipboards, traffic citations, or any other equipment or tools in your strong hand or gun hand.

Key Terms

TRIAD officer: A member of the community, in most cases an employee of the police department, who has received training from the AARP in the reduction of victimization and vulnerability of senior citizens.

Your Assignment—Results

As the TRIAD officer, it is your responsibility to follow up on any police reports that have been submitted to you from officers in the field. In this case, the first thing you should do is to return to the house and speak with the wife, alone. You should then speak with the husband. You would look for any inconsistencies in their stories. What you discover in the interviews determines whether further action is necessary. Other agencies or people that may be involved in this case include the following:

- Family members
- Family doctor
- Department of Elderly Affairs
- Department of Social Services
- If there is reason to believe a criminal act was committed, the District Attorney or prosecutorial agency should be contacted.

Your Next Assignment

You are assigned to the detective unit, and you have just been given a copy of a preliminary burglary report, submitted by a patrol officer from the previous evening shift.

As you read over the report, you discover that in the burglary that was reported, a DVD player and numerous DVDs were taken. The time frame of the housebreak was between 11:00 A.M. and 3:00 P.M. As the lead investigator in this case, which of the following actions would you take? Based on your selections in the following statements and using your own imagination, write a follow-up report that details what you have done with this case.

1. What would you look for at the location you have selected? Why?

2. Would you check local pawnshops or secondhand stores? Why or why not?

3. Let's say that you have a suspect in mind who you have arrested for the same types offenses in the past. What would you do? Why?

Call for Service

The previous chapter on preliminary reporting included a scenario regarding the Martin family. Using the following information that was obtained after the initial report was filed, write a follow-up report to add to the preliminary report. As with the assignment in Chapter 5, what you say is your decision. Make sure that your follow-up report is orderly, organized, and understandable.

- You have received additional information from Mrs. Martin's sister, who lives in another state. She tells you that that five years ago, while her sister and brother-in-law were vacationing, the police department in the vacation community responded to a call where Mrs. Martin told the police that her husband had hit her. The department in that community is the Happy Woods Police Department, and the investigating officer was Officer Mark Sherman. The sister's name is Meredith Stouffer of 77 Elm Street, Smithfield, Kansas. Her date of birth is August 9, 1958. Her phone number is (555) 433-9090.

You have spoken with Officer Sherman of the Happy Woods Police Department. He tells you that he was the one who investigated the call. He stated that he had observed some marks on Mrs. Martin's face and arms. He also stated that she was visibly upset and crying when he arrived. Mr. Martin was brought to the station and was to be detained until the following Monday (the incident occurred on a Saturday night) for a court appearance and arraignment. He was to be charged with domestic abuse. Officer Sherman further stated that Mrs. Martin dropped the charges the next day after returning to her home. She did not wish not to pursue the matter. She also stated that she would not testify against him and that she would not return to the state for any court appearances. Officer Sherman stated that the department had no choice but to drop the charges and release Mr. Martin. Mr. Martin was never formally charged in the matter and returned home.

Taking the Police Report to the Next Step—Court

Knowledge Objectives

- Review the preliminary report.
- Review the follow-up, or supplemental, report.
- Define the following terms: disposition, summons, subpoena, bail, personal recognizance, hold for trial, motions, pretrial conference.

Skills Objectives

- Demonstrate the ability to compile information from different sources.
- Demonstrate the ability to prepare a completed case file in an orderly manner.
- Demonstrate the ability to communicate with other agencies and/or departmental personnel to complete an investigation or reported incident.

You have just completed a thorough investigation of a motor vehicle accident in which there were serious personal injuries. You are the investigator assigned to the case, and you arrive on the scene approximately 20 minutes after the responding officer arrived. You get the responding officer's field notes. These notes describe what the officer observed when he arrived on the scene and detail any actions he took.

As you review the report, you notice that he had been approached by a witness. You, too, spoke with this same witness in your investigation. However, the witness gave two different accounts of what she had seen.

- What would you do?

Introduction

This chapter examines how to prepare for a court case and describes the other agencies that play an important role in the prosecution of an offense. We will also review what happens from the time an arrest is made until the case goes to trial.

You will see that with some cases, no matter how well you prepare for court, the issues presented in court may not even be related to the offense being charged. You will see how courts and juries make their decisions based on what is presented by the prosecution and the defense.

Preparing for Court

We now examine the final phase of the reporting process, the "conclusion." However, let's first review the first two steps of the police reporting process: the preliminary report and the follow-up report.

Preliminary and Follow-up Reports

The *preliminary report* is the first written record that explains the events that have occurred and the parties involved. A preliminary report should include the following information about an incident: the who, where, what, why, when, and how.

The *follow-up,* or *supplemental,* report is completed following the initial contact. The follow-up report includes any subsequent evidence, records, reports, or other forms of documentation that develop or are discovered after the initial investigation. Follow-up information may also come from other law enforcement, social, or government agencies. Keep in mind that in some cases a call may be completed or resolved during the initial contact. If so, then a follow-up report or investigation is not required.

If we look at the basic fundamentals of any story, they all have a beginning, a middle, and an end. Police reports have basically the same format, except that the parts are preliminary, follow-up, and conclusion. All three aspects of the police report may be contained in one preliminary report. The preliminary report may document the entire situation and include the conclusion of the incident. In such a case, a separate conclusive document is unnecessary.

When discussing the conclusion, it is important to realize that we are not always looking for a written police report with the word *Conclusion* as a heading. A conclusion can be whatever documents are needed to conclude the investigation or take it to the next level. A conclusion can be a warrant issued by the court for an arrest, a determination that no further police action should be taken and that the case or investigation is over, or that the facts presented define the suspect from a known person to an unknown. In the case where there may be a confession, or a written statement from the suspect, or some other conclusion of fact, then the Prosecutor or District Attorney would present this case to the next level or in this case, court or trial.

Where an Officer's Responsibility Ends

It is important to realize that when a police officer conducts an investigation, makes an arrest, or removes a child from the care and custody of his or her parents, the officer's job has been accomplished. The officer has used all the tools that he or she has been provided with to do this. He has received information from outside agencies when applicable. These outside sources may include the Board of Probation, other police departments, Department of Social Services, etc. These agencies supply additional or supporting documentation for the officer to make or build his case for presentation to the next step. For example, the Board of Probation will provide any criminal history, regardless of which jurisdiction the past offenses may have been committed in. However, once a suspect is brought before the court for arraignment or to be formally charged with the crime that he or she is being accused of, the police officer's job is done, except for the testimony the officer will present. This prosecution of the suspect is now in the hands of the courts, the attorneys, and the judges.

Whatever the court decides to do with the case, or the **disposition** of the case, is up to the court and the jury. Once a case goes to court, the police officer has no further jurisdiction or control. The matter is now in the hands of the federal, state, county, or local courts.

Unfortunately, many officers feel that if the person they brought forward is found "not guilty," then it is their fault. An officer may feel that he or she must have messed up or made mistakes. However, the court and the jury may not know all of the information that the police officers do. Remember, a police officer has firsthand knowledge of the laws, what transpired, and what was reported. The jury only hears what the judge and the attorneys want them to hear. Let's look at an example case.

Say that a small business owner calls the station to report that he had left his manager in charge of the store during a month-long vacation. This occurred seven months ago. Since that time, the owner has transformed his old archaic recordkeeping system of shoeboxes of receipts and handwritten ledgers into an elaborate computer system capable of modern recordkeeping.

The owner relates that a customer came in to have a product repaired that was under warranty. The customer hands the owner a handwritten transaction receipt for the purchase. The owner notes that the purchase was made during his month-long vacation. The owner looks for the record of the sale, but cannot find it. He attributes this to his past shoddy recordkeeping practices and the transition to the computer-based recordkeeping system. He honors the customer's warranty and makes the repair.

A few days later, a second customer comes in from the same purchase period and relates the same story, and again the owner cannot find any record of the transaction. It should be noted that both purchases were cash transactions. Over the next several months, the owner finds out that the parts for that particular product were defective, and as a result, there were 32 returns under the warranty. Of the 32 returns, 27 were purchased during his vacation and absence. Of those 27 returns, 16 were cash purchases. The other 11 were made either by check or credit card. For the 11 purchases made by check or credit card, the owner was able to find the transaction receipts in his old records. No receipts were found for the 16 cash transactions.

As a result of an investigation, the manager is charged with larceny (stealing) in the amount of $3,200.00 ($200.00 for each of the cash transactions that occurred during the vacation). It is important to note that the manager who was charged was the only person working at the business during that month. It is also important to know that for all 27 purchases made during that time period—the 16 in cash and the 11 by checks or credit cards—the customers who are now witnesses—were able to testify that the accused manager was the one who transacted the purchase.

The court proceedings take place, and the witnesses are called to testify on their experiences with the manager. The owner testifies about the poor recordkeeping system that was in place at the time. The prosecutor shows that no one other than the manager could have taken the money. All of the receipts in question were initialed by the accused.

The defense attorney presses the issue of the shoddy records and has the boxes brought to court and entered into evidence. The defense attorney asks the owner to find a record from the period that he was on vacation. After much shuffling through paperwork, going from one box to another, he finally, by chance, finds the paperwork. Of course the jury observed the lack of organization and frustration that the owner went through to find the record.

The defense rests without putting the accused manager on the stand. The prosecution cannot call him to the stand and question him. Since he is the defendant, he cannot be compelled to take the stand unless the defense puts him on the stand to testify. The prosecution cannot call him to the stand to ask questions of him. In closing arguments, the defense attorney focuses his closing statements on the owner's poor recordkeeping. The prosecution reiterates that no one else could have done it and that that all the witnesses testified that they gave the manager cash. The jury returns with a verdict of not guilty.

While the police know what actually transpired, the defense attorney had complete control of what the jury heard and saw and focused on the owner's poor recordkeeping. The defense attorney was able to plant seeds of doubt in the minds of the jury.

This is an instance where the outcome of a case was not representative of the investigation or the facts involved. You should realize that the games attorneys play are perfectly legal. The reason for this example is to demonstrate that the detective or police officer did everything correctly. What occurred in the trial was not under the officer's control. Although the outcome of the case was frustrating, it should not deter an officer from conducting as thorough an investigation as possible.

By now you may understand that the "conclusion" does not mean the end of a situation. It may mean the end of the police reporting function, but the incident may now have a new beginning in the court system.

From Arrest to Sentencing

The process of arrest to sentencing is as follows once the person has been arrested: he may be bailed depending upon the crime committed and his prior record and whether or not he has defaulted or not shown up at a previous court date or if he is a likely risk of fleeing. After he gets bailed or not the next step is the arraignment, where he will be formally charged with the crime for which he has been brought before the court. Sometimes there is a "show cause" hearing to determine if there is enough probable cause to go forward with the charges; this is held prior to the arraignment. After the arraignment there are motions. One type is a discovery motions, where the attorneys can ask for specific documents such as a police department policy to determine if the officer has in fact followed department protocol in order to make the arrest; copies of other past similar incidents. In the case of a motor vehicle accident he may request a printout of the accident location to see if it is a high risk area, trying to put the blame on the municipality for negligence by not addressing the danger of the location; etc. Other forms of motions can be for a continuance or for more time. These motions must be pretty precise as to what you are looking for and why. There may be other hearings for a plea bargain where a suspect may plead guilty to a lesser crime in order to avoid trial for the greater crime. These are all considered pre-trial hearings and take place prior to the actual trial. These hearings can take months.

As mentioned earlier, the disposition of the case is up to the court and the jury. For cases that are set to go to trial or sent to another agency, the paperwork has only just begun. If the next step is the courts, summonses and subpoenas must be sent out. A **summons** is a notice that requires the accused to come forward to face the court for possible impending charges. A **subpoena** is a notice to a person that she must come forward to act as a witness either for the prosecution or for the defense.

Arraignment

Complaint forms must be filled out depending upon the jurisdiction and responsibilities, these may be filled out by the police officer, the police department prosecutor, or the county or court prosecutor or District Attorney. At this time they are filed in the courthouse so that the clerk or magistrate can officially charge the person with the offense for which he is to be arraigned. An **arraignment** is when the person is brought before the judge and formally charged. At this time, any records of past offenses are brought to the attention of the judge by the probation department. At the arraignment, the police department prosecutor or court officer will most likely read the police report as it has been submitted before the court. The judge can now hear arguments from the prosecution and the defense attorneys as to whether bail should be set, whether the person is to be held for trial, or if the suspect is to be released on his personal recognizance. The following are all important court terms that you should be familiar with:

- **Personal recognizance.** A person being charged is released on his personal recognizance when the court has no reason to hold the accused until the trial date. For example, the person being charged may have a job, a family, be a respected member of the community, have strong ties to the area, have no record of previous offenses, and so on. In these cases, the person usually signs a document where he promises to be in court at the appointed time.

- **Bail.** The judge imposes bail when there is a possible likelihood that the person will not show up to court on the date of the court case. The bail amount is set based on risk factors. If the judge believes that the accused will skip out on the trial, then the bail may be equal to the person's mortgage or home value so that the accused has to put the house up for collateral. Most states or jurisdictions have bail companies or bail bondsmen. These people put up the bail for the offender for a fee. In most cases, the fee is a **surety**, or token of the total bail amount. For example, the bail company many require a $10.00 surety for every $100.00 of the bail amount. The rest of the bail amount would be covered by a promissory note to the court and a signed contract by the parties who procured the bail.

- **Held for trial.** In some cases, the crime committed is so serious that the court will not let the accused remain free until the trial date. The judge may want the person to remain in custody because the accused may be of harm to himself or herself or others or is very likely to flee. In cases where the mental state of the accused is an issue, the judge will usually send the person to a secure location for a psychological evaluation to determine if the accused is mentally capable of standing trial.

In cases in which the offense is minor (e.g., traffic violations, shoplifting, larcenies, etc.), the court may allow the person to go to trial at the same time or date as the arraignment. During the arraignment, the judge will ask the person if he wishes to plead guilty or not guilty. If the person pleads guilty, the judge or some other court official will make sure the person understands the consequences of the guilty plea. The judge or court official then determines if he will allow the accused to proceed with the guilty plea.

Usually, if a person pleads guilty, the court will not allow any appeals. This is to dissuade the accused from changing his plea if the sentence is longer or the fine is in excess of what he thought it would be. If guilty pleas could be appealed, the accused wouldn't have anything to lose by changing his plea to not guilty and appealing the case, hopefully getting a lighter disposition the second time around. The courts realize this; judges do not want to tie up the courts by giving everyone a second trial.

Continuance

The period of time between the trial and the arraignment is called the *continuance*. This is because from the time of arraignment until the next court date, the case has been continued.

It is very likely that when a trial date is set, that date may also be continued. The reasons for a continuance are many: motions of discovery, time needed for lab or test results, or time needed to retrieve documents.

Motions   A **motion** is the process by which either attorney can ask for additional time or information. A defense attorney can request that evidence, statements, and other information that may have been obtained illegally be eliminated from the court proceedings. Note that motions take place prior to the trial.

The attorneys for both the defense and the prosecution may ask for a continuance. A *motions of discovery* means they are asking for extra time to gather all of the relevant information about a particular case. A motion of discovery is a type of motion that can be requested, usually by the defense, as the prosecution has sufficient information to make the case.

For example, the defense attorney may have discovered during the review and reading of the police report(s) that he wants copies of the police department's policies and procedures manuals. The defense attorney would file a motion of discovery to obtain these documents. The policies and procedures manuals outline exactly what the officer is allowed to do in various instances. The defense attorney may try to use these documents to prove that the officer acted wrongly—whether or not that is in fact the case.

Other issues brought up before the court during the motions process are the legality of evidence seizure, the actual arrest, if all of the elements of a crime were met to justify an arrest, and so on. At a motions hearing the judge will decide whether to allow or deny the motions. The judge may allow all entered evidence, deny the attorney copies of department manuals, and so on.

Lab Results   A continuance may be granted to obtain the lab results or psychological evaluations. Lab results are necessary when the evidence depends on DNA results or lab tests for the chemical analysis and positive detection of drugs (e.g., to make sure the white powder was cocaine or heroin or some other drug, not baking soda). Lab tests and psychological evaluations take time and may not be completed by the original trial date. Waiting for such results is a valid reason for a continuance.

Other Information   In addition, continuances may be granted when copies of police reports or probation records from other jurisdictions must be retrieved from archives.

Pretrial Conference

The next step in the trial process may be **pretrial conference**. At the pretrial conference, the attorneys and the court official, who may be a judge, a clerk, a mediator, or a magistrate, sit down and see if they can work out any deals to eliminate back ups in the court system. Both sides of the case, the defense *and* the prosecution, must agree on the outcome of any negotiations.

Trial

After all of these pretrial meetings and motions, the trial eventually takes place. Regardless of what has occurred, the suspect still must go before the judge for a disposition. The disposition can be informal, where the charges are read and the judge decides, or it can be a full trial with a jury and witnesses.

The police officer's role in the trial is to testify as to what he saw and the actions he took, and the reasons he took those actions. He will be subject to cross-examination from the defense who will try to confuse the officer to make him appear to be unsure of himself. The police officer's written report is incredibly useful if written well. The police officer can refresh his memory based on the report that may have been written years before. These are the facts that allowed the incident to be brought to court and there was evidentially enough probable cause for the court to allow this.

Keep in mind that the time period from arrest to trial can be months or even years. If you look at the dates that some trials occur and compare that date with the date that the offense took place, you may be surprised at how much time lawyers need and judges allow.

After the trial, if the accused is found to be guilty, the conviction can be appealed. If the accused is found to be innocent, the prosecution cannot appeal the ruling. Note that the accused can only be placed on trial once for the offense that he is charged with committing, hence the term *double jeopardy*.

If the accused is found to be guilty and decides to appeal, the judge can determine if the accused should be confined or released until all appeals have been exhausted. In most cases, the accused is confined after being found guilty.

The next and final step in the trial process is the sentencing. At the sentencing, the judge assigns the punishment. The punishment can be jail time, fines, or both.

The trial process can vary. States and even specific courts have their own processes. This discussion served to familiarize you with the police reporting process and how it relates to the trial process.

Chapter Wrap-Up

Key Terms

arraignment: The first stage of a formal charging of an individual with a crime or offense.

bail: Collateral that is usually submitted as an assurance for the defendant's appearance before the court at the next proceeding. Bail can be in cash or in a surety.

disposition: The outcome of a court proceeding. The disposition could be guilty, not guilty, not guilty by reason of insanity, or continued without a finding.

held for trial: When a judge orders a defendant to be held in custody until the trial. The decision is based on the suspect's past record, whether the suspect is a flight risk, as well as the severity of the crime and whether there is a likelihood of the suspect committing a similar crime while free awaiting trial.

motion: The process by which the defense attorney can request evidence, statements, and other information that the attorney feels may have been obtained illegally and should be eliminated from the court proceedings. Motions take place prior to the trial.

personal recognizance: A person being charged is released on his or her personal recognizance when the court has no reason to hold the accused until the trial date.

pretrial conference: When the attorneys, both defense and prosecution, meet with the judge to outline the court case before them. If there are any plea bargains or deals to be made, this is where they will be presented.

subpoena: A notice to a person that he must come forward as a witness either for the prosecution or for the defense.

summons: A notice that requires a person to come forward to face the court for possible impending charges.

surety: A token of the total bail amount, or collateral. Can be a mortgage or a deed that has a substantial value that covers the cost of the bail.

Your Assignment—Results

With regard to the two conflicting statement from the same witness, you should first speak with the responding officer who spoke with the witness initially to make sure that the officer accurately recorded what she said. If the officer states he recorded it correctly, your next move would be to contact the witness to try and clarify what she was trying to say each time and why there was a discrepancy between the two accounts. In any case, you should report the statement as initially reported by the responding officer as well as how it was reported to you the second time. You must also include the results of the third interview you conducted as well. The facts must be reported as they occurred. It is not up to you to determine what she meant at which time. This particular case may end up in civil court as well as criminal court if any charges are filed. The judge or the jury must hear the events of what happened as they happened; they will then decide how to interpret them themselves.

Your Next Assignment

For each of the following calls, place an "F" on the blank if you feel that follow-up information is needed. If you feel that no formal report is required, place an "N" on the line, for "no report." Leave the line blank if you feel that a preliminary report is all that is needed. Be prepared to defend your answers.

_____ 1. A burglary occurred in which jewelry was taken.

_____ 2. An officer gives a traffic citation for a red-light violation, there is no confrontation between the operator of the car and the officer.

_____ 3. There was an attempted housebreak and the suspect did not gain entry.

_____ 4. A bank is held up in an armed robbery.

_____ 5. An irate citizen calls to complain about a traffic ticket.

_____ 6. You responded as a back-up officer to a motor vehicle accident. You had to accompany the ambulance to the hospital with an injured operator and stand by until the investigating officer showed up at the hospital.

_____ 7. When issuing a parking ticket for an overtime violation at a parking meter, the owner of the vehicle comes out after you have placed the violation on the windshield and begins to argue or complain.

_____ 8. You issue a parking ticket for an overtime violation at a parking meter.

_____ 9. While on patrol, you investigate graffiti that was painted on the side of a building.

_____ 10. You observe that a traffic light is not functioning properly.

Call for Service

Using all the information you have been provided in Chapters 5, 6, and 7, create a report with any follow-up data and prepare it for submission to the court for the arraignment as a completed package. You can make up the particulars as far as statements, reports, and so. However, use the following information when drafting your report:

- **The call for service:** A report of a loud argument in an apartment
- **Reporting parties:** A husband and wife
- **Witnesses:** The couple's 15-year-old son and his 15-year-old friend who was also at the house

Your report should include statements by all four parties if you feel that they are necessary. Whether you include all four will depend on what determine has occurred. Did you make an arrest? Do not be concerned with the legality of the arrest at this time, just state whether an arrest was made and why.

The purpose of this exercise is to record information accurately. The emphasis should be on completeness, organization, and the presentation of the facts.

Interviews and Interrogations

Knowledge Objectives

- Define *interview* and *interrogation*.
- Describe *Miranda* rights.
- Discuss issues involved with questioning people on the street.

Skills Objectives

- Demonstrate the ability to control a conversation.
- Demonstrate the ability to extract the information needed from a suspect.
- Demonstrate the ability to decipher responses.
- Demonstrate the ability to formulate an orderly statement.

You have just made an arrest for a handbag-snatch incident, which is sometimes classified as an unarmed robbery, depending on state law. The suspect matches the description of suspects in other, similar incidents. The suspect has been brought to the station and is in the process of being booked. Booking is the process of administratively entering a person into the criminal justice system. This is where he is photographed, printed, given his Miranda rights, and processed initially by having an arrest record filled out. He most likely will be placed in a jail cell at a holding facility until his appearance in court or he will be bailed out. After obtaining the suspect's personal information (i.e., name, address, etc.), you advise the suspect of his rights (Miranda). The suspect states that at this time he does not wish to answer any questions without an attorney present.

- Do you continue with the booking process, which may include asking the suspect for additional personal information?
- Can you ask the suspect questions about other incidents of handbag snatches that he may have been involved in?

■ Introduction

This chapter explores interviewing and interrogation and how they differ. The chapter also presents information about *Miranda* rights. You will learn when a suspect should be read his rights and whether questioning must stop after a suspect has been read his rights. You will also learn what information can be obtained without reading *Miranda* rights.

■ Interviewing and Interrogation

Police officers learn about the circumstances of a call, what any witnesses saw, what the victim was faced with, and what the suspect did and why through interviewing and interrogation. A police officer should always control the conversation; he should be asking the questions and listening to the answers. The subject being questioned should not have the opportunity to take that role. The ability to control the interview is an indication of a good interviewer and one not as good. The control can be maintained by asking yes or no questions or questions that would elicit a particular type of response (i.e., instead of how tall was he? ask, was he taller or shorter than me?). These responses give clearer, better, and more accurate detail of the incident being questioned about.

Interviews and interrogations differ specifically in the manner that interviews are any conversation with witnesses, victims, or other involved parties such as neighbors and friends who may be able to provide information. Whereas an interrogation is specifically designed as a solicitation of information from a suspect who the officer believes has committed a crime or is involved in some manner and there may be some form of prosecutorial action taken, an interview can turn into an interrogation as a result of the information provided if some form of involvement has been determined.

Both interviews and interrogations are voluntary; any person can refuse to speak with an officer either as a suspect, witness, victim, etc. In the case of a suspect, a refusal to speak may be an indicator of some involvement, as a reasonable and prudent person who had nothing to hide wouldn't necessarily refuse to speak to the police. Officers should make these notes in their report.

Interviews

An **interview** is a voluntary conversation that is usually performed at the start of an investigation to help an officer determine what has transpired. The purpose of the interview is to determine if a crime has in fact occurred, and if so, who may have committed the crime. In some cases, the interview may just help the officer determine what has happened and may not necessarily involve a crime and a suspect. For example, when a citizen calls to report a power outage or a malfunctioning traffic signal, the purpose of the interview is only to gain information—it does not involve a crime. However, in the case of a missing child, an interview will be required to determine information about the child and any suspects who may have abducted the child.

Any two-way conversation in which questions from one party are asked of another is an interview. In the chapter on preliminary reporting, you learned what information a police officer needs to gather right at the start of an investigation. This information is gathered through interviews. The information gathered in these preliminary interviews greatly affects what transpires in the ongoing investigation.

When conducting an interview, it is important to let the person talk and explain what has occurred. The officer should direct the conversation by asking pointed questions. Oftentimes when trying to remember information about a suspect's description, a witness may draw a blank and not remember. One technique an officer can use to help the witness or victim remember is to ask: "Is the person taller or shorter than me?" From there, the next question could be: "Is the suspect older or younger than me?" By directing the interview, the officer can then gather information that may help to identify or apprehend the suspect.

If the person being interviewed may in fact be a suspect, or may develop into a suspect, then the interview has to take a different course. Once the officer has acquired information from the suspect, either through answers or statements made by the "suspected" individual, that leads the officer to determine probable cause *the interview must stop immediately.* Probable cause is when the officer has reason to believe that the person may have committed an offense or have been involved in the commission of the crime. Once probable cause is established, the interview now takes on a whole new life.

Probable cause requires that the officer invoke *Miranda* and advise the suspect of his rights. The suspect's rights, as defined by the courts, are that the suspect must be informed of and acknowledge that he has been informed of the following:

- *"You have the right to remain silent."*
- *"If you give up the right to remain silent, anything you say can and will be used against you in a court of law."*
- *"You have the right to speak with an attorney and to have the attorney present during questioning."*
- *"If you so desire an attorney and cannot afford one, an attorney will be appointed for you with out charge before questioning."*
- *"You can decide at anytime to exercise these rights and not answer any questions or make any statement."* (This statement is added in some jurisdictions.)
- *"Do you understand each of these rights as I have explained to you?"*
- *"Do you wish to give up the right to remain silent?"*
- *"Do you wish to give up the right to speak to an attorney and have him present during questioning?"*

After a suspect has been read his *Miranda* rights, the suspect is given a form that has the written version of what has been read to him. The suspect must initial each statement and sign and date at the bottom of the form, acknowledging that the suspect understands his rights and whether he wishes to answer questions or remain silent.

If a suspect invokes his rights and states that he does not wish to talk, and then later decides to talk, the officer is best advised not to question the suspect unless the suspect's attorney is present. *If a suspect states that he doesn't want to say anything, then the interview is over.*

Note that you are not required to read a suspect his *Miranda* rights unless you intend to ask the suspect questions about the incident for which he is being charged. However, if a suspect voluntarily makes statements that are relevant and incriminating, then you must stop the suspect and advise the suspect of his rights. Routine information gathered at the scene of a crime, such as the person's name, address, whether or not they own the vehicle, and so on, do not require the reading of *Miranda* rights.

Additionally, when conducting a field interview or inquiry, you do not need to read *Miranda* rights to simply ask: "Who are you?" "Where are you going?" or similar questions. A *field interview* (FI) is when you stop and ask questions of an individual or group of individuals who are out at a late hour hanging around where they shouldn't be or in an area prone to crime or gang activity. Information that can be obtained during a field interview without the reading of *Miranda* rights includes the following:

- Name
- Subject's nicknames
- Gang names or "tags"
- Date of birth
- Address
- Driver's license information
- Physical description: height, weight, eye color, hair color, race, scars, deformities, tattoos, etc.
- Occupation
- Vehicle information
- Clothing description
- Intended destination and where he has just come from
- If the person has a criminal record or is on parole/probation

Interrogation

An **interrogation** is when you question a person you believe to be involved in the crime you are investigating. An interrogation can be conducted anywhere, but it should usually be held in a controlled area, such as an "interview" room at the station. Such interview rooms are used for both interviews and interrogations, but the term *interrogation* is intimidating and does not need to be advertised with signage on the door of the room.

Interview rooms are usually equipped with a table and three chairs: one for the subject being interviewed and two for the officers conducting the interview or interrogation. Additional chairs may be brought in for parents, when the suspects are juveniles; attorneys; or additional advocates, as needed or required by local or state law. Usually, the room is equipped with an audio or video recording device. In some cases, a hidden viewing window, or one-way glass, which separates the interview room from an observation room may have audio capabilities in the room where the observations are being made.

When interrogating a suspect, you should let the suspect talk as much as he wants. Don't interrupt the suspect; let the suspect say what he has to say in response to a question. If you have facts that you wish to use to rebut any statements made by the suspect, use them. He will now know that you know some of the elements that he was trying to hide or deny. Use the information you have in a way as to be able to extract what information you can from the suspect, that is, if he is willing to talk to you and give you the answers you seek. When the suspect has answered all of your questions, have the suspect write out his own statement. Or you many write the statement, using the suspect's words exactly. Do not paraphrase what the suspect has said. After the statement has been written, you should have the suspect date and sign it.

Body language is an important part of the interrogation process. Many investigators take great credence in body language and use it to determine if the suspect is lying or telling the truth. Body language and the physical actions of the person interviewed can be revealing of whether the subject is telling the truth or lying. A person who is lying will not usually look the interviewer in the eye, and will instead look away or downward. Other actions from a subject may be how he responds to questions and accusations; a person who is guilty may respond in a timid and cooperative manner in order to be nice and feel as if he is gaining the trust of the interviewer by cooperating. Whereas a subject who is not guilty will reply to accusations very abruptly and angered, as his personal integrity is being attacked and he takes pride in protecting his own values.

Based on the results of the interrogation, the investigators' suspicions about the suspect's role in the crime will either be enhanced or the investigators will determine that the person is no longer a suspect.

All interrogations do not result in a confession. However, a confession is not required to charge a suspect with a crime and take the case to court. Most cases require evidence from the crime scene, statements from the victim and witnesses, and statements made by the suspect during interviews and interrogations.

When dealing with juveniles, an interested party, ideally a parent or guardian, should be present to act on the juvenile's behalf. The police should not display a show of force, such as having several officers present during questioning, when interrogating a juvenile.

These statements that have been recorded in the interview or in the interrogation should be transcribed to paper as a written statement. Regardless of the sequence or order of the statement, the officer should, using his notes, write the statement in an orderly fashion for the individual who gave it to sign. Remember, people don't always talk in chronological sequence, but it is extremely important to make order out of disorder.

Questioning Suspects on the Street or During Motor Vehicle Stops

Once an officer stops a motor vehicle, any questioning of the suspect should be conducted at the location of the stop. Investigative stops are intended to be on-the-spot inquiries. During such stops, you may need to verify the information obtained from the suspect. In such cases, it may be necessary to move a short distance in order to use a radio or a telephone. Under special circumstances, such as the gathering of a hostile crowd, heavy traffic, or the necessity to use the police radio, you many place the suspect in the rear seat of the police vehicle.

As part of a threshold inquiry, an officer may detain a suspect for a short time so that an eyewitness may be brought to the scene to make an "in-person" identification.

An officer may also bring a suspect back to the scene for a one-on-one identification; this is where a victim or witness may be asked to identify the individual as the one who committed the crime. This can also exonerate an innocent person who looked like the suspect. One-on-one confrontations conducted promptly after the commission of a crime are not considered a violation of due process rights despite the absence of exigent circumstances. Due process are the rights we all enjoy as provided by the U.S. Constitution, and address the right to a fair and speedy trial, the right to face our accusers, and the right to be free from double jeopardy (i.e., cannot be tried for the same offense twice).

If a stopped person is told to move to another location or if the person tries to leave but the officer orders the person to stay where he is, the person may, at that point, be considered "in custody" (although not under arrest). Once a person is in custody, any additional questioning by police must be preceded by reading the *Miranda* warning and eliciting a waiver from the suspect.

Chapter Wrap-Up

In-Service Training

When conducting an interview or an interrogation, do not overpower the subject by having numerous officials present; two interviewers are usually adequate for a given situation. If more than two officers are present, the defense attorney may say that you used intimidation to coerce a confession from the suspect. When interviewing or interrogating a juvenile, a parent, guardian, or interested party should be present.

From the Experts

When a suspect is being interviewed and begins to talk, let the suspect continue; don't interrupt to ask questions. Interrupting the suspect may throw off his train of thought, causing the suspect to become confused and get sidetracked. Let the suspect talk, then ask questions.

Caution

No matter how well an interrogation is going or how comfortable you feel in the presence of a suspect, *never drop your guard*. Always be alert, cautious, and ready to respond. Once the suspect feels that he has been cornered either by a confession or an admission, the suspect may realize that his freedom is in jeopardy. The suspect may not be ready for that and act out accordingly.

Key Terms

interrogation: When you question a person you believe is involved in the crime you are investigating.

interview: A voluntary conversation that is usually performed at the start of an investigation to help an officer determine what has transpired. The purpose of the interview is to determine if a crime has in fact occurred, and if so, who may have committed the crime.

Your Assignment—Results

With regard to the opening assignment, you advise the suspect of his rights (*Miranda*). Those rights include the right to an attorney and the right to remain silent. If the suspect exercises his rights and requests an attorney, then all questioning relative to the crime for which he is being charged with or any crimes you may associate him with *must cease immediately*. However, you may continue with procedural questions that are associated with the booking process. For example: in a case of driving under the influence, where the suspect has refused to speak after his rights have been given, you cannot question him relative to the incident or accident, or arrest for which he is being charged. If you have other questions to ask him, as in his right to take or refuse a breathalyzer test or a field sobriety test in the station, you may ask these.

Your Next Assignment

You have made an arrest for a motor vehicle break-in. The suspect was caught inside of someone else's vehicle and was attempting to steal a radio. You bring the suspect to the station and book him. You read him his rights; he invokes his right to remain silent and will not speak without an attorney present. He is placed in a jail cell, because he cannot make bail. A few hours later, he tells you that he is willing to talk now.

- Do you question him now that he is willing to talk to you?
- Can you question him about the crime he is being charged with?
- Can you ask him what he does with the stolen property?
- Can you question the suspect in any way?
- Can you question him if he signs a waiver, relinquishing his rights to remain silent and to have an attorney present?

Call for Service

You are at the station waiting for a witness to arrive who observed a hit-and-run motor vehicle accident that resulted in serious personal injury to a pedestrian. You are an investigator on the Accident Reconstruction team. You have been trained to reconstruct the scenes of automobile accidents. As the lead investigator of this team, you have prepared a list of questions to ask the witness when she arrives. Using common sense, identify and list the questions that you would ask the witness.

CHAPTER

9

General Searches and Searches of Persons

Knowledge Objectives

- Discuss the Fourth Amendment as it relates to searches.
- Define the following: abandoned property, administrative search, body cavity search, consent search, open fields, search incidental to an arrest, stop-and-frisk search, strip search, threshold inquiry.
- Identify the grounds for making a stop.
- Describe how to conduct a search.

Skills Objectives

- Understand the ability to physically control a person in order to conduct a search.
- Be alert to identify movement by a subject being searched that may be threatening.

You are on patrol, and it is 2:00 A.M. You are checking the downtown business district, which has experienced several breaking and entering incidents over the last few weeks. While patrolling the area, you observe a male who appears to be lurking in a darkened doorway of a business. As you approach in your cruiser, he sees you and ducks deeper into the doorway, further into the darkness. You stop your cruiser and get out and approach him. You observe and recognize him to be someone who has been arrested previously for breaking into businesses. As you approach him, you observe a bulge in his front pocket. You look around, approaching with your flashlight, but do not see any signs of a break-in or attempted break-in.

- Can you question this person about his presence and actions?
- Can you search him?
- Do you need to administer him his Miranda rights prior to questioning him?

Introduction

In this chapter, you will learn what rights and restrictions the police have with regard to questioning and searching people. You also will learn how the U.S. Constitution and the Bill of Rights protect citizens from unreasonable searches and seizures of their person or property. You also will examine some of the various court cases that have been brought before the U.S. Supreme Court and the supreme courts of individual states that further protect those rights. You will also gain a clear understanding of what constitutes suspicion and when the police have probable cause.

Search and Seizure

Thus far, you have learned about the primary functions of the police, police officers' duties, the tools and equipment needed and used by police officers, how incidents are reported, and how the police question and interview people. We now move on to another area of police work—the physical contact an officer has with a subject or suspect. This text does not discuss defensive tactics for dealing with hostile or aggressive people. This text will assume that we are dealing with people who are fairly compliant.

In this chapter, you will read about several court cases that have determined when an officer is allowed to search a person. You will also learn where the police's authority to conduct searches and seizures is derived from. You will also learn about a number of terms that refer to various aspects of searches and seizures. The following excerpt from the Waltham Police Department Manual (Waltham, Massachusetts) provides a good working definition of *searches and seizures:*

> *The term searches and seizures includes examination of persons or places for the discovery of property stolen or otherwise unlawfully obtained or held, or of evidence of the commission of crime, and the taking into legal custody of such property or evidence for presentation to the court. Failure to comply with the legal technicalities, which govern these procedures, results in more failures to obtain convictions than any other source. The Fourth Amendment to the United States Constitution has been interpreted by the United States Supreme Court to require that, whenever possible and practicable, with certain limited exceptions, a police officer should always obtain a valid search warrant in advance. [Mincey v. Arizona, 437 U.S. 385, 89 S. Ct. 2408 (1978).]*

You also should be familiar with what the Fourth Amendment of the U.S. Constitution declares about searches and seizures:

> *The right of people to be secure in their persons, houses, papers, and effects, against unreasonable searches and seizures, shall not be violated, and no warrants shall issue, but upon*

probable cause, supported by oath or affirmation, and particularly describing the place to be searched, and the person or things to be seized.

The following terms and court cases will aid in your understanding of lawful searches and seizures and where the police derive their powers to conduct them.

Abandoned Property

Experienced police investigators recognize that highly incriminating evidence may often be found in wastebaskets, trash receptacles, or garbage barrels. Garbage or trash that has been left in an area particularly suited for public view and inspection for the express purpose of having strangers take it and dispose of it no longer enjoys the protection associated with the property that individuals associate with a reasonable expectation of privacy. Such garbage or trash is considered **abandoned property.**

In *Abel v. United States,* the U.S. Supreme Court observed that once Abel had vacated the premises (a hotel room):

> In Abel v. United States, 362 U.S. 217, 4 L. Ed. 2d 668, 80 S. Ct. 683(1960), the petitioner had been arrested by the Immigration and Naturalization Service (INS), on the basis of [*816] an administrative warrant that, he claimed, had been issued on pretextual grounds in order to enable the Federal Bureau of Investigation (FBI) to search his room after his arrest. We regarded this as an allegation of "serious misconduct," but rejected Abel's claims on the ground that "[a] finding of bad faith is . . . not open to us on th[e] record" in light of the findings below, including the finding that "'the proceedings taken by the [INS] differed in no respect from what would have been done in the case of an individual concerning whom [there was no pending FBI investigation],'" id., at 226-227. But it is a long leap from the proposition that following regular procedures is some evidence of lack of pretext to the proposition that failure to follow regular procedures proves (or is an operational substitute for) pretext. Abel, *moreover, did not involve the assertion that pretext could invalidate a search or seizure for which there was probable cause . . . that it was not unlawful to seize (without a warrant) the entire contents of a wastebasket, even though some of the contents had no connection with the crime. So far as the records show, the petitioner (Abel) had abandoned these articles. He had thrown them away. So far as he was concerned they were abandoned goods. There can be nothing unlawful in the Government's appropriation of such abandoned property.*

In *California v. Greenwood,* the U.S. Supreme Court held that the Fourth Amendment to the U.S. Constitution does not prohibit the warrantless search or seizure of garbage left for collection outside the curtilage of a home. The court also ruled that there is no Fourth Amendment protection once one exposes his or her garbage to the public.

With regard to abandonment of premises such as an apartment or hotel room, the courts have noted that abandonment consists of the act of leaving coupled with an intention not to return.

Administrative Searches

Under certain circumstances, the police may engage in warrantless searches or inspections as part of their administrative functions. These searches are termed **administrative searches.** For example, it is proper to search a person who is about to visit an arrestee in a jail cell if the visitor would otherwise be able to smuggle a weapon or contraband to the arrestee.

Body Cavity Searches

A **body cavity search** is an intrusive search. A body cavity search is a search that includes some degree of touching and probing of the anus and/or vagina. It allows the searcher to examine a person's body cavities in order to retrieve or search for contraband or *fruits of the crime.* Fruits of the crime are additional evidence of an illegal act.

In most jurisdictions, a warrant is required to conduct a body cavity search, and the search must be conducted in a medical facility by a physician and conducted in such a way as to prevent and/or limit the humiliation of the person being searched. The Massachusetts Supreme Judicial Court commented on body cavity searches in *Rodriques v. Furtado*:

> *It is difficult to imagine a more intrusive, humiliating, and demeaning search than one conducted inside a [person's] body. Where an officer seeks to conduct a search in someone's body, a warrant must be issued by a judge, supported by a strong showing of particularized need and a high degree of probable cause.*

The police must have probable cause to believe that the contraband or other items of evidentiary value is actually inside the cavity, independent of whether there is probable cause to believe that the individual being searched is hiding contraband elsewhere in his or her home or on his or her person.

The warrant for a body cavity search must be authorized by a judge, not by an officer of the court (i.e., a clerk magistrate cannot approve a search). Once a search warrant has been obtained, the body cavity search shall take place as soon as practicable.

Strip Searches

A Massachusetts court has defined **strip searches** as "an inspection of a naked individual without any scrutiny of his or her body cavities." Strip searches are conducted only when the circumstances and/or nature of the arrest causes the booking or arresting officer to have probable cause to believe that a weapon, item of evidentiary value, and/or contraband may be concealed upon the prisoner in such a manner that it would not be discovered by a conventional prisoner inventory search or search incident to arrest.

Such searches are usually limited as to who can conduct them. Usually, a supervisor or commanding officer must authorize that such a search is needed. If authorized, the search must be performed by members of the same sex as the prisoner being searched and conducted in a private room or area.

Strip searches are distinguishable from body cavity searches. The difference is that a strip search is limited to examining the prisoner's body as it exists. The prisoner is naked to ensure that a weapon, an item of evidentiary value, and/or contraband are not concealed under the person's garments. The searching officer is allowed to separate the prisoners buttocks to ensure that nothing is being concealed just outside the anus. If items are visible and inside the anus, then the search becomes a body cavity search, and the relevant laws and rules apply.

Consent Searches

With a **consent search**, an individual gives his or her consent for the police to conduct a search of his or her property. A consent search is a voluntary surrendering of a fundamental constitutional protection and will be closely looked at by the courts if it is used. In many cases, it is a recognized exception to the search warrant requirement. It may be the quickest and easiest way for the police to gain lawful access to the premises, whether a residence or business, in the investigation of crime.

One issue that arises with regard to consensual searches is who is allowed to give lawful consent to the police for an entry and search. In addition, whether the consent was given voluntarily may be a factor in a trial, in motions, or in the pretrial conference. However, when properly used, consent to search may speed up a criminal investigation.

In fact, the police may participate in a warrantless search after they have obtained consent even in circumstances where they do not have probable cause. The U.S. Supreme Court summarized this police procedure as follows in *Schneckloth v. Bustamonte*:

> *In situations where the police may have some evidence of illicit activity, but lack probable cause to arrest, a search authorized by valid consent may be the only means of obtaining important and reliable evidence. A search pursuant to consent may result in considerably less*

inconvenience for the subject of the search, and properly conducted, is a constitutionally permissible and wholly legitimate aspect of effective police activity.

Consent is a question of fact to be determined by the circumstances in each individual case. For a consent search to take place, and for any evidence found to be admissible in court, two conditions must be met:

- First, the consenting party must have the lawful authority over the premises or property in order to be able to give consent to a search of the premise or property in question. For example, a landlord may give consent to searches of common areas such as hallways, stairwells, and so on, but, generally, the landlord has no legal right to give consent to a police search of a tenant's apartment.
- Second, consent must be freely and voluntarily given.

Although there is no legal requirement that a person be advised of his or her right to refuse to give consent to a police search, this is one of the factors that the court will consider in determining whether the consent was voluntarily given.

A person's consent to search may be given orally, but it is preferable that it be in writing. In addition, the person's consent must be specifically and intelligently offered. The police cannot assume consent if the person remains silent when he is asked for consent. The person's consent must be voluntary and free of any coercion, intimidation, or threat (officers must avoid even the appearance of intimidation or duress). The person's consent must be obtained free of misrepresentations or fraud. It can only be obtained prior to the search and after the police officers have identified themselves.

Consent may be obtained from any person who has the right of ownership, possession, or control of the premise or property. If there is serious doubt as to whether the person is able to grant consent, a search warrant should be obtained. Generally, if the property is a house, an apartment, or a business and is owned jointly by two or more persons, any one of them may consent to a search of the common areas of the premises. For example, a spouse may give consent to a police search of a jointly owned home. However, if the police receive consent from a suspect's roommate, that roommate may be able to give consent to a police search of common areas of the apartment, but the roommate probably cannot give consent to a search of areas exclusively reserved for the suspect, such as his bedroom, luggage, or closet. Generally, a landlord cannot give consent to a search of a tenant's apartment; nor can a hotel or motel owner or manager give consent to a search of a guest's lodgings.

A consent search is limited to the area specified. Consent may be revoked at any time and the search stopped by the person who gave consent. If a person wants the search stopped, the search should cease upon revocation, unless additional factors or information have come to light which justify a continued warrantless, nonconsensual search. For example, evidence found prior to revocation of consent may be retained and used as a basis for an immediate arrest or as probable cause for a further search (if exigent circumstances exist) or for obtaining a search warrant.

Contraband is anything that is illegal to possess. Examples of contraband include illegal drugs, drug paraphanalia, betting slips where gambling is illegal, child pornography, dangerous weapons (if so stated by local laws or state or federal statutes), and so on. **Plain view** is exactly what it sounds like; it is something that is observable by a normal person under normal circumstances. For example, if you were walking by a storefront and observed an article of contraband in the window display (e.g., drug paraphanalia), then it would be in plain view. Therefore, action could be taken against it. Another example of plain view would be if officers respond to a call at a house for a loud party, and upon entering the house, they observe a bag of marijuana on the kitchen table. In this case, the marijuana is in plain view, and the officers could take action on it.

However, in the case we described earlier, the officers are looking for clothing that the suspect has worn in the commission of the crime or that places the suspect in the vicinity of the crime. The officers have obtained a warrant. Therefore, they can search the house for the clothes. Clothes can be hidden in many different places, because they can be crumpled up. Legal places to look for the clothes would be in a dresser, hamper, washing machine, dryer, closet, trash bag, and so on. It would be illogical to look for clothing in a desk drawer, a jewelry box, or an empty coffee can. Search locations must be limited to where the object could be hidden or located.

The so-called plain view doctrine is often relied upon by both state and federal courts to uphold the seizure of evidence by police officers legitimately carrying out their duties. This plain view exception of the warrant requirement is permissible if the following conditions are met:

- The officer is lawfully on the premises.
- The item is in plain view.
- The discovery of the item is inadvertent.
- The item seized must be immediately apparent as contraband or evidence of a crime.

The term *inadvertent* has been interpreted to mean that a police officer did not have probable cause to believe or suspect that such evidence would be found on the premises in question. To satisfy the condition of being *immediately apparent* as seizable evidence, the officer must have probable cause to believe that the evidence observed in plain view was incriminating.

For example, say that an officer lawfully enters a private residence to execute a valid search warrant for designated property or articles (which is required by the warrant). While conducting the lawful search, he inadvertently discovers other items in plain view that he immediately recognizes as incriminating. These items may be properly seized as evidence.

The courts have upheld the seizure of incriminating evidence inadvertently found in plain view when a police officer has entered the premises to make a lawful warrantless arrest, has entered as a result of lawful consent, or has entered in an emergency to render necessary aid or assistance. When a police officer lawfully enters a dwelling, the officer may seize objects in plain view if such a seizure was not anticipated and if the officer has reasonable cause to believe that there is a connection between the objects seized and criminal behavior.

Items discovered by a police officer inadvertently and without particular design and reasonably believed by the officer to be connected with criminal activity may be seized if in plain view even if it is not mentioned in the search warrant. When an officer enters a private premise as authorized or required by his duties, the officer is not a trespasser. Therefore, anything that he inadvertently observes in plain view is subject to seizure and may be seized without a warrant. In such cases, the usual requirements for search and seizure are not necessary, because no "search" was conducted. A "search" implies a prying into hidden places for concealed items, but it is not a "search" to observe articles that are open to plain view. It is also permissible for an officer to use a flashlight to make such observations. Using this plain view doctrine, officers can often be successful in recovering stolen property, seizing contraband, or confiscating weapons used, or intended to be used, in the commission of a crime.

A simple rule to follow when trying to decide if it is proper to search a location or if you need to establish probable cause is the *reasonable and prudent person rule*. The courts take a lot into consideration when determining what a reasonable and prudent person (a normal or average citizen) would do in a similar circumstance that you are trying to decipher. Would a reasonable and prudent person look for a pair of jeans in the silverware drawer?

Open Fields

Open fields may be searched without a warrant even if the terrain in question is not easily accessible to the public and even if the owner has posted "No Trespassing" signs and has a locked gate.

Search Incident to an Arrest

It is well accepted that a **search incident to a lawful arrest** is a traditional exception to the warrant requirement of the Fourth Amendment. A police officer is allowed to conduct a warrantless search of an arrested person if the following conditions exist:

1. The arrest is lawful and the search is reasonably related to the circumstances of the arrest
2. The search is conducted only for the purpose of:
   - To seize the fruits, instrumentalities, contraband, and other evidence of the crime for which the arrest was made
   - To prevent the destruction or concealment of evidence
   - To remove any weapons that the arrested person might use to resist arrest or to effect his escape

The search is limited in scope to the person of the arrestee and to the immediate surrounding area. *Immediate surrounding area* means that area from which an arrestee can either obtain a weapon or destroy evidence. In addition, such a search must be substantially contemporaneous with the arrest and conducted in the immediate vicinity of the arrest. However, if safety requires, the officer may delay the search and conduct it at a safe location. Also, there is a separate exception to the search warrant requirement, which allows police to conduct a warrantless search of a person who is about to be incarcerated in a police lockup.

An officer conducting a search incident to an arrest (or by search warrant) may use the degree of force reasonably necessary to:

- Protect himself and others present
- Prevent an escape
- Prevent the destruction of evidence

A search also may be made of articles in the possession of the arrested person and of the clothing worn at the time of arrest if the search is related to the offense for which the arrest was made.

The courts have recognized that in addition to a careful search of the area within the arrested person's immediate control, a search of the entire premise may also be justified at that time or immediately following a valid arrest if there is a reasonable belief that it was imperative for the officers safety because of the presence of others in the house or apartment. The courts found in *Commonwealth v. Flowers* that:

> *This search, often termed a "protective sweep," is limited to areas where an accomplice or other person who might come to the aid of the arrestee might reasonably be hiding. Any item or object recognizable as criminal evidence discovered in plain view during a justifiable "protective sweep" may be properly seized.*

Other cases, including *United States v. Bowdach* and *Commonwealth v. Bowden*, have also ruled in favor of protective sweeps.

It should be noted that an arrest must not be used as a reason to make a search. The Court found in *South Dakota v. Opperman* that "If the arrest is unlawful, the search is also unlawful." The courts also have ruled that a lawful arrest must not be used as a reason to search a suspect in order to uncover evidence of a totally unrelated crime.

Any search made under a false or fictitious warrant or under any pretended legal authority is unlawful, even if consent for the search is obtained as a result. Any evidence seized under such circumstances will be declared invalid.

Stop-and-Frisk or Searches

Stop-and-frisk searches, or **pat searches**, are conducted based on the person, time, location, and other circumstances. These "stops" give the officer the ability to do a pat-down, or a frisk-type, search. Such searches are not intrusive and may be conducted on people of the opposite sex if the officer has reason to believe that the person may have a weapon or contraband. If a stop-and-frisk search is to be conducted, the officer must be able to articulate why the stop and the search was justified.

If a police officer reasonably believes that his or her own safety or that of others is in danger, the officer may frisk the person stopped and search the area within that person's immediate control to discover and take control of any weapon that may be used to inflict injury (**FIGURE 9-1**). The officer does not have to be absolutely certain that a person is armed, but the officer must perceive danger to himself or others because of the events leading to the stop or those that occurred after or during the stop. If the officer has a reasonable belief or suspicion, based upon reliable information or personal observation, that a weapon is being carried or concealed in some specific place on the person of the suspect, the officer should immediately check that area before performing a general pat-down.

A frisk should not be a pretext to search for evidence of a crime; it must be of a protective nature. The frisk must initially be limited to an external pat-down of the suspect's outer clothing. If such outer clothing is bulky, such as a heavy overcoat, these garments may be opened to permit a pat-down of inner clothing.

If the officer feels an object that could reasonably be a weapon, the officer may conduct a further search for that particular object in order to remove it. If, after completing the pat-down, the officer does not feel any object that could reasonably be a weapon, the officer should discontinue the search.

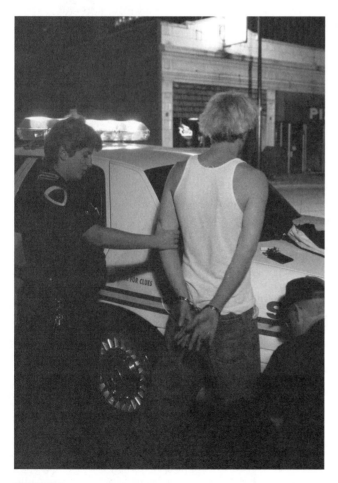

FIGURE 9-1
Police Officer conducting a frisk.

If while frisking a stopped person, the officer discovers an illegal firearm, contraband, stolen property, or evidence of a crime, and probable cause to arrest develops, an arrest should be made and a full-scale search incident to that arrest should be made.

When a police officer makes a decision to stop a person for an investigative purpose, the officer should identify himself as a police officer (unless the officer is in uniform) as soon as it is safe and practical to do so. The officer should also announce the purpose of his inquiry unless such information is obvious.

A stop-and-frisk search of a person of the opposite sex can be done even when no officers of the same sex are available. When searching a person of the opposite sex, the officer must be sure to use either the edge of an opened hand or the back of an opened hand to do the search. This will eliminate any accusations of improper touching.

When are stop-and-frisk searches justified? If there is a large group, a fight, or something that would make the officer believe that there were some type of weapon on the person(s), the officer could justify the search. Consider the following example.

Say that senior citizens were being robbed in front of banks on the day Social Security checks were received and that you have a description of the suspect who robbed an elderly woman after chasing her at knifepoint. As you patrol the area, you observe a person who has some of the same characteristics as the suspect, based on the witnesses' descriptions. You can approach the person and conduct a stop-and-frisk search. You can justify the search based on the description of the suspect and your safety. However, the search is limited to the person's immediate area and to locations on the person where the weapon (knife) in this case could be concealed.

The search cannot be intrusive, but you can pat-down the suspect to see if you can feel a knife. If you come across a hard object in his pocket that could be a knife, you can reach in and remove it. You can grab at an object through the person's clothing to see if that helps to identify the item. Of course, you can always ask the person to empty his pockets in a consent search.

However, you *cannot* do the following. If you feel a baggie of "something," you cannot remove it if you are looking for a knife. The courts do not allow officers to go on "fishing trips."

What level of force can the police use when performing a stop-and-frisk search? If a suspect fails or refuses to stop when so directed by a police officer, reasonable force and physical restraint may be necessary, depending upon the circumstances. When combined with the observations and information that led the officer to reasonably suspect criminal activity may be afoot, if the suspect runs or tries to evade the officer, that additional factor may give probable cause for arrest. Reasonable force in such cases is the minimal amount of physical force required to overcome the resistance offered, but it does not include the use of firearms or other weapons. If an officer is attacked, however, the officer may use sufficient force to defend himself or herself and to ensure his or her personal safety.

Threshold Inquiry

A police officer, in appropriate circumstances and in an appropriate manner, may temporarily stop and briefly detain a person for the purpose of inquiring into possible criminal behavior even though the officer does not have probable cause to make a lawful arrest at that time. The **threshold inquiry** is the process of determining whether or not the subject in question is up to no good or not. This is based on several factors such as where he is, what time of day or night, what type of recent activity is there in the area. An example is if there is a series of "peeping toms" or voyeurs in a particular neighborhood, is this person in the area late at night? Is he wearing dark clothing? Is he from a different section of town? He may be questioned as to why he is in that part of town.

In addition, an officer may frisk such a person for weapons as a matter of self-protection when the officer reasonably believes that his or her own safety, or that of others nearby, is endangered. The purpose of this temporary detention for questioning is to enable the police officer to determine whether to make an arrest, whether to further investigate, or whether to take no police action at that time.

Investigative Detention

Investigative detention is commonly referred to as stop-and-frisk and is very similar to threshold inquiry. Although stop-and-frisk and threshold inquiry procedures refer to the same types of police activity (the warrantless stopping, questioning, and frisking of suspicious persons), those phrases refer to different sources of law to justify such police actions. Investigative detention is the act of holding someone for a reasonable period of time in order to determine if he is involved in some type of illegal activity. The phrase *stop and frisk* is derived from the case of *Terry v. Ohio*. In *Terry v. Ohio*, the U.S. Supreme Court recognized the authority of the police to engage in warrantless stopping, questioning, and frisking of suspicious persons. The Court based that authority on the Fourth Amendment. The phrase *threshold inquiry* refers to the same type of police action. A search for weapons is permissible when an officer has reason to believe that he is dealing with an armed and dangerous individual, regardless of whether the officer has probable cause to arrest for a crime. The officer does not need to be absolutely certain that the individual is armed, but whether a reasonably prudent person in similar circumstances would believe that his safety, or that of others, was in danger.

Investigatory stops are essentially considered to be forcible rather than voluntary. Therefore, such stops are considered seizures under the Fourth Amendment. The degree of force appropriate to enforce a stop in a particular case depends on the surrounding facts and circumstances.

If an officer fails to adequately enforce a stop, it could result in the escape of a dangerous criminal or pose a serious threat to the lives and safety of other persons. The use or threatened use of actual force to carry out an investigatory stop, when such force is not justified under the circumstances, could result in a finding by the court that an arrest had occurred without the necessary element of probable cause, and any evidence obtained as a result might be excluded.

Note that a premature or unnecessary stop can sometimes destroy a good investigation that could have resulted in a subsequent valid arrest and a successful conviction.

Although officers should never hesitate to make an investigatory stop and a necessary frisk under appropriate circumstances, they should avoid the indiscriminate or unjustified use of their authority. The courts do not only frown upon inappropriate police action, but it also detracts from the professional image of the police among the citizens of the community in which they serve.

Grounds for Making a Stop

It is a basic police duty to check on suspicious persons or circumstances, particularly at night and in high-crime areas. A brief investigative stop and inquiry is warranted under the following circumstances:

- When an officer knows that a crime has been committed
- When an officer reasonably believes that a crime has been or is being committed
- When an officer seeks to prevent a crime that he reasonably believes is about to be committed

A police officer has the authority to stop a person for an investigative inquiry in any place where the officer has a right to be, including:

- Any public place
- Any place or area open to the public
- Any private premises entered with valid warrant, by consent, or under emergency circumstances

There is no precise formula for determining the legality of an investigatory stop. However, a stop must be based upon a reasonable belief or suspicion on the part of the officer that some activity out of the ordinary is taking place, that such activity is crime related, and that the person under suspicion is connected with or involved in that criminal activity.

An investigatory stop does not require probable cause for arrest. It may be based upon the officer's own observations or information supplied by others. The information on which the officer acts should be well founded and reasonable. A hunch, guesswork, or an officer's unsupported intuition are *not* sufficient.

If the information provided to the police is from an anonymous caller, the police must satisfy the Aguillar and Spinelli two-prong test. The police need to establish that the anonymous caller (1) is reliable and (2) has a basis of knowledge. The reliability of the caller may be verified when the responding officers are able to corroborate the information provided by the anonymous caller (e.g., confirm description of clothing or vehicle as provided by anonymous tipster). An anonymous caller's basis of knowledge may be satisfied by obtaining information on how the anonymous tipster knows the information that is being provided (e.g., the anonymous tipster is witnessing the reported crime).

In *Illinois v. Gates,* the Court replaced the two-prong test of Aguilar and Spinelli with a "totality of the circumstances" requirement. (However, in Massachusetts, police must satisfy the requirements of both *Illinois v. Gates* and *Aguilar and Spinelli*). The Court stated:

> *On May 3, 1978, the Police Department of Bloomingdale, Ill., received an anonymous letter which included statements that respondents, husband and wife, were engaged in selling drugs; that the wife would drive their car to Florida on May 3 to be loaded with drugs, and the husband would fly down in a few days to drive the car back; that the car's trunk would be loaded with drugs; and that respondents presently had over $100,000 worth of drugs in their basement. Acting on the tip, a police officer determined respondents' address and learned that the husband made a reservation on a May 5 flight to Florida. Arrangements for surveillance of the flight were made with an agent of the Drug Enforcement Administration (DEA), and the surveillance disclosed that the husband took the flight, stayed overnight in a motel room registered in the wife's name, and left the following morning with a woman in a car bearing an Illinois license plate issued to the husband, heading north on an interstate highway used by travelers to the Bloomingdale area. A search warrant for respondents' residence and automobile was then obtained from an Illinois state court judge, based on the Bloomingdale police officer's affidavit setting forth the foregoing facts and a copy of the anonymous letter. When respondents arrived at their home, the police were waiting, and discovered marihuana and other contraband in respondents' car trunk and home. Prior to respondents' trial on charges of violating state drug laws, the trial court ordered suppression of all the items seized, and the Illinois Appellate Court affirmed. The Illinois Supreme Court also affirmed, holding that the letter and affidavit were inadequate to sustain a determination of probable cause for issuance of the search warrant under Aguilar v. Texas, 378 U.S. 108, and Spinelli v. United States, 393 U.S. 410, since they failed to satisfy the "two-pronged test" of (1) revealing the informant's "basis of knowledge" and (2) providing sufficient facts to establish either the informant's "veracity" or the "reliability" of the informant's report.*
>
> *The rigid "two-pronged test" under Aguilar and Spinelli for determining whether an informant's tip establishes probable cause for issuance of a warrant is abandoned, and the "totality of the circumstances" approach that traditionally has informed probable cause determinations is substituted in its place. The elements under the "two-pronged test" concerning the informant's "veracity," "reliability," and "basis of knowledge" should be understood simply as closely intertwined issues that may usefully illuminate the common sense, practical question whether there is "probable cause" to believe that contraband or evidence is located in a particular place. The task of the issuing magistrate is simply to make a practical, common sense decision whether, given all the circumstances set forth in the affidavit before him,*

there is a fair probability that contraband or evidence of a crime will be found in a particular place. And the duty of a reviewing court is simply to ensure that the magistrate had a substantial basis for concluding that probable cause existed. This flexible, easily applied standard will better achieve the accommodation of public and private interests that the Fourth Amendment requires than does the approach that has developed from Aguilar and Spinelli.

The judge issuing the warrant had a substantial basis for concluding that probable cause to search respondents' home and car existed. Under the "totality of the circumstances" analysis, corroboration of details of an informant's tip by independent police work is of significant value. Here, even standing alone, the facts obtained through the independent investigation of the Bloomingdale police officer and the DEA at least suggested that respondents were involved in drug trafficking. In addition, the judge could rely on the anonymous letter, which had been corroborated in major part by the police officer's efforts. 85 Ill.2d 376, 423 N.E.2d 887, reversed.

The reliability prong may be satisfied when the responding officers are able to corroborate the anonymous caller information (e.g., confirm description of clothing or vehicle as provided by anonymous tipster).

No single factor alone is normally sufficient, but the following factors may be considered in determining the reasonableness of an investigative stop by a police officer in the field:

- Personal observations by the officer and the officer's police training and experience
- The officer's knowledge of criminal activity in the area
- The time of day or night and the place of observation
- The general appearance and demeanor of the suspect and any furtive (suspicious) behavior that indicates possible criminal conduct
- The suspect's proximity to the scene of a recently reported crime
- The knowledge of the suspect's prior criminal record or of his association with known criminals
- Visible objects in the suspect's possession or obvious bulges in his clothing
- Resemblance of the suspect to a person wanted for a known crime
- Information received from police sources or from other reasonably reliable sources of information

The fact that an individual has aroused a police officer's suspicion should cause the officer to make his approach with vigilance and to be alert for any possibility of danger. A routine police check of suspicious circumstances may uncover the commission of a serious crime or the presence of a dangerous criminal. If the stopped suspect has just committed a major crime, the suspect may be an immediate threat to the officer's safety or the suspect may suddenly attempt to flee from the scene.

No hard-and-fast rule can be formulated to determine the period of time required for an investigative detention, but it should be reasonably brief under the particular circumstances. Generally, it should be no longer than the period of time necessary to check the suspect's identity and the reliability of his story, unless information is obtained which establishes probable cause to make an arrest. If the answers given by the suspect are unsatisfactory because they are false, contradictory, or incredible, they may serve as elements or factors to establish probable cause. The period of investigative detention should be sufficiently brief so that the "stop" cannot be construed as an "arrest," which would require probable cause.

Chapter Wrap-Up

For safety reasons, it is always best to have two officers conduct a search of a person. Law enforcement agencies use a variety of search techniques, and new ones are being developed every day. All search techniques have one thing in common: the welfare of the police officer(s) is the utmost concern. A search as a result of an inquiry is much different then one from an arrest. In the instance of a search whether an arrest or an inquiry, if there are two officers:

- Each officer should control one arm of the subject. The subject's legs should be situated so that he is slightly off-balance.
- With each officer controlling one arm, each officer should use his free hand to pat-down the subject.
- The search should begin at the head and work down.
- If a suspicious object is detected, the officer may remove the item for closer inspection.
- The officers should pat and grab the subject's pockets and clothing.

If a pat-down search must be conducted on a subject of the opposite sex, and no officers of that sex are able to respond, the searching officers should conduct the pat-down using the back of the hand as opposed to the palm or open hand. This will allow the officers to physically control a person in order to conduct a search. Any gestures or movements will be detected as the officer will feel the muscles tightening or the movement of the suspect and should be able to react quickly if and when needed. Officers will, by using the defensive tactics they have learned, be able to maintain control over the suspect or subject who is under their control.

From the Experts

It is always better to have two people conduct a search. The presence of two officers will deter the suspect from trying anything defensive or retaliatory against the officer(s).

Caution

When conducting a search on a person, always consider the "plus-one rule." If one weapon is found, you should assume that the suspect has two weapons. If two weapons are found, you should assume that there are three, and so on.

Key Terms

abandoned property: Garbage or trash that has been left in a public area no longer enjoys the protection associated with property that individuals associate with a reasonable expectation of privacy.

administrative searches: Under certain circumstances, the police may engage in warrantless searches or inspections as part of their administrative functions.

body cavity search: A search that includes some degree of touching and probing of the anus and vagina. Allows the searcher to examine a person's body cavities in order to search for contraband or fruits of the crime.

consent search: When an individual gives his consent for the police to conduct a search of his property.

contraband: Anything that is illegal to possess.

open fields: An open field may be searched without a warrant even if the terrain in question is not easily accessible to the public and even if the owner has posted "No Trespassing" signs and has a locked gate.

plain view: Something that is observable by a normal person under normal circumstances.

search incident to a lawful arrest: A traditional exception to the warrant requirement of the Fourth Amendment. A police officer is allowed to conduct a warrantless search of an arrested person if the following conditions exist: the arrest is lawful and the search is reasonably related to the circumstances of the arrest; the search is conducted only for the purpose of seizing fruits, instrumentalities, contraband, and other evidence of the crime for which the arrest was made; to prevent the destruction or concealment of evidence; to remove any weapons that the arrested person might use to resist arrest or to effect his escape.

stop-and-frisk searches (pat searches): Searches based on the person, time, location, and other circumstances. These searches are not intrusive and may be conducted on people of the opposite sex if there is reason to believe that there may be a weapon or contraband.

strip searches: A Massachusetts court has defined strip searches as "an inspection of a naked individual without any scrutiny of his or her body cavities."

threshold inquiry: A police officer, in appropriate circumstances and in an appropriate manner, may temporarily stop and briefly detain a person for the purpose of inquiring into possible criminal behavior even though the officer does not have probable cause to make a lawful arrest at that time.

Your Assignment—Results

With regard to the opening assignment, you have the right to make a threshold inquiry. A police officer, in appropriate circumstances and in an appropriate manner, may temporarily stop and briefly detain a person for the purpose of inquiring into possible criminal behavior even though the officer does not have probable cause to make a lawful arrest at that time.

In addition, an officer may frisk such a person for weapons as a matter of self-protection when the officer reasonably believes that his own safety, or that of others nearby, is endangered. In this case, you observed a bulge in the subject's pocket. If you patted the bulge and found it to be soft and did not suspect it to be a weapon or a tool for breaking in, you cannot remove it. However, you can inquire about it, and the answers or gestures that the suspect makes may cause you to believe that he is hiding something, giving you probable cause to remove the soft bulge. If the item is a solid object, then by all means you have the right to remove the object.

You do not have to administer any *Miranda* rights at this time unless you develop information to believe that he is about to commit or has committed a crime. As soon as you feel that he is responsible for or involved in some incident, you must administer them. If the suspect makes any incriminating statements as a result of your questions, then you must give him his rights. If his statements are just voluntary and not the result of any questioning, then you can let him talk as long as you don't ask him any questions.

Your Next Assignment

You are on patrol in the business district; it is 1:30 A.M. on a Saturday night. Area businesses have experienced a few attempted breaking and enterings, but no actual break-ins. As you are driving through the area, you observe an individual in one of the alleys. You shine your light in the alley, and the man, who is startled, walks towards you.

You see that his hands are free of any objects; he does not appear to be concealing anything. As he approaches, you stop him a few feet from you in order to ask him some questions. He states that he lives in the area and has just left a local bar. He was walking home and stopped to relieve himself in the alley.

1. Can you pat him down and check for weapons?
2. Can you search inside his pockets for any drugs or other contraband?
3. What could you do to verify that he is who he says he is and lives close by?
4. How would you verify his story?
5. Would you write a report on what transpired or just fill out a field interview report?

Call for Service

You have just arrested two people—one male and one female—for selling drugs. Prior to placing them into custody, you (a male officer) observe the male suspect remove something from his pocket and give it to the female, who then places the object under her clothing. She is now handcuffed. Several male and female officers are currently on duty. Considering that the female suspect may have concealed some of the drugs or contraband on her person, explain the steps that should be taken to conduct each of the following:

- A pat-down search
- A search incident to the arrest
- A strip search, if warranted
- A body cavity search, if warranted

Reference

Waltham Police Department. 1997. Waltham Police Department Policy Manual, Waltham, MA.

Motor Vehicle Searches

CHAPTER 10

Knowledge Objectives

- Describe the various types of motor vehicle searches that do not require a warrant.
- Define exigent circumstances and plain view observations.

Skills Objectives

- Demonstrate the ability to search a motor vehicle.

You have just made a motor vehicle stop for a traffic violation (running a red light). As you approach the vehicle, you observe an underage passenger in the rear seat trying to conceal a can of beer.

- Can you search all of the passengers in the vehicle? If so, what are you searching for?
- Can you search both the front and back passenger compartments of the vehicle?
- Can you search the trunk?

■ Introduction

This chapter explores when an officer can search a motor vehicle and how such searches should be conducted. You will also examine a number of court cases that have determined when and how the police can search a vehicle. In addition, you will learn what is meant by *exigent* circumstances and other situations that provide for a warrantless search.

■ Motor Vehicle Searches

You will examine several issues with regards to motor vehicle searches. First, we will determine exactly what a motor vehicle is as defined by the courts.

Although motor vehicles are considered "effects" within the meaning of intent in the Fourth Amendment, the courts have not considered motor vehicles to be in the same category as other property and have upheld searches of motor vehicles where searches of a dwelling house or other structure would have been prohibited. This is because a motor vehicle is a moveable object rather than a fixed object, such as a house.

In *Arkansas v. Sanders* the Supreme Court stated that:

> . . . the inherent mobility of automobiles often makes it impracticable to obtain a warrant and, in addition, the configuration, use, and regulation of automobiles often may dilute the reasonable expectation of privacy that exists with respect to differently situated property.

Of course, whenever it is possible and practical, the police should always obtain a search warrant before conducting a search. If evidence results from a warrantless search, the courts will look at the scope of the situation and determine if a warrant could have been obtained.

When the Police Can Search a Vehicle

If a person is stopped for a motor vehicle infraction, the police have several options if they want to search a vehicle. First, the police may search the immediate area or the passenger compartment of the vehicle, including the front and back seats and the glove compartment. Basically, the police can search anywhere that is within "reach" of the subject.

Second, if during the course of an arrest the suspect's vehicle must be towed for some reason, the police can conduct an inventory search. Inventory searches are examined in detail later in this chapter.

Third, the police can get permission to search a vehicle by obtaining a search warrant. When an arrest is made and the officers believe that contraband or evidence may be located in the motor vehicle, the officers may have the vehicle towed to the police station and then apply for a search warrant. The warrant will state what the officers are looking for and where in the vehicle the officers can search for this item. This is based on the size of the item they are looking for.

Warrantless Searches

The practical considerations of police work often require that a warrantless search of a motor vehicle be conducted under the following circumstances:

- **Warrantless stopping, questioning, and frisking of a motor vehicle operator or occupants.** A stop-and-frisk type of protective search determines whether a suspect is armed. The search is confined to the area of the motor vehicle from which a suspect

FIGURE 10-1
Police will search this suspect's vehicle once he has been placed securely in the cruiser.

might gain access to a weapon. The search is limited to the passenger compartment. However, in circumstances when the operator or subject is outside the vehicle and standing at an open trunk, the trunk falls under the "immediate area" rule.

- **Search of a motor vehicle incident to the arrest of an occupant or operator.** A search incident to a lawful arrest is limited to the area from which the person could obtain a weapon or reach any destructible evidence (**FIGURE 10-1**). If it is not practical to conduct a full search immediately at the scene, then the vehicle can be towed to a police facility to be searched later. In this case, you have proven that there is no immediate rush to search the vehicle to prevent the loss or destruction of evidence. Therefore, the courts usually prefer that the police obtain a warrant before conducting the search.
- **Exigent circumstances. Exigent circumstances** are present when moving the vehicle will result in the loss or destruction of evidence. If there is probable cause that the vehicle contains incriminating evidence and exigent circumstances exist, then a

warrantless search is justified.

- **Consent.** A warrant is not needed if the person in lawful control of the vehicle voluntarily consents to the search.
- **Roadblocks.** In some states, roadblocks (e.g., to detect drivers under the influence of alcohol or for seatbelt checks) are permissible if the selection of motor vehicles to be stopped is not arbitrary. The officers must set forth the procedures for a "specific" random stop (e.g., every third vehicle in traffic, etc.). In addition, if police have a description of a suspect vehicle, they may stop all vehicles fitting that description.
- **Plain view.** If an officer has lawfully stopped a motor vehicle and is in the process of questioning the operator of the vehicle and the officer notices an incriminating item in or on the vehicle in **plain view**, including anything observed with the use of a flashlight, then the officer has probable cause to search the vehicle and seize the items observed without a warrant.

Random stops of motor vehicles in the absence of reasonable suspicion of criminal activity or a motor vehicle violation constitute an unreasonable seizure that violates of the Fourth Amendment. Any evidence obtained as a result of such random stops is subject to exclusion in the court and most likely will be thrown out as an illegal seizure. Any testimony or subsequent information derived from that seizure is also invalid and will not be accepted by the courts.

Inventory Searches

In must jurisdictions, a vehicle is towed if there is no other licensed driver to take the motor vehicle. The purpose of the inventory search is to protect the property of the owner of the vehicle being towed. During an inventory search, officers are allowed to search and inventory all property inside the vehicle. The purpose of the search is to list all items of value in the motor vehicle to be towed. The list of articles inventoried will be presented to and signed by the tow-truck driver. This protects the driver and the police from claims of theft of the items by the owner.

The courts permit inventory searches if two key conditions are met:

- The department has a written policy that states when inventory searches can be conducted
- The department inventories all vehicles in the same manner

The following is an example of an inventory policy that has been accepted and approved by the courts:

An inventory search shall be conducted on all motor vehicles brought into police custody to protect the property of persons and to protect the officers and department from false claims of loss or theft of property.

Officers conducting the inventory are to check the entire motor vehicle, including: passenger compartment; under the seats; glove compartments; consoles; trunk, when officers are in possession of the keys to the trunk; any containers found within the above areas of the vehicle. Any container (or any item reasonably appearing to be a container, including the trunk, glove compartment, and console) found in the motor vehicle shall be opened and its contents inventoried; any locked container for which the prisoner has a key among his other personnel belongings shall be opened and its contents inventoried; any locked container for which the prisoner does not have a key among his other personal belongings shall be opened only if the police have reasonable suspicion to believe that the container contains any items posing a threat to the safety and security of the police station or its personnel.

After Completion of Inventory: In most cases, after the inventory is completed, valuables can be secured in the trunk of the motor vehicle. Items of high value and any weapons found SHALL be transported to the station for safekeeping. Such items shall be turned into the Property/Evidence Officer. Papers, documents, or any other writings found in the motor vehicle or within any container searched may be examined only to the extent necessary to ascertain the identity of the vehicle's owner, effect the removal of items dangerous to the police station or its personnel, and protect the department from false claims of theft. (Waltham Police Department, 2000)

Chapter Wrap-Up

In cases when there is a subject or person standing by the motor vehicle, it is best to have two officers present during the search. One officer should conduct the search, the other should monitor the subject(s). Of course, if there is more than one person or subject, more than two officers should be present. If getting an extra officer on the scene is not possible, the person(s) should be secured in the cruiser.

The bottom line is that an officer should not take any unnecessary risks. If additional officers are needed, the officer should wait for backup to arrive before conducting any search.

Any and all searches should be conducted in an orderly manner. If only one officer is available to search the vehicle, the search should begin at the driver's side front. The officer should check the floor, under the seats, the center console, the dashboard, the visors, under the dashboard, and any compartments in the area and on the door. The officer should then search the rear driver's side, checking under the seats and between the seats and the cushions. If it is a two-door vehicle, the officer should check between the seats and the side panel and the rear dashboard or rear deck. Starting from the other side, the passenger front, the same process should be repeated.

If two officers are present to do the search, then each officer should take half of the vehicle, front and back. They should search in the same manner just described. However, they should overlap their search areas so as not to miss the middle.

From the Experts

If you are not sure if exigent circumstances are present and you feel that the vehicle needs to be inventoried, it is best to be safe and secure a search warrant for the vehicle. You should have the car towed to the station. You do not want to lose a case on a motion to suppress evidence from a defense attorney that the area searched was not associated with the arrestee's control (e.g., trunk, rear bed of a pickup truck, any compartments in the rear, under the rear seats, etc.) or that the conditions were not urgent (i.e., the suspect was in police custody and therefore was not in close proximity of the vehicle and there was no reason for the officer to search areas that were not in the suspect's immediate control).

Caution

Do not search a vehicle if you are alone and there is an operator and multiple passengers. If you must perform a search, secure the subjects in your cruiser or wait for backups to arrive. Never turn your back on a suspect.

Key Terms

exigent circumstances: A police officer is authorized to conduct a search without a warrant when faced with an emergency situation whereby a delay would endanger his or the public's safety or might result in the escape of the offender or the destruction of evidence.

plain view: If an officer has lawfully stopped a motor vehicle and is in the process of questioning the operator of the vehicle and the officer notices an incriminating item in or on the vehicle in plain view, including anything observed with the use of a flashlight, then the officer has probable cause to search the vehicle and seize the items observed without a warrant.

Your Assignment—Results

With regard to the opening assignment, in order to search the passengers and the motor vehicle, you must be able to verbalize and explain what you are looking for. The only thing you have noticed is a can of beer. Thus, you are only allowed to search the vehicle for beer. You can search anywhere you believe that beer may be hidden.

Practically speaking, in such cases you will be able to view any beer inside the car. You can ask the occupants where the rest of the beer is; they will most likely cooperate and divulge any hidden beer. If they do not cooperate, then you have the right to look in the trunk and any place inside the vehicle where beer or liquor may be hidden.

If you believe that the occupants may have drugs, based on smell or any paraphernalia, then you may search them. However, you must be able to articulate the reason why you feel that such a search was necessary. If you have no indications of anything else other than the beer, then you cannot go into the occupants' pockets to look for drugs.

Note that you do not need consent to search the vehicle or the occupants.

Your Next Assignment

You have just made a motor vehicle stop for speeding. The vehicle has two occupants: a passenger and the operator. As you approach the vehicle, the operator rolls down his window to speak with you. As he does this, you smell the odor of marijuana. You ask the operator for his license and registration, and while looking in the vehicle you observe that the inside is slightly "smoky" and a plastic bag on the console between the seats appears to contain some plant matter.

Both occupants deny any knowledge or ownership of the alleged marijuana. What is your course of action?

- Can you remove both of the occupants from the vehicle?
- Can you search each of the occupants of the vehicle?
- Can you search the vehicle?
- Can you search the trunk?
- Can you arrest both occupants?
- Can you still write a ticket for the speeding violation if you determine you can arrest the operator for the marijuana possession?

Call for Service

You are on patrol in a one-officer unit (cruiser). A car has just sped past you. You pull your cruiser into traffic behind the suspect vehicle. As you are about to activate your emergency equipment, which are blue lights and a siren, the rear-seat passenger turns and looks at you. As he turns back around, it appears as though the driver passes something to him. The rear-seat passenger seems to be stuffing something down his pants, or at least hiding something. You activate your blue lights and siren and stop the vehicle in a remote rural area. Three people are inside the car: a male and female in the front and a male in the back seat. You are a male officer.

Assume that you have made the stop and you have not yet exited your vehicle. You have informed the dispatcher that you have made the stop. You have provided the station with the following information, as is proper protocol: the make and model of the vehicle; the license plate number; the location of the stop; the reason for the stop; and the number of occupants. You are now exiting the cruiser.

Describe in a narrative essay what you would do. Do not be concerned with tactics or with the proper use of techniques. This is an exercise in common sense. Use what you have learned so far, life experiences, and so on. Be as specific as possible in your description.

Reference

Waltham Police Department, 2000. Waltham Police Department Policy Manual, pp. 18–19. Waltham, MA.

Building Searches

Knowledge Objectives

- Discuss building searches that require warrants.
- Define probable cause.
- Discuss building searches that do not require warrants.
- Describe searches made during emergencies or exigent circumstances, including hot pursuits.
- Describe building searches that result from a call for service.

Skills Objectives

- Demonstrate the ability to search a building.

You have just been assigned to investigate a possible break-in of a building that is closed for the evening. When you arrive on the scene, you see an open door.

- What is the first thing you would do before entering the building?

Introduction

In this chapter, you will learn about building searches. You will learn when a building can be searched and the techniques you can use to conduct a search. You will also learn about fresh and continued pursuits, which enable an officer to enter a building or residence without a warrant.

Building Searches

Searches with a Warrant

A general rule is that searches and seizures are reasonable and proper if they are based on a valid search warrant. A warrant indicates that the police have demonstrated that probable cause exists and that evidence of criminal activity will be uncovered by the search. With certain limited exceptions, a search should always be conducted with a search warrant issued by a court that has control or jurisdiction over the subject of the warrant.

A warrant will be issued if the probable cause is set out in front of the judge, clerk, or magistrate by the presentation of a properly executed affidavit. The affidavit must contain the facts, information, and circumstances that have led the police to have probable cause to believe that a crime has been, is being, or is about to be committed and that seizable evidence relating to that crime is present in the place or on the person to be searched.

Probable cause is a phrase that describes the facts observed, information obtained from others, and personal knowledge and experience that is sufficient to lead a *reasonable and prudent person* to believe that seizable evidence of crime exists and that it will be found in a specific location or on the specific person. The information presented must be strong enough for a judge or magistrate to issue a search warrant. Many cases have been lost because an officer had sufficient basis for probable cause but did not furnish enough information in the affidavit. Any fact that is not set out in the affidavit cannot be inserted or used later for the purpose of establishing probable cause for a search.

The affidavit must provide specific information about the objects to be seized. The resulting search warrant must be sufficiently definitive so that the officer(s) serving the warrant will not seize the wrong property. The warrant must be sufficiently descriptive so that an officer can identify the property to be seized with reasonable certainty.

In some states, the legal procedure specified for the issuance of a search warrant is as follows:

> *A court or justice authorized to issue warrants in criminal cases may, upon complaint on oath that the complainant believes that any of the property or articles hereinafter named are concealed in a house, place, vessel, or vehicle or in the possession of a person anywhere within the commonwealth and territorial waters thereof, if satisfied that there is probable cause for such belief, issue a warrant identifying the property and naming or describing the person or place to be searched, and commanding the person seeking such warrant to search for the following property or articles (Waltham Police Department, 1997):*
>
> - *Property or articles stolen, embezzled, or obtained by false pretenses, or otherwise obtained in the commission of a crime;*
> - *Property or articles which are intended for use, or which are or have been used, as a means or instrumentality of committing a crime, including, but not in limitation of the foregoing,*

any property or article worn, carried, or otherwise used, changed, or marked in the preparation for or perpetration of or concealment of a crime;

- *Property or articles the possession or control of which is unlawful, or which are possessed or controlled for an unlawful purpose; . . .*
- *The dead body of a human being;*
- *The body of a living person for whom a current arrest warrant is outstanding.*

The word "property" as used in this section shall include books, papers, documents, records, and any other tangible objects.

A search warrant may also authorize the seizure of evidence.

A search warrant shall designate and describe the building, house, place, vessel, or vehicle to be searched and shall specifically describe the property or articles to be searched for; . . . and shall be directed to the sheriff or his deputy or to a constable or police officer, commanding him to search in the daytime, or if the warrant so directs, in the nighttime, the building, house, place, vessel, or vehicle where the property or articles for which he is required to search are believed to be concealed, and to bring such property or articles when found, and the persons in whose possession they are found, before a court having jurisdiction.

The first objective when executing a warrant is for the officers to gain entry to the building as peacefully as possible. Forcible entry is authorized if, after waiting a reasonable time, it becomes apparent that the officers will not be admitted voluntarily; that the officers or any other persons are in danger of physical harm; that the occupants are escaping; or that evidence is being, or is in danger of being, destroyed.

What constitutes a *reasonable time* before making a forcible entry depends upon the circumstances of each case and the best judgment of the searching officers.

It is always a good police practice to gain entry without force. In addition, the police should avoid gaining entry by means of deception or by means of a ruse. If the resulting deceptive entry will allow officers into the house and not to use force enter, causing unnecessary damage, such as using a ram to smash a door, etc., then that method is acceptable.

In all such cases, the manner of entry shall be made with the least possible destruction of property and a copy of the warrant should be left in a conspicuous place on or in the property.

Even if not specified in the search warrant, the following articles may be lawfully seized by an officer who observes them in plain view while serving a search warrant:

- Instrumentalities or means by which any crime was committed (e.g., weapons, masks, tools, etc.)
- Contraband (articles that may not be legally possessed, such as counterfeit money or controlled substances, narcotics, etc.)
- Fruits of any crime (e.g., stolen property)
- Other evidence of any crime (e.g., clothing or other items fitting the description of the criminal offender)
- Any property that bears a reasonable relationship to the purpose of the search (e.g., documents establishing who owns the premises searched if ownership is an element of the crime)

Any item not named in the search warrant may be seized only if the police have probable cause to believe it is contraband, stolen property, or evidence of a known crime.

If during the execution of a search warrant it appears that there is probable cause to believe that the seizable property is located in an area of the premises outside the scope of the present warrant, a new warrant should be obtained immediately, unless consent is granted or exigent circumstances are present. While the new warrant is being sought, any occupants of the premises may have their activities restricted.

Searches without a Warrant
The Fourth Amendment to the U.S. Constitution prohibits unreasonable searches and seizures, and the Supreme Court has consistently held that unless they come within one of the few carefully limited exceptions to the search warrant requirement, warrantless searches and seizures are unreasonable.

Searches in Emergency or Exigent Circumstances
A police officer is authorized to conduct a search without a warrant when the officer is faced with an emergency situation where delay would endanger the officer's or the public's safety or result in the escape of the offender or the destruction of evidence.

Many emergencies that justify a warrantless entry and search do not necessarily involve criminal acts. For example, when an officer hears a call for assistance, when an officer observes smoke or flame, or when an officer learns of an actual or potential natural or manmade calamity or disaster, the officer has the duty and obligation to respond immediately.

Searching as a Result of a Call for Service
Conducting a search in a building as a result of a call for a break-in or an alarm report is an entirely different set of circumstances. In these cases, the police are responding to check a building in which either an intruder alarm has gone off, a witness has observed someone enter a building illegally, or an officer has observed or heard something to warrant further investigation.

Factors to Consider Before Searching a Building
A number of factors should be considered when determining whether a building should be searched:
- Why does the building need to be searched?
- Is there a suspect inside the building?
- If, so, what is the suspect suspected of?
- How many suspects are in the building?
- Does the suspect(s) have a weapon? If so, what type of weapon?
- Are backup units available? If so, how much backup can be provided?
- What type of building is it?
- Is there anything inside the building that the suspect can use as a weapon?

Common Building Targets
The following are some of the buildings and/or establishments that are commonly targeted for crimes: jewelry stores, liquor stores, firearms stores, pharmacies, banks, gas stations, hardware stores, and variety stores.

The Weather
Sometimes storms or power outages will set off many false alarms. Officers who are assigned to respond to a spate of alarms should check each alarm as though it may be in response to a break-in. During a storm, criminals know that the police sometimes do not check as thoroughly as they should. Officers should still request backups and check these buildings.

Searching Outside the Building
When beginning the search, the officer should look at and identify if windows and doors were used for entry or tampered with.

Police cruisers are usually equipped with spotlights that can be adjusted to provide additional light in an area. These lights are called *alley lights*. An officer should shine these lights on all windows and doors to identify the "obvious" point of entry by the suspects. The check should include all alcoves and locations where windows or doors are present.

Note that in many cases, a building may not have a driveway or parking lot beside it; in such cases, an officer will have to physically leave the cruiser to check the building.

If possible, when checking the windows and doors from the outside of the building, the officer should try to see inside the building to see if there is any disturbance or signs of an illegal entry.

An officer can use a flashlight to determine if a door's deadbolt is engaged. The fact that a deadbolt or a door is locked does not conclusively mean that a break-in or illegal entry has not occurred. Sometimes criminals lock doors behind them once they are inside. Officers should also jiggle and shake the doors to make sure they are not just closed to look like they are locked.

If a criminal or suspect enters a building and then locks the door behind him, an alarm will still sound. Officers should be aware of this. It is always a good idea for the owner of the building/establishment or someone in charge of it to respond and check out the alarm system. When an alarm is activated, it is usually a good idea to have the owner respond with a key so the officers can make an accurate check of the premises. If the officers do not check the building and a second alarm sounds, it could be that the suspect has just left the building.

In addition to doors, criminals may enter a building through vents; fire escapes; upper-story windows, using ladders and ropes; the roof; and so on.

Checking Nearby Vehicles

When checking a building as a result of an alarm or possible break-in, officers should check out the parking lot and any vehicles present. Officers should look inside the vehicles.

Sometimes criminals will set off a building alarm on purpose to time the police response and observe their actions. The criminals will often take note of the following:

- Did the officers check the building?
- Did the officers call the owner?
- Did the officer wait for the owner to arrive and check the building with him or her?
- How long did it take for the owner to arrive?
- How long did it take for the police to arrive?

Suspects will sometimes record and log this information on several occurrences to see how the police respond.

If vehicles are seen in the parking lot of a closed business, an industrial park, or a similar area, the officer should:

- Check the vehicles
- Run computer checks on the vehicles' registration plates to determine who owns the vehicles and whether the vehicles are stolen
- Make a record of the vehicles' license plates
- Check to see if the vehicles are there on subsequent visits

Officers should keep this information for at least a day or until the next business day to make sure that the business was not broken into, because it might not be until the next day until the business owner discovers that a break-in has occurred. It is not a bad idea to keep this information just in case the vehicle turns up later at another location of an alarm.

Roofs

One of the most difficult types of entries for an officer to observe is roof entries. It is difficult for the officer to determine if this type of entry has been made from outside the building. A few indications of whether a roof entry has been made or not would be if there was observed damage to drain pipes or on the building roof line or eaves and/if there is any stacked pallets, ladders, boxes, or other objects that would assist a suspect to gain access to the roof. In addition, officers can look through windows from outside the building to see if there are damaged ceiling tiles and debris on the floor.

Adjacent Buildings

Sometimes criminals will use an adjacent building to enter their target building, using the walls as a means to get in. Older buildings and even newer ones, such as those commonly found in strip malls, usually have thin walls between adjacent establishments. In these cases, the actual target building will seem to be secure when checked by the officer.

Wires

Most buildings have electrical and telephone wires; whether the building has an alarm will determine if there are alarm wires. During some break-ins, criminals will cut these wires. Sometimes criminals will cut the wires and then reattach them so that it looks as if they have not been tampered with. If the cut wires are not discovered by the police or the owner, the criminals may return to burglarize the unprotected building.

In some cases, criminals cut alarm wires and replace them in order to see how long it takes the police to respond to the scene and whether the police wait for the owner to arrive with the keys before checking the building. The criminals may record and log how long it takes an owner to fix the alarm. This information enables the criminals to plan future burglaries.

Loading Docks

Loading docks are common sites of suspicious activity at a business. While a truck may be backed up against a building legitimately, a truck, car, or van that is backed to a building's loading area with its doors open and engine running should be considered suspicious if it is after the business's hours. Officers should also make sure that the loading doors are secured and that there is no gap on the bottom that may indicate that the door is unlocked or has been tampered with.

Suspicious Persons

Anyone at the scene after normal business hours should be considered suspicious. However, keep in mind that employees do stay late. In addition, there may be a new late shift or some special project going on such as inventory, a large order going out, and so on.

Suspicious activities that should alert officers to check out a building include the following:

- A person is parked outside of the building in a motor vehicle with a raised hood
- A person is standing outside the building speaking on a pay phone or a cellular phone (they may be calling accomplices or acting as if they are making a call while actually observing the officer)
- A person who is hanging around who does not seem to have any purpose for being there

Searching Inside the Building

Once the officers have been assured that the perimeter of the building is secure and that the owner of the building has arrived with the keys, they can enter the building (FIGURE 11-1).

When preparing to search the interior of a building, the police officers at the scene should assess the location and determine what would be considered adequate backup. How many officers do we need? How many officers are available? Is a K-9 unit available?

Buildings are best searched with a K-9 unit. If a K-9 unit is available, the officer should take some preliminary steps to make the K-9's search more effective. The officer should secure the perimeter of the building and stay out of the building to avoid contaminating the subject's scent. The longer the subject stays in the building, the stronger the scent. In addition, officers should avoid looking in windows while the canine searches so as not to distract the dog.

When the K-9 unit is in the building, a second officer should accompany the K-9 dog and officer to watch the dog handler's back during the search and to act as a cover officer.

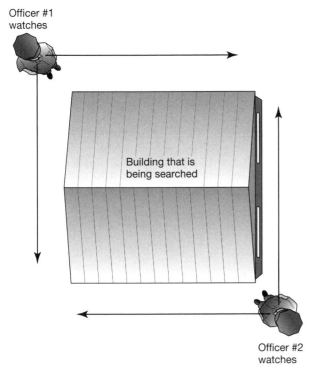

Officer #1
watches

Building that is
being searched

Officer #2
watches

FIGURE 11-1
Two officers cover the perimeter of a building.

A **cover officer** is on hand to protect the primary, or lead, officer, keeping alert to any dangers or threats that may arise from an officer's unguarded side.

If the department does not have a K-9 unit or one is not available from a neighboring community, then the officers should begin the search without the K-9 unit. The search should have no less than two and no more than five officers.

All of the officers on the search team should coordinate their search efforts. Each officer should know where the other officers are to avoid any "surprises." The officers should gather as much related information about the incident as possible, including the subject's identity, the nature of the incident, the subject's means of entry, and the building's layout. The officers should assume that the subject knows the building's layout and that the subject(s) has a weapon(s).

Officers assigned to the call will have areas of responsibility. The areas of responsibility will be assigned by a supervisor or by the initial responding officer. After entering the building, each officer will secure his or her position and take responsibility for the location.

Entering the Building

When entering the building, the officer(s) should use the owner's keys (if the owner has provided them) to enter a door of the building at a location away from the suspect's **point of entry** or **point of exit**.

Officers when entering a building should try to identify any **cover** or **concealment**. Cover is some sort of protection that an officer can use to protect him or herself from gunfire. The cover object should be solid, such as a tree, building, cement wall, motor vehicle, and so on. Concealment is when an object can prevent the officer from being seen, but that cannot protect an officer from a suspect's bullets. For example, bushes, trashcans, darkness (shadows), and picket or stockade fences offer concealment.

It is dangerous to enter the building at the suspect's point of entry. The subject may be near the point of entry and thus be able to ambush the incoming officers. This point of entry is considered a **fatal funnel** for the officer because the subject is aware that the officer(s) may enter the building at this location and the suspect can prepare an attack. In addition, the officers should avoid using elevators because in addition to doors, they, too, are fatal funnels. Once the elevator door is opened, the officer is limited on his exit to seek out cover or concealment. The officers should bring any elevators to the first floor and secure them so they cannot be used or summonsed to other floors.

In general, officers should avoid entering the building through a window. If a window is the only alternative, then the officers should:

- Secure their firearms in their holsters
- Designate a cover officer to watch any areas the entering officer cannot see
- Clear the room visually

In addition, when entering through a window, the officers should be aware of building hazards as well as any suspect(s). The entering officers should be on the lookout for broken glass from the window, if the suspect had entered in this manner, and furniture (e.g., desks, shelving, chairs, radiator covers, tables, etc.) that may not support an officer's body weight.

When making an entrance, the officer should get inside as quickly as possible and locate cover. If it is dark, the officer should try to allow time to gain his "night eyes" or "night vision." The officer should then secure the room.

The officers should communicate silently through hand signals. However, when communicating, the officer should not look away from his area of responsibility.

Once inside the building, the officer should scan the room at firearm point (i.e., checking the room with the weapon in the ready position, which is in front of the officer).

Searching and Clearing the Room

To search and clear the room, the officer should **run the walls.** To run the walls, the officer should place his firearm in a position, known as "ready," that is not pointed at anything but down and ready to use if needed, and move around the perimeter of the room with his back against the wall. The officer should avoid and brushing or scraping against the walls to eliminate any unnecessary noises or sounds so as to prevent the subject from hearing the approach.

When entering, or penetrating, a room, the officer enters with, *not ahead of,* his partner. The officer should move with his partner unless they are each responsible for clearing a different area of the room. When clearing a specific area of the room, the officer should make sure that his partner has adequate cover. The officer should avoid all **crossfire** situations.

When moving around the room, the officers should make sure they do not move or touch anything that looks suspicious or out of place (e.g., radio playing). The officers should not turn off normal building noise (e.g., radio), because this may alert the suspect as to the officers' position. The suspect knows the radio is on and where it is, and the sudden silence of the radio turned off will alert the suspect of the officer's location or that others are in the building.

Once the room of entry is secure, the officers can then move carefully and quietly into the hallway or next room, depending on the building.

Entering a Hallway

Upon entering the hallway and before the officer moves on, the officer should stop and listen for any noises. In addition, the officer should pause frequently to listen during the building search.

Listening is the safest way for an officer to determine if a subject is in an area. It also enables the officer to adjust to noise in the building. By listening, the officer may hear the subject breathing heavily, moving, or running, actions associated with the break-in such as sounds of prying, smashing, or bumping into furniture as he moves.

The following is an important fact that may save your life: *A bullet can follow a path 6 to 12 inches from the wall.* This means that a bullet fired at a target against the wall may cause the bullet not to deflect at the same angle, but instead run along the wall parallel to the wall surface. Keep this in mind as you move around the building.

At corners of hallways, use the **quick-peek** or the **slice-the-pie** technique. The quick-peek technique enables the officer to "look before leaping." To perform the quick-peek technique, the officer should look quickly around the corner or through the crack of an opened door with one eye. The officer should never peek at the same height twice. The officer's partner should provide cover. This will prevent the suspect, if he observed the officer doing the quick peek, from lining him up for a target.

The **slice-the-pie technique** offers a means of rounding the corners and softening rooms. To perform the slice-the-pie technique, an officer should be 6 feet from the corner, moving away from the wall. This allows the officer to observe the unknown a little at a time, in a safe manner. The officer should place his firearm in the "third eye" or "belt tuck" position. (To assume the third-eye firearm position, the officer should hold the firearm in the two-handed grip in front of the belt buckle, keeping the firearm close to the body. This ensures that the slide of the weapon has room to function.) The officer should then shuffle-step sideways toward the opposite corner of the hallway wall (on a diagonal), taking small steps at a time. As the corner becomes visible, the officer should slowly clear it by peeking quickly and leaning the upper body forward. The officer should make all movements slowly and in 1-inch or smaller increments. The officer should also mentally "paint" the hallway or room while viewing it.

Before taking a corner or entering a doorway, the officer should not walk into an unknown situation and needs to see who or what is on the other side of the corner or the door. Some officers will use a mirror to accomplish this; however, most police officers do not carry one. An officer should be aware of his or her partner's position, avoid any crossfire, and avoid bunching (staying close together) to ensure safety on the corners or doorways. Officers may tend to group together for a feeling of safety.

Controlling the Lighting

To control the lighting during a building search, the officers should turn on all possible lights to minimize the subject's hiding areas. The officers will try to prevent exterior lights from betraying their approach (shadows arriving into the next search area before the officers' approach if the lights are behind them). If possible, the officers should extinguish all exterior lights.

The officers should be careful in their use of the flashlight. The officers should avoid silhouetting themselves or other officers with the flashlight. In addition, the officers should avoid shining the lights in the direction of themselves or others which may cause the reflection of shiny objects, equipment, and badges, on their uniforms.

If necessary, if a suspect is seen, the officer can use light from the flashlight to blind the subject temporarily, which may cause confusion or disorientation. The officer can then change position after a short burst of light to avoid being an easy target for a hidden subject.

The officer should avoid entering a dark room from a lighted hallway or room, because the eyes need time to adjust to low-light conditions. It takes approximately 20 minutes for night vision to develop fully.

Note, however, that some officers prefer to search a room in darkness. They feel the lighting of the room gives away their positions.

Keep in mind most rooms have a light switch next to the door, so if an officer turns on the light, it automatically gives his position away.

Take a moment to consider the following two examples and picture them in your head. After doing so, you may have an idea as to why there is a difference in opinion on these techniques.

Say that an officer is searching a large warehouse and enters the darkened area where the suspect is hiding. The officer has no idea what the inside layout of the building is (i.e., shelving, partitions, lofts, etc); the suspect does. What happens when the lights come on? Who has the advantage when the lights come on? What if the suspect has a firearm?

Consider the same scenario but say that the officer is searching an office building that has a number of smaller rooms and offices. The officer has no idea what the inside layout of the building is (i.e., shelving, partitions, lofts, etc); the suspect does. But in this case, the area to be searched is much smaller and more confined. What happens when the lights come on? Who has the advantage when the lights come on? What if the suspect has a firearm?

Some officers believe that "lighting it up" enables them do a quick scan of a room for cover. Once the officer is in a secure location, he has a clearer and quicker view of the room and can observe any suspect movement or identify the location of any suspicious sounds.

Entering Rooms

In order to enter a room safely, the officer should try and determine the direction the door opens by learning to read and understand the door hinges. The door hinges will indicate if the door opens in or out.

If the door is unlocked and opens outward, then the officer on the side of the door knob should stay low and the partner should stay at the opposite side of the door (hinge side). The first officer should throw the door open to the partner. The partner should then grab the door and make sure it stays open.

If the door is unlocked and opens inward, the officer positioned the same as above should open the door slightly, step backward, and listen. The officer should then push the door hard enough to open it against the wall; this will expose any subject who may be hiding behind it. The door will strike the suspect if the suspect is hiding behind the door.

Once the door is opened, the officers should use the slice-the-pie technique from the doorjamb. When using the slice-the-pie technique to observe the area beyond the open-door situation, the officer should stay approximately 3 feet from the doorway and move toward the opening. The officer should check the room while he is moving. Keep in mind that structurally, the wall on either side of the door may not be adequate cover to stop a bullet.

Officers can use the *wraparound,* or *buttonhook, technique* to enter the room. To perform the wraparound technique, the officers should stand on either the opposite sides of the door or on the same side of the door. Keeping their backs to the wall, the officers should wrap around the wall and into the room one at a time. Speed and fluid motion are important with the wraparound technique. Officers want to avoid any stops in the door-way where they may be silhouetted. Officers should be prepared to keep moving into the room if it is darkened and there is furniture or some other obstacle preventing them from positioning themselves immediately inside the door.

Another technique for entering a room is the *diagonal technique.* To perform the diagonal technique, the officers stand on the same side of the doorway and at same time both rush crosswise through the door and into the room to positions of cover. The diagonal technique requires speed.

Officers may also use the *"X" technique* to enter a room. To perform the "X" room-entering technique, the officers stand at opposite sides of the doorway (one on the knob and the other on the hinge side) and then enter the room at almost the same time in a crisscross fashion.

Navigating Stairways

Clearing the stairways is also known as *stairway navigation.* Officers should use the leapfrog technique to navigate a stairway. With the leapfrog technique, one officer moves first and then provides cover to the other officers.

If searching a multistory building, the ideal search should have enough officers to cover all stairwells in the building as well as any unsecured elevators. Covering stairwells and elevators prevents the subject from moving between floors. However, in most cases this alone would require a significant number of officers as well as those securing the outside and used for the search.

In order to ascend stairways safely during the building search, the officers should use the *foot-drag method* to avoid tripping. With the foot-drag method, the officer takes one step at a time. The officer should avoid rubbing any walls or making noise that would betray his or her position.

When descending stairways safely during the a building search, the officer should maintain a low stance, keeping the head as close to the feet as possible, or as in a crouched position.

Where to Search

When conducting a building search, the officers should search all places a small adult or child could hide. The officer conducting the search should make sure not to overlook an area of the building. The search should include all parts of the building—from the basement to the roof. In addition, officers should remember to look up, especially in warehouses, where suspects could be hiding on top of boxes or shelving as well as on overhead pipes and vents. Many officers fail to look upward when searching. When searching residences, officers should also make sure to check on closet shelves and attic entrances as well as crawlspaces on top and under a house.

Locating the Subject

If and when a subject has been located in the building, the officer should maintain his cover and have the subject walk backward toward him. The officer should handcuff and search the subject (**FIGURE 11-2**). Once the subject has been secured and searched, the officer should move to a secure area with the suspect.

The officer, who is with the suspect, should never remain alone in an unsecured area. It is not known if there are additional subjects elsewhere in the building. The officers should search any areas left unsecured to check for additional suspects. Remember the "plus one" rule: there may be more than one subject at any time. Always expect one more then what you find. This applies to suspects and weapons alike.

FIGURE 11-2
Police officers make an arrest of a suspect in a break-in at a warehouse.

Chapter Wrap-Up

When searching a multistory building, once the outside of the building has been secured, you should start your search from the top floor and work your way down. If there is a suspect on a lower floor and he is flushed out of the building after hearing or seeing you skip his floor as you proceed upstairs, your backup officers outside the building will apprehend him on his exit of the building.

■ From the Experts

Always search everywhere; don't assume that "no one would or could hide in there." Small adults and children can hide almost anywhere. They have been found in kitchen and bathroom cabinets, laundry baskets, washing machines and dryers, refrigerators, and so on.

■ Caution

Never assume that a hiding place is too small for someone to hide. Never walk by an "unknown" or any place that a suspect could hide. Suspects can hide in the least obvious locations, as well as small spaces such as cabinets, chests, etc. Never forget to look on top of cabinets, shelving, and stacked boxes in commercial or residential searches.

■ Key Terms

concealment: When an object can prevent the officer from being seen, but that cannot protect an officer from a suspect's bullets.

cover: Some sort of protection that an officer can use to protect himself from gunfire. The cover object should be solid, such as a tree, building, cement wall, motor vehicle, and so on.

cover officer: Protects the primary, or lead, officer, keeping alert to any dangers or threats that may arise from an officer's unguarded side.

crossfire: A situation when an officer and one or more officers are positioned in such a way that other officers, bystanders, or others will be in the direct line of fire in the event that the officers have to fire their guns.

fatal funnel: Any location where an officer is vulnerable to an attack from an unknown source.

point of entry: The location where it is believed that the suspect may have illegally entered the premises.

point of exit: The location where it is believed that the suspect may have exited the premises.

probable cause: A phrase that describes the facts observed, information obtained from others, and personal knowledge and experience that is sufficient to lead a reasonable and prudent person to believe that seizable evidence of crime exists, and that it will be found in a specific location or on a specific person.

quick peek: A technique that enables an officer to "look before leaping." With this technique, the officer with one eye looks quickly around the corner or through the crack of an opened door.

run the walls: A search technique whereby the officer places his firearm in "ready" position and moves around the perimeter of the room with his back against the wall.

slice the pie: A means of rounding the corners and softening rooms.

Your Assignment—Results

With regard to the opening case study, the first thing you would do is notify the police dispatcher of what you have observed (open door, etc.). You should request that the dispatcher send additional officers. You may have the police station contact the building owner.

Your Next Assignment

You have just stopped a motor vehicle that has been reported as being stolen. As the stolen vehicle comes to a stop, the operator opens the door and flees. You begin a foot pursuit of the suspect; there are no other passengers in the vehicle. The suspect is heading toward a nearby house.

- Can you shoot the suspect in order to stop him? Justify your answer.
- Can you follow the suspect inside the house? Explain why or why not.
- Do you need to get a warrant before entering the house? Explain why or why not.

Call for Service

You have just responded to a report of a break-in in progress. This usually means that a witness has seen someone enter a building who should not have. It is 3:00 A.M. Explain your use, or nonuse, of the lights in the building for each of the following scenarios. Defend your positions.

1. You have arrived at the scene and observe that the building in question is a large warehouse. The business is a storage facility for a moving company. You observe an open door on one side of the building. Closer inspection reveals that the padlock securing the building has been cut off with a pair of bolt cutters that you see lying on the ground. You have called for backup and the building owner. The backup units arrive and secure the outside of the building. You and your partner are ready to enter the dark building.

2. You have arrived at the scene and observe that the building is a small day-care center. The day-care center is located in a residential area and was once a single-family, one-story residence. You observe an open window at the rear of the house and some scuff marks on the vinyl siding under the window. You call for backup and the building owner. The backup units arrive and secure the outside of the building. You are assigned as a single-unit cruiser, and you are ready to enter the darkened building.

References

Massachusetts Criminal Justice Training Council (MCJTC), 1998. Patrol Response Module. South Weymouth, MA.

Waltham Police Department, 1997. Waltham Police Department Policy Manual, pp. 14–28. Waltham, MA.

Putting it Together

In Part II, you will complete the scenarios. These scenarios can be conducted in one of three ways, depending upon the learning environment and the format selected by the course instructor. The formats are as follows:

1. The student can simply read the situation presented. The student may then respond orally or complete a written assignment as to how he or she would respond to the situation.

2. The situation can be set up in the classroom, using desks and chairs as needed, and the students can take on the roles of the subjects described.

3. The scenario can be acted out with props in a location that is suitable for the specific situation, such as using vehicles in a parking lot, using rooms or a building, and so on.

Note that there should be no physical confrontations when conducting the role-playing situations. All enactments and situations should be presented at a walk-through pace.

CHAPTER 12

Motor Vehicle Stops: Minor Infractions and Traffic Violations

Knowledge Objectives

- Describe the proper procedure and technique for making a motor vehicle stop.
- Understand the basic rules for making a motor vehicle stop.
- Know how to conduct a basic motor vehicle stop safely and effectively.

Skills Objectives

- Describe the interaction between a law enforcement official and a citizen during a traffic stop.
- Demonstrate the ability to handle a verbal or a suggested physical confrontation by an irate citizen.
- Demonstrate the powers of observation when approaching a stopped vehicle.
- Demonstrate the ability to locate and identify visible contraband.

■ Introduction

In this chapter, you will learn how to make a motor vehicle stop for a minor traffic infraction and how to deal with offenders.

■ Investigative Stops

When a police officer makes an investigative stop that involves a motor vehicle, the vehicle may be stopped and the occupants (driver and passengers) may be briefly detained and questioned if there is a reasonable suspicion of criminal activity based on specific and articulable facts that justify the need for immediate police action. In other words, if a police officer makes a stop, the officer must have a reason why he wants to make the stop and must be able to articulate that reason. An officer *cannot* just stop a vehicle because it looks suspicious or because the operators are of a particular race or ethnic group that would make them fit a "profile" of a suspect.

An officer can stop a vehicle for a number of different reasons. An officer can stop a vehicle for an equipment violation, such as a burnt-out headlight, a loud muffler, an expired inspection sticker, and so on. An officer may also make a stop for a traffic violation, also called a *moving violation,* which may be a red light or stop sign violation, speeding, and so on. Infractions such as expired license plates or expired or suspended drivers license may fall under be considered criminal offenses depending on the laws and ordinances of the jurisdiction.

Motor vehicle stops are extremely dangerous for police officers. When they make such stops, officers are dealing with unknowns in a constantly shifting environment. Police officers must be especially alert and watchful when making an investigative stop of a motor vehicle; many officers have been seriously injured, some fatally, in taking this police action.

When making such stops, officers should take reasonable protective precautions for their own safety, such as directing the occupants to exit the vehicle and frisking them for weapons when justification for such frisks exists.

The occupants of a stopped vehicle may be frisked if the officer has reasonable belief that they may be armed and dangerous and that the police officers or others nearby may be endangered. Even after frisking the occupants, if the officers have reason to believe that there is still a possible danger, they should inspect those areas of the motor vehicle that are "readily" accessible to an occupant that may contain a dangerous weapon.

A protective search of the interior of a motor vehicle must be limited to what is minimally necessary to determine whether the suspect is armed and to remove any weapon discovered. A protective search for weapons in a motor vehicle must be confined to the area from which the occupant might gain possession of a weapon.

It should be noted that "random" stops of motor vehicles in the absence of reasonable suspicion of motor vehicle violations or criminal activity constitutes an unreasonable seizure in violation of the Fourth Amendment. Any evidence obtained as a result of such impermissible stops is excludable in court.

Conducting the Motor Vehicle Stop

A motor vehicle stop for a minor motor vehicle or traffic infraction involves several different steps on the part of the officer. These steps are presented here; they are followed by a series of scenarios where you can apply what you have learned about conducting motor vehicle stops.

Step 1

When an officer has decided to stop a motor vehicle for a minor infraction, the officer must make some decisions and take some actions.

First, the officer should identify a safe location for the stop, making sure that the stop does not take place on a hill; a curve; a narrowed lane, as may be the case on a bridge; or obstruct an intersection. The stop should be in a well-lit area that is safe enough for the officer and the occupants.

FIGURE 12-1
A cruiser in the offset position.

FIGURE 12-2
Turning the cruiser's wheels to the left will offer additional protection to the officer.

When the officer determines where the stop is to be made, the officer should turn on her emergency equipment, such as the blue lights and siren, as necessary. Activating these too soon may cause the vehicle that is being stopped to pull over in an unsafe location.

As the officer makes the stop, the officer should notify the station or dispatcher and provide the dispatcher with the following information:

- Location of the stop
- Vehicle license plate number
- Vehicle model
- Vehicle make
- Vehicle color
- Reason for the stop
- Number of occupants in the vehicle. (The officer may request any additional backup or help at this time. If backup is called, the officer should wait for the backup to arrive before approaching the vehicle.)

Once the vehicle is stopped, the officer should position the cruiser in an offset position (**FIGURE 12-1**). The cruiser should be positioned so that the right front headlight is aligned with the center of the trunk of the stopped vehicle. The cruiser's wheels should be turned to the left. This will afford the officer additional cover or protection, if needed. Also, if the cruiser gets struck from behind, with the wheels turned to the left, the impact will cause the struck cruiser to swerve to the left, away from the officer who may be standing alongside the stopped vehicle (**FIGURE 12-2**).

Step 2

Once the vehicle has been stopped in a safe location and the dispatcher has been notified, it is time to approach the vehicle and operator. However, before exiting the cruiser the officer should make the following observations:

- What are the occupants in the stopped vehicle doing? Do they appear to be hiding something? Are they moving or acting suspiciously?
- Is the trunk lock popped out? (This may indicate a stolen vehicle. The trunk would be popped to gain access to the contents.)
- Is the vehicle clean and the license plate dirty? Or is the plate clean and the vehicle dirty? (This may indicate a stolen car with a stolen, attached plate.)
- Does the age of the occupants match the type of vehicle? (Of course, a juvenile operator could be driving his parents' car, but it may also be an indication of a stolen car or a "joy ride" incident.)
- Is the license plate attached by screws or is it wired or tied on? This would indicate a hastily attached plate.

Step 3

Once the officer makes these preliminary observations and has determined that it is safe to approach the vehicle, the officer may proceed to the next step: approaching the vehicle. When approaching the vehicle, the officer's attention should be focused on the occupants. An officer may approach a vehicle in a number of different ways depending on the circumstances of the stop.

Daytime Stops

When approaching a vehicle during the daytime, the officer may use the driver's side approach, the passenger side approach, or the two-officer approach:

- **Driver's side approach.** With this approach, the officer exits the cruiser and walks to the operator's side of the vehicle. This position offers the officer the advantage of the operator having to turn to respond to the officer. The officer can then make some observations on the operator and any passengers.

- **Passenger side approach.** With this approach, the officer walks to the passenger side of the vehicle. This is usually a surprise to the operator, who is most likely expecting the officer to approach on the driver's side. This affords the officer a more visible view of the operator and the center console of a vehicle if there is no passenger. (It should be noted that most people are right handed, which may be a disadvantage to the officer in some circumstances.)
- **Two-officer approach.** If there are two officers making the stop, each officer will take one side of the vehicle.

Nighttime Stops

When approaching a vehicle during the nighttime, the officer may use the driver's side approach, the passenger side approach, or the two-officer approach. However, if a nighttime stop is of a nature where a higher level of caution is needed, then other factors regarding motor vehicle stops come into play; these will be discussed in greater detail in the subsequent chapters.

If the officer wishes to use the element of surprise, she may approach the vehicle from the passenger side. When it is dark outside, the officer may choose to exit her vehicle very quietly, making sure not to slam the cruiser door, and then walk behind the cruiser to the right side of the vehicle and approach the stopped vehicle from the passenger side. The officer would go behind the cruiser to avoid walking across the cruiser headlights between the two cars. This keeps the operator of the vehicle off guard, if that is a needed or desired effect.

The Approach

Regardless of the time of day, the officer should check the following during her approach:
- **Trunk.** As the officer approaches the rear of the stopped vehicle, the officer will check the trunk to make sure that it is secure. Although the occasion of a person hiding in the trunk may seem remote, you want to make sure all is secure before you pass it. Keep in mind that a secured trunk may be opened from a lever in the passenger compartment from the operator.
- **Rear-passenger compartment.** During the approach, the officer should look into the vehicle as he moves forward. If there are occupants in the rear of the car, the officer should observe their hands, the floor (if possible), between their legs, and so on. The officer should observe any place where something may have been stashed.
- **Front-passenger compartment.** The officer should observe the operator, the operator's hands, and any objects within reach of the operator, including the console, sun visors, door pockets, and glove compartment. If you cannot see an area because of the layout of the vehicle's interior, then keep your eyes on the person's hands.

Step 4

Once the officer is at the vehicle, the officer should position her body in relation to the vehicle and the operator. Depending on the circumstances, the officer may choose to stand at the doorpost between the front and rear windows on the driver's side of the vehicle. This makes the driver reach back awkwardly to his left to hand information to the officer as well as to speak with her. This places the officer at a greater positional advantage.

If there are rear-seat passengers, the officer may feel more comfortable standing behind the rear-window doorpost. In this case, the operator has to pass the information to the rear passenger who then passes it to the officer. This enables the officer to keep her eyes on the occupants in the front and rear compartments.

In some jurisdictions, officers prefer to have the operator step out of the vehicle. The officer then conducts the business of the stop either at the rear of the stopped vehicle, between the vehicle and the cruiser, or at the right shoulder of the road or the sidewalk.

Step 5

Once the officer has positioned herself in relation to the vehicle, the officer initiates the interaction or conversation. The officer should always be cordial and polite, not demeaning. Police officers are professionals. They should afford the citizens they deal with the same respect that they demand. When conversing with the public in any forum, officers should not belittle, scream, yell, argue, or use profanity.

Step 6

Sometimes an officer will return to the cruiser during the stop. Some officers will move to the rear of the cruiser to write a citation or warning or to conduct a computer check. When walking back to the cruiser, the officer should take an occasional glance at the occupants and the stopped vehicle.

If the officer returns to the cruiser, the officer should always be observant of the occupants of the stopped vehicle. While in the cruiser, the officer should not write citations on her lap; the officer should use the steering wheel in order to keep paperwork at eye level to enable better observation.

When returning to the stopped vehicle, the officer should take the same precautions as with the initial approach and watch for anything that is different or out of place from the initial approach.

Step 7

After the officer has conducted the business of the stop, the officer should return to the cruiser, cautiously watching the stopped vehicle. The officer should watch the stopped vehicle so that it can return to the flow of traffic safely.

The officer should then notify the dispatcher that the stop has been cleared and that the officer is back in service. The officer should return to the flow of traffic and turn off the vehicle's emergency lights.

Your Assignment 12-1

It is a sunny and warm Sunday morning at 9:45 A.M., and traffic flow is light. You are parked in a marked police cruiser. You were parked in a parking lot of a closed business at the intersection of Maple and Elm Streets, watching the traffic lights at the intersection for violations. You are now entering the intersection to continue your patrol. As the traffic light turns green (you are heading north on Elm Street), you observe a motor vehicle traveling west on Maple Street proceed through the intersection, running the red light.

In your community, the red light infraction is a violation punishable with a $100.00 fine. The insurance company imposes a surcharge for the offense if the driver is found to be responsible. The surcharge is $75.00 a year added onto the premium for four years.

As you pull into traffic westerly on Maple Street, you activate your emergency lights and siren to stop the vehicle. The operator observes you in his rearview mirror and immediately pulls over to the side of the road.

You have positioned your cruiser properly, the location of the stop is safe, and you have provided the dispatcher with the proper information (location, vehicle description, plate number, number of occupants, and reason for the stop).

You exit the cruiser and approach the stopped vehicle, making all of the proper observations. As you approach the rear-passenger compartment, you observe three small children, all wearing seatbelts and/or in car seats. They are approximately ages 4, 6, and 8 years. As you approach the front-passenger compartment, you observe a male operator and a female passenger dressed in proper church clothing, a suit and a dress.

You approach the car. Once you are in speaking distance, the operator rolls down his window to speak with you. He asks if he did something wrong and at the same time hands you a valid driver's license, vehicle registration, and proper proof of insurance.

As an officer, you have certain discretions. You may either write a citation, write a warning, or give a verbal warning.

1. Describe what you would do in this case. Be specific as to how you would deal with the operator of the vehicle, the wife, and the children.
2. Would you write a citation for the red light violation? Explain why or why not.
3. Would you write a warning for the red light violation? Explain why or why not.
4. Would you give a verbal warning for the red light violation? Explain why or why not.
5. After returning to your vehicle after the motor vehicle stop, what would you do next?

Your Assignment 12-2

It is a sunny and warm Monday morning of a long holiday weekend. It is 11:00 A.M. You are traveling through an intersection when the vehicle to your left runs a stop sign and enters the intersection in front of you, causing you to stop suddenly to avoid a collision.

The operator sees you. As soon as he is in his proper lane, he immediately pulls over before you even have to activate your blue lights or siren.

You pull in behind him and turn on your blue lights for visibility and safety. You make all the proper notifications to the dispatcher and observations of the stopped vehicle.

As you approach the vehicle, you observe that there is a 10-year-old girl in the back seat; she is properly belted in. As you move forward toward the vehicle, you notice that the driver is an 18-year-old male. He states that he is the girl's older brother and that he is dropping off his sister for soccer practice and was running late.

He acknowledges the stop sign violation and he has all the proper paperwork, such as driver's license, vehicle registration, and proof of insurance.

In your jurisdiction, the stop sign violation is punishable with a $100.00 fine. The insurance company imposes a surcharge for the offense if the driver is found to be responsible. The surcharge is $100.00 a year added onto the basic insurance premium for four years.

As an officer, you have certain discretions. You may either write a citation, write a warning, or give a verbal warning.

1. Describe what you would do in this case. Be specific as to how you would deal with the operator.
2. Would you write a citation for the stop sign violation? Explain why or why not.
3. Would you write a warning for the stop sign violation? Explain why or why not.
4. Would you give a verbal warning for the stop sign violation? Explain why or why not.
5. After returning to your vehicle after the motor vehicle stop, what would you do next?

Your Assignment 12-3

It is a Saturday evening at 10:00 P.M. The outside temperature is a cool and breezy 54°F degrees. You are patrolling in your jurisdiction and are assigned to a two-officer cruiser. You and your partner are back in service after clearing a call for a group of youths causing a disturbance.

While driving eastbound on Main Street, you observe a vehicle traveling westbound, also on Main Street, with only one headlight operating. As the vehicle passes you, you also hear the stereo blasting loudly from inside the vehicle, which has its windows rolled down. The vehicle is occupied by two males between the ages of 17 and 19.

You turn your cruiser around and pull in behind the vehicle and activate your blue lights and siren. After several seconds pass, the vehicle acknowledges the cruiser and pulls over to the right-hand side of the road.

1. What do you do now? Explain all the steps you would make up until the point of exiting the cruiser.
2. Explain what steps you and your partner will take as you exit the cruiser and approach the vehicle. Make sure to explain all the steps and observations you make up until the verbal communication begins.

You are now positioned properly and are about to begin speaking with the operator of the vehicle. The occupants of the vehicle have, upon your approach, turned down the radio. The operator has his registration for the vehicle and proper proof of insurance. He does not have his wallet, which contains his driver's license. He gives you all the information you need to run a check on his license through the computer (i.e., name and date of birth).

In your jurisdiction, the following laws apply in this case:

- You may issue a traffic citation for the violation of operating the vehicle without a headlight. The fine is $50.00, and there is no insurance surcharge attached to this offense.
- You may issue him an equipment violation, which is a ticket. The operator then has 10 days to have the defective equipment repaired. The operator must bring the vehicle to the issuing police department in order to verify the repair has been made. There is no fine attached to this option. Failure to have the repair on the defective equipment fixed and inspected will result in the issuance of a ticket.
- You may issue a summons or file a complaint for a violation of the noise ordinance in your jurisdiction for the loud stereo. This is punishable by a $100.00 fine.
- You may arrest the operator of the vehicle for not having his license in his possession.

You have returned to your cruiser and are awaiting a response to the inquiry into the status of the operators license. The dispatcher notifies you that the license on the operator is valid and active, there are no warrants, and the registration of the vehicle is also active and valid.

3. Based on the information presented, what actions will you take, if any? Explain your reasoning and why you used your discretion to make the choices you did.

Your Assignment 12-4

It is 4:00 P.M. on a cold and snowy Wednesday afternoon. The roads have been plowed regularly, but the snow is covering the road at a pace that the snowplows cannot maintain. You are parked in a parking lot, observing traffic and awaiting any calls for service that may be dispatched to you.

You know that on nights like this it is sometimes better to be a visible stationary deterrent to traffic offenders then it is to be a mobile one. People will tend to slow down and be more cautious if they see a cruiser. This intersection is one of high traffic volume, and your presence is conspicuous.

As you observe the intersection you see a vehicle approaching. As the light turns yellow, the driver accelerates the vehicle to beat the light before it changes to red. The driver then decides that she will not make it through the light and begins to apply the brakes enough to stop for the light, now red. In doing so, the vehicle enters into a skid and rotates 180 degrees, spinning through the intersection. The vehicle, which is operated by a young female approximately 20 years of age, comes to rest on the opposite side of the intersection, facing north in the southbound lane. (The vehicle is facing the wrong direction, against the curb.)

The young woman appears to be shaken up, but is uninjured. You position the cruiser with the blue lights on in order to afford as much protection as possible. The vehicle is fully operable with no damage.

In this case, you have the following violations. It is up to you to choose your options:

- It is a violation to operate a vehicle at a speed that is greater than the road or traffic conditions will allow.
- You can issue a red light violation, because she did go through the intersection when the traffic light had turned red.

1. What will you do? In a narrative report, explain all of the actions you would take and why. Be complete; cover all of your actions up until the time you return to service.

Your Assignment 12-5

It is a Saturday night at 11:15 P.M. on a cool moonlit evening. You have been assigned to respond to a residential neighborhood where there has been a report of a speeding motor vehicle, which has been burning rubber with its tires. You are in a two-officer cruiser. Neighbors have described the vehicle as being dark in color with several occupants in the vehicle.

The following offenses are all misdemeanors and must be committed in your presence in order to take any action. The laws of this jurisdiction are as follows:

- Improper starting or stopping (screeching the tires) is punishable by a $100.00 fine and a four-year $100.00 per year surcharge added to the insurance premium.
- Driving as to endanger, or reckless driving, carries a maximum penalty of a $500.00 fine and may also result in the loss of a driver's license for 90 days. This also comes with a four-year insurance surcharge of $250.00 per year. You, the police officer, must be able to prove some degree of recklessness or willful and wanton negligent behavior or actions on the part of the operator. In other words, the operator must know that the action is dangerous and have total disregard for the public at large, which includes any passengers.
- Speeding carries a maximum penalty of a $50.00 fine for speeding and an additional $10.00 per mile for every mile per over the speed limit, after the first 10 miles per hour over.
  - If the speed limit is 30 miles per hour and the vehicle is clocked at 39 miles per hour, the fine is $50.00, because the speed was 9 miles over the limit.
  - If the speed limit is 30 miles per hour and the vehicle is clocked at 41 miles per hour, then the fine would be $60.00. This amount is represented by the initial $50.00 fine plus an additional $10.00 for the 41st mile, which is one over the base 10 miles per hour given by statute.

1. What would be the fine for a vehicle that is stopped for speeding at a speed of 57 mph in a 35-mph zone?

As you and your partner approach the residential area, you hear tires screeching and proceed in the direction of the noise. As you turn a corner, you can see the remnants of smoke clearing from the area; the smell of burnt rubber permeates the air. You observe what appears to be fresh tire marks in the pavement. This is clearly visible form the well-lit streets.

You drive around the area for a while. You observe a dark-colored vehicle parked on the side of the road. Five young men between the ages of 18 and 19 are standing around the vehicle. The vehicle is not running. You pull up behind it and approach the group standing outside the car.

2. Before speaking with any of the individuals, what could you do, or what observations could you make to determine if this was the vehicle making all the noise and operating in an unsafe manner?

As you approach the group, you ask who owns the vehicle. One of the young men steps forward and says that he is the owner.

3. What do you need to determine?

4. What would you do if the operator denies doing anything wrong? Explain in detail what you would do and justify your actions.

5. What would you do if the operator admits that he is the one who was driving in that manner? Explain in detail what you would do and justify your actions.

Chapter Wrap-Up

In-Service Training

When starting your tour of duty, always inspect your vehicle, especially the rear-passenger compartment. Check the seat cushions and floor for any contraband that may have been dumped by a prisoner on a previous shift.

From the Experts

When approaching a vehicle you have stopped, if the vehicle is still running, watch the rear lights. If the brake lights are illuminated, the car may still be in drive. If the white backup light flashes, the operator may have shifted from park to drive.

Caution

Use caution when exiting your vehicle to approach a stopped vehicle. Remember that your cruiser is parked at an offset to the car in front of you. Your right-front headlight should be lined up with the center of the trunk of the stopped vehicle in front of you. Always make sure you check your rearview and sideview mirrors. The driver's side of the vehicle is much closer to the flow of traffic.

Reference

Massachusetts Criminal Justice Training Council (MCJTC), 1998. Motor Vehicle Stop Module. South Weymouth, MA.

Motor Vehicle Stops: Driving Under the Influence–Drugs or Alcohol

Knowledge Objectives

- Determine the proper procedure and technique for making a motor vehicle stop for a driver suspected of operating under the influence of drugs or alcohol.
- Identify the signs that a driver is operating under the influence of drugs or alcohol.
- Know the proper precautions to take when making motor vehicle stop under these conditions.
- Conduct a motor vehicle stop safely and effectively.

Skills Objectives

- Describe the interaction between a law enforcement official and a citizen during a traffic stop.
- Demonstrate the ability to handle a verbal or a suggested physical confrontation by an irate citizen.
- Demonstrate the powers of observation when approaching a stopped vehicle.
- Demonstrate the ability to locate and identify visible contraband.
- Understand drug and alcohol detection phases, clues, and techniques.
- Understand requirements for organizing and presenting testimony and documentary evidence in DWI cases.
- Recognize and interpret evidence of DWI violations.
- Administer and interpret standardized field sobriety tests.
- Know and recognize typical vehicle maneuvers and human indicators symptomatic of DWI.
- Know and recognize typical sensory and other clues of alcohol and/or drug influence that may be seen during face-to-face contact with DWI suspects.
- Know and recognize typical behavioral indications of alcohol and/or drug use when a suspect steps out of a motor vehicle.
- Write a narrative report that describes your observations and the operator's actions and reactions.

■ Introduction

In this chapter, you will learn how to make a motor vehicle stop for a driver who appears to be under the influence of alcohol or drugs.

■ Highway Safety

The police focus on motor-vehicle-related arrests and traffic tickets in order to enforce public compliance with traffic laws. The purpose of enforcing compliance with traffic laws is to reduce motor vehicle collisions, which oftentimes result in death and injuries.

The National Highway Traffic Safety Administration (U.S. Department of Transportation) states:

> There are over 40,000 highway fatalities each year in the United States. This number puts highway death and injury in a category with other major public health issues. By collecting data regarding causes and conditions of collisions, analyzing the data, and formulating actions to reduce the number of collisions, police display problem solving in one of the most serious quality-of-life issues. (Technology can be of great assistance in this effort.)
>
> In Massachusetts, 80 percent of fatalities occur on secondary roads where posted speed limits are 45 mph or less. This fact indicates that highway safety is clearly not an exclusive high-speed phenomenon. Municipal police can expand their attention beyond radar and tickets to include public service education regarding seat belts, speed, alcohol, and vehicle maintenance (Massachusetts Criminal Justice Training Council, 1998).

Educating the public has become a primary police strategy in reducing highway collisions and subsequent injuries. Speed, seat belts, responsible alcohol use, and vehicle maintenance are all key factors that are within the control of drivers.

Motor vehicle stops are an important tool in educating the public about highway safety. They also are an important opportunity to demonstrate civility and respect to the public. A motor vehicle or traffic stop offers an officer an opportunity to create a change in the performance of the operator for the better, not to punish him or her for wrongdoing. In some cases, a warning will be more effective than a citation.

In Chapter 12, you learned the basic procedure for making a motor vehicle stop. All of these procedures will carry through this into this chapter. However, in this chapter we go a step further and discuss motor vehicle stops involving suspected impaired drivers.

Impaired Motor Vehicle Operators

Many traffic accidents, particularly those involving a fatality or personal injury, are directly attributable to persons who are driving under the influence of alcohol and/or drugs. In all motor-vehicle-related incidents, officers should be aware of the possibility that the driver may be under the influence alcohol or drugs. If the officer determines that the operator is under the influence of alcohol or drugs, the officer should take appropriate enforcement action. Appropriate enforcement action consists of immediate arrest or, if the circumstances do not allow for an arrest (e.g., if an operator is admitted to a hospital, the officer has no means to effect an arrest), the officer should issue a citation.

It is important to understand that there are several possible reasons for the impairment. An operator may suffer from a medical problem, such as diabetes, shock, heart attack, stroke, and so on. A motor vehicle operator may be overtaken by a sudden incident or episode and that will at first glance make the operator look as if he or she is driving under the influence of drugs or alcohol. These drivers may even appear to be incoherent. You may also smell strong odors from their breath, such as an acetone or a sweet smell, which may appear to be alcohol.

Other operators may be on a medication and may not realize the effects it has had on them. Although technically these operators are driving under the influence of drugs, the officer needs to look at the intent and knowledge of the person and the medication taken. Did the person take the medication knowing how he or she would be affected? Was the medication just prescribed or just picked up from a pharmacy?

A third type of impaired operator is the person who has ingested drugs, whether legally or illegally obtained, and the person has chosen to operate a vehicle, regardless of the consequences and without respect of the rights of others.

The fourth and last type of impaired operator we will discuss is the person who has decided to have alcoholic beverages and feels that he or she is able to operate a motor vehicle. Like the operator who uses drugs, this person also is not concerned with the consequences of his or her actions or the rights of others.

Signs of Impairment

This chapter focuses on drivers who are impaired due to drug or alcohol use. However, the signs that an operator is or may be impaired are the same for all impaired drivers, regardless of the cause of their impairment. What are some of the signs that indicate that an operator is under the influence or impaired for some other reason?

Erratic Operation

Erratic operation of a motor vehicle is indicated when the operator slows down or accelerates in ways that do not reflect road or traffic conditions. For example, say an operator is driving down a straight roadway in a 30 mph speed zone and then suddenly slows down to 15 mph or repeatedly applies the brakes. The driver may continue this way or speed up unexpectedly where the road or driving conditions may not warrant such response. Any type of unexpected driving behavior indicates erratic operation.

Crossing Center Lines

Another indication of impairment is when an operator begins to drift over the center line either into oncoming traffic or toward the right side or shoulder of the road where parked cars or pedestrians may be.

Turn Signals

An impaired driver may leave his or her turn signals on after making a turn or may signal to make a turn and then not make the turn. This is also a stereotypical sign of an elderly driver or someone who is oblivious to what is going on. It is a common oversight—and improper use of turn signals alone does not determine that an operator is impaired. However, when coupled with other observations, this behavior may lead the officer to make determine that the driver is impaired.

Swerving

Swerving is similar to crossing the center line, which we discussed earlier. With swerving, the operator may appear to be driving fine and then make a deliberate and obvious swerve or adjustment of the vehicle. The operator may try justify his or her actions by telling the officer "a dog ran in front of my car" or "there was something in the road," or some similar story.

Wide or Narrow Turns

Another indication of an impaired operator is an operator who makes wide turns, crossing over the center line into ongoing traffic or, if at an intersection or traffic light, who comes too close to a vehicle that has stopped and is waiting for the light to change. An impaired driver may also make narrow turns, striking or running over the curbing or shoulder of the road. These operators may also strike cars parked close to the intersection on the right-hand side of the road.

No Lights or Other Equipment

Some impaired drivers forget to put on their headlights on in the dark or turn their wipers on in the rain.

It should be noted that these indicators are just indications of an impaired driver. We do not mean to suggest that every person who crosses a center line, who swerves, or who forgets their headlights is impaired. These occurrences should just draw an officer's attention to the operator. These signs, when coupled with other observations of the vehicle and the driver, will determine the outcome of the observation and/or the stop.

Making the Motor Vehicle Stop

Once an officer makes the motor vehicle stop and pulls the vehicle over, additional indicators may be presented: Did the operator pull the vehicle over in a rational manner? Was the vehicle positioned properly, as it would be with a normal driver? Did the vehicle come to a complete stop? When the officer activated her emergency lights and siren, did the operator of the vehicle notice right away? Did the driver acknowledge the officer promptly? Did the driver pull right over in an area where it was suitable?

It is important that the officer document any observations with regards to the impaired driver's actions and behavior, because they will determine the officer's subsequent actions. The documentation of this incident will be the written narrative report that coincides with the arrest.

Once the vehicle is stopped, the officer must make a few more observations. The officer must now determine whether the operator is impaired, ill, or under the influence of medication, drugs, or alcohol. If the driver does appear to be under the influence, is it from medication, too much alcohol, or the smoking or ingestion of illegal drugs?

In previous chapters, you learned how to approach a vehicle. As with other types of stops, officers look for items in the vehicle that may indicate what type of activity is going on. With regard to a stop of an impaired operator, the officer will look for empty or full beer bottles, cans, liquor bottles, or other indications of substances that may have affected the driver's ability to operate the vehicle properly.

The officer will also observe the driver: Are the driver's actions that of a rational and normal person? The officer should observe the following:

- **Breath.** Does the driver have alcohol on his breath?
- **Speech.** Is the driver's speech slurred? Is he running words together? Do sentences make sense?
- **Eyes.** Are the driver's eyes glassy?
- **Stance.** Is the driver steady on his feet? Is the driver able to maintain his posture and stance without staggering?

Field Sobriety Test

The officer's observations can be tested and documented in what is called a *field sobriety test*. The field sobriety test is a set of several individual tests that can assist an officer in determining the stability and coordination of the person in question and how it relates to his ability to operate a motor vehicle. The determination as to which individual tests are used and how many should be used is usually determined by department policy or protocol or court interjection or precedence. This battery of tests includes some of some of the following:

- **Ability to understand and follow directions.** The officer shall instruct the operator verbally as to how to perform all of the tests. The ability of the operator to understand and follow verbal instructions, with no visual examples, is part of the sobriety testing.
- **Alphabet test.** Can the operator recite the alphabet correctly?
- **Walk-and-turn, heel-to-toe test.** This tests the ability of the operator to balance and listen to and follow instructions given by the officer. The officer instructs the operator to stand on the solid line, with one foot in front of the other, no more than one-half inch apart. The officer then explains to the operator that he is to walk the line, one foot in front of the other. While walking, the operator is to count aloud from one to

nine. The operator is to walk heel to toe with his hands at his side. After taking nine steps, the operator is to pivot and repeat the procedure, ending at the starting point.

- **One-leg stand.** This tests the ability of the operator to maintain. The operator is instructed to raise one foot (either foot may be raised, the decision is left to the operator) six inches off the floor while counting to 30.
- **Finger-to-nose test.** This test enables the officer to test the operator's coordination. The operator is instructed to stand with his feet together and the head tilted back. While in this position, the operator is instructed to close his eyes and fully extend both arms outward in a horizontal position. The operator is then told to touch the index finger of one hand to the tip of his nose. The same instructions are then given for the other arm.
- **Horizontal-gaze (Nystagmus) test.** An officer makes certain and specific observations of the eye based on the operator's eye movement in following a moving object, such as a pen or pencil. This test is used to test the response and ability of an individual who is suspected to be under the influence.

Custody

Once the officer has determined that an operator is under the influence of either alcohol or drugs, an arrest should be made. In a situation requiring medical attention, as in the case of an accident with injuries, the operator as well as any or all passengers should be transported to the nearest medical facility by emergency personnel.

Once arrested, the operator should be transported to the police station or the detention center, whatever the protocol is for that jurisdiction. The operator will then be processed and booked. He will be afforded his rights and offered an opportunity to take a breathalyzer test and possibly to repeat the field sobriety tests. In some jurisdictions, this process is videotaped, including the field sobriety tests. Some departments have cruisers that are equipped with video recording devices; these are used to record any field observations made as well. Some of these cameras are set up to be activated as soon as the cruiser turns on the emergency equipment (blue lights) and continue recording until the lights are turned off and/or the police officer turns the camera off. Officers with such cameras are usually equipped with a remote portable battery-operated microphone.

From this point, the police officer's arrest process is complete. The next phases of the arrest are up to the courts and the legislative protocol of the jurisdiction.

Your Assignment 13-1

It is a Saturday night at 1:00 A.M.; you are in a one-officer cruiser. You are patrolling the outskirts of your town. The neighborhood is rural and remote and very sparsely populated. Houses are far apart, and there is very little, if any, traffic.

You observe a motor vehicle driving toward you with the headlights off. The vehicle is partially on your side of the road—it has crossed the center line of the two-lane roadway.

As you get closer, you have to pull over to the right to avoid being struck. As the vehicle passes you, you observe in your rearview mirror that the vehicle has applied its brakes, slowed down, pulled back into the proper traffic lane, and is proceeding on its way.

You turn your cruiser around and activate your blue lights, pulling up behind the now slow-moving vehicle. Turning on the blue lights also turns on the in-cruiser video camera. The operator in front of you has slowed down considerably more and is extremely deliberate in his driving. You observe two hands on the steering wheel and very precise movements. The driver, though driving slowly, is still proceeding forward and not stopping.

You activate your siren for a short blurt to gain the attention of the driver. The driver appears to see you in his rearview mirror and gestures his arm as if to signal either "up ahead" or "to the right." The driver eventually, after about another half mile of this 20-mph pursuit, pulls into a driveway at a residence. When doing so, he cuts the turn short and strikes the fence around the yard, hitting a car parked in the driveway. The driver then brings the vehicle to a stop and turns it off.

After stopping, the operator opens the door of the vehicle. He has a big smile on his face and almost falls out of the car; however, the driver's side front door saves him from falling. As he exits the vehicle he says, "Shee, I knew I could make it."

When he had initially refused to pull over, you ran a license check and a registration check on him based on the vehicle's plates. The driver lives at the address that he has pulled into.

You tell him to stay where he is as you approach him. As you approach, you observe that the vehicle does not have any other passengers and that he does not appear to have any weapons on him. You smell a strong odor of alcohol emanating from his breath. He is unsteady on his feet, and his speech is slurred.

While conducting your observations, a woman comes out of the house and asks what is going on. She identifies herself as the driver's wife. She informs you that he does live here and owns the house and the other car parked in the driveway.

Based on your observations of the driver, you feel that you have enough probable cause to believe that he was driving under the influence of alcohol.

1. Would you ask him any questions? If so, what would you ask him?
2. Would you advise him of his *Miranda* rights prior to asking any questions?
3. Would you administer any field sobriety tests? Remember, you already feel he is driving under the influence and your cruiser video camera is still on.
4. What would you do with him? Arrest him? Leave him in the custody of his wife? Explain what you would do.
5. What else might you do for this incident, regardless of your above decisions?

Your Assignment 13-2

It is around 2 P.M. on a Thursday afternoon. It is a clear sunny day, and you are patrolling in the downtown area. You observe a motor vehicle pulled over to the side of the street. The vehicle is pulled over at a precarious angle against a telephone pole and is still running. As you pull the cruiser over, you observe the driver (no other passengers) sitting behind the wheel, facing forward. From what you can see, there is no damage to the vehicle or to the pole. The airbag did not deploy.

You observe the driver to be a woman in her mid-40s. She is staring forward. You speak to the driver, she very slowly turns her head toward you and stares. You observe her eyes to be glassy, and she seems to be confused. You ask her if she is hurt or injured, and she shakes her head "no."

You ask her to put the vehicle in park and to turnoff the ignition, which after some coaching, she does. You cannot determine if she has any alcohol on her breath, because she is not directly facing you.

You do not observe any skid marks on the road, which would indicate that she may have applied the brakes prior to impact. You speak with a store merchant who is outside of his business. He states that he saw her just pull up on the sidewalk; the car rested against the pole and she just sat there. He was about to come out to see what happened and that's when you pulled up, about 15 seconds after she had stopped.

You ask her to step away from the vehicle, but she just has a blank stare on her face. She finally turns to you and states that she is on some pain medication for arthritis and that it has never acted like this on her before. She then adds that she wonders if it was the two glasses of wine she had with lunch that may have done this.

1. What will you do? Explain.
2. Would you have her perform any field sobriety tests?

3. Would you press charges on the operator? Explain why or why not.
4. What would you do regarding the telephone pole that was struck?
5. What additional information would you obtain regarding the events?

Your Assignment 13-3

It is 11:30 P.M. on a Thursday night. You have just received a radio call for a one-car motor vehicle accident on a side street in a residential neighborhood. The dispatcher informs you that the accident was called in by a passing motorist using a cell phone. When you arrive on the scene, you observe a single motor vehicle down the embankment on the left shoulder of the road. The operator is sitting in the driver's seat, and the car is still running.

The driver is not injured and is able to respond. As you approach him, you ask him if he is hurt, he states he is not. You ask him for his driver's license and his registration. As he reaches into his back pocket to retrieve his license, you observe a badge in his wallet. He hands you his license and a police identification card from a neighboring community.

He states that he got off work around 9:00 P.M. and then stopped off for a few drinks at the local club. He was on his way home. He states that he must have dozed off and that he couldn't be drunk, because he only had a few beers and some shots. He then states that because this is no big deal, that no other cars involved, and that no property was damaged. He would like you to call a tow truck for his car. He also asks if you could give him a ride home, which is about 2 miles away.

He then proceeds to get out of the car. You have already noticed a strong odor of alcohol on his breath and that his eyes are glassy. As he steps out of the car, he staggers a bit and falls back against his rear driver's side door.

In this state, for the purposes of this scenario, a police officer must have a valid driver's license in order to maintain his job. The punishment for driving under the influence, aside from the monetary fines, alcohol abuse classes, court costs, lawyers fees, and insurance surcharges, is an automatic loss of license for 90 days.

1. Would you arrange to have the vehicle towed?
2. Would you give him a ride home? Explain why or why not.
3. Would you arrest him for driving under the influence of alcohol? Explain why or why not.
4. Would you, as a professional courtesy, attribute the accident to his tiredness from work and not pursue any other charges, especially because there was no damage to persons or property other than his own motor vehicle?
5. Knowing that he could lose his job for the driving under the influence of alcohol, would you just give him a traffic ticket for some other offense, such as operating left of the center line, driving to endanger, impeded operation (tired), or other offenses in order to cover yourself because there was a call and, although anonymous, there was a witness?

Your Assignment 13-4

Use the same situation as in Your Assignment 13-3, but with some differences, to answer the questions.

It is 11:30 P.M. on a Thursday night. You have just received a radio call of a one-car motor vehicle accident on a side street in a residential neighborhood. The dispatcher informs you that the accident was called in by the resident of the house where the accident occurred. When you arrive on the scene, you observe a single motor vehicle down the embankment on the left shoulder of the road. The operator is sitting in the driver's seat, and the car is still running.

The driver is not injured and is able to respond. As you approach him, you ask him if he is hurt, he states that he is not. You ask him for his driver's license and his registration. As he reaches into his back pocket to retrieve his license, you observe a badge in his wallet. He hands you his license and a police identification card from a neighboring community.

The resident who had called from the house across the street comes over to you and states that the driver of the car struck his parked car on the right side of the road and then swerved off to the left, landing in the ditch where it is now.

The witness also states that he went over to him and saw that he was okay and uninjured. The witness also noticed the smell of alcohol on his breath. That is when he went inside and called the police.

You ask the witness for the information on his motor vehicle for your report. You notice that the damage to the witness's motor vehicle is minor, most likely under a $1,000, which in this state does not mandate any reporting to the police or the State Department of Motor Vehicles.

After speaking with the witness and getting all of the pertinent information and giving him the driver's information for insurance purposes, you return to the vehicle down the embankment and speak with the driver.

He states that he got off work around 9:00 P.M. and then stopped off for a few drinks at the local club. He was on his way home. He states that he must have dozed off and that he couldn't be drunk, because he only had a few beers and some shots. He then states that this is no big deal, that no other cars were involved, and that no property was damaged. He would like you to call a tow truck for his car. He also asks if you could give him a ride home, which is about 2 miles away.

He then proceeds to get out of the car. You have already noticed a strong odor of alcohol on his breath and that his eyes were glassy. As he steps out of the car, he staggers a bit and falls back against his rear driver's door.

In this state, for the purposes of this scenario, a police officer must have a valid driver's license in order to maintain his job. The punishment for driving under the influence, aside from the monetary fines, alcohol abuse classes, court costs, lawyers fees, and insurance surcharges, is an automatic loss of license for 90 days.

1. Would you arrest the driver for driving under the influence of alcohol? Explain why or why not.

2. Would you, as a professional courtesy, attribute the accident to his tiredness from work and not pursue any other charges?

3. Knowing that he could lose his job for the driving under the influence of alcohol, would you just give him a traffic ticket for some other offense, such as operating left of the center line, driving to endanger, impeded operation (tired), or some other offense in order to cover yourself since there was a call and a witness?

4. Would you return to the witness and update him on what you did? If so, what would you tell the witness? Would you mention that the driver is a police officer? Why or why not?

Your Assignment 13-5

It is 1 A.M. on a Friday night. You are stopped at a red light. As the light turns green, you observe a motor vehicle pass in front of you, crossing the intersection through the red light.

You turn right behind the vehicle and activate your cruiser's blue lights. The operator sees you in his rear view mirror and pulls over to the side of the road. As he does this, he bumps the curb a little; other than that he has not shown any signs of impaired operation.

You pull in behind the vehicle and give the dispatcher all the information pertinent to the stop. You observe two passengers in the car, a male operator and a female passenger.

You approach the vehicle and speak with the operator. There is a strong odor of alcohol from his breath, and his eyes are glassy. Between his legs is an open bottle of beer. You ask him to get out of the vehicle and ask for his license and registration.

He staggers a bit and then composes himself. His paperwork is in order. He states that he is coming home from a wedding and did have a few drinks. His wife speaks to you, stating that she can drive home, because she hasn't been drinking.

1. What will you do? In a narrative answer, write out what you would do in this case. Make sure to include all of the factors you used in making your decision.

Chapter Wrap-Up

In-Service Training

When you start your tour of duty, if your cruiser is equipped with video recording equipment, make sure that you have ample free tape space on the tape you are using.

From the Experts

Before exiting your cruiser, make sure you check for oncoming traffic before opening the door and stepping out, blue lights and the sight of a police car can sometimes distract oncoming drivers and cause them to sway in closer without realizing it.

Caution

Exercise extreme caution if a vehicle has been involved in an accident in which a utility pole has been struck. Before you exit your vehicle, make sure that there are no power lines down, whether on the vehicle involved or on the ground. If there are downed wires, instruct the driver and passengers to remain in the vehicle and to not make any attempt to leave until they are told it is safe to do so.

Reference

Massachusetts Criminal Justice Training Council (MCJTC), 1998. Motor Vehicle Stop Module. South Weymouth, MA.

Motor Vehicle Stops: Dangerous Situations

Knowledge Objectives

- Describe the proper procedure for making a motor vehicle stop in which there is the potential for danger from a known or unknown threat.
- Identify the signals and signs that may alert an officer to a possibly dangerous situation.
- Know what precautions to take when making a dangerous motor vehicle stop.
- Know how to conduct a motor vehicle stop safely and effectively.
- Understand the following special circumstances when making a motor vehicle stop: tinted glass, vans, tractor trailers, motorcycles, violators who do not speak English, argumentative violators, violators who exit their vehicles.

Skills Objectives

- Demonstrate the ability to handle a verbal or a suggested physical confrontation by an irate citizen.
- Demonstrate powers of observation when approaching a stopped vehicle.
- Identify and locate visible contraband in a stopped vehicle.
- Understand detection phases for contraband or unlawful activity, clues, and techniques.
- Recognize any suspicious movements or activities that may indicate that a stop is not a routine motor vehicle stop.
- Conduct an aggressive-action motor vehicle stop safely and effectively.
- Conduct a high-risk or felony motor vehicle stop safely and effectively.
- Write a clear narrative report that describes your observations and the operator's actions and reactions.

■ Introduction

In this chapter, you will gain an understanding of the potential and actual dangers that officers face daily when making motor vehicle stops. These dangers may be real or perceived, but nonetheless, they are a realistic part of the process of making a motor vehicle stop.

■ Dangers Associated with Motor Vehicle Stops

As you have seen in previous chapters, a motor vehicle stop may be a low-risk event or it may escalate into a medium- or high-risk situation. Activities may occur during a low-risk stop could that may threaten an officer's safety and thus initiate more aggressive action on the part of the officer.

Some of the factors that can cause a motor vehicle stop to escalate to a higher risk level are observations that the officer makes coupled with some overt act that does not amount to a high-risk or felony situation. Some different types of circumstances that increase the risk level of a motor vehicle stop to aggressive-action level include:

- **Threats or gestures.** An operator may make a threat or gesture that is obviously directed at the officer. For example, a suspect may, without batting an eye, say, "Come on Pig, bring it on." An officer should take all threats seriously.
- **Multiple occupants.** A higher level of risk is indicated when there are multiple occupants in the vehicle, especially if the occupants are loud, boisterous, or of some unsavory character.

Conducting Medium-Risk Motor Vehicle Stops

When attempting to conduct a medium-risk stop, the police officer should (1) call for backup, (2) contain the suspects in the vehicle, and (3) be on guard for any threatening actions by the suspects.

In a medium-risk motor vehicle stop, the police officer should not issue a ticket or check for contraband until backup arrives on the scene or the situation has returned to a low-risk situation. Some jurisdictions insist that officers keep the suspects seated in the vehicle. Other jurisdictions believe that it is safer to remove the occupants from the vehicle and have them step to the side of the road in between the cruiser and the stopped vehicle.

Officers should position the patrol vehicle a safe distance from the suspect vehicle. The most common practice is have 15 and 25 feet between the two vehicles. This allows the officer to observe the vehicle and react, if needed, or to place the cruiser in reverse to create more distance.

The officer should keep chemical spray and her baton readily available. The officer should not use or display firearms during a medium-risk stop. If the officer needs a firearm, the stop has elevated to a high-risk or felony level. If the stop has escalated, other actions need to be initiated.

Conducting High-Risk or Felony Motor Vehicle Stops

A medium-risk motor vehicle stop has progressed to a high-risk situation once the officer has reason to believe that her life or well-being is in imminent danger or there is a threat of serious bodily harm or death. The police officer should determine if circumstances indicate a threat of serious bodily injury or death. If so, then actions other than ordinary self-protection are needed.

Indications that a motor vehicle stop may be a high-risk or felony situation include the following:

- **Overt actions.** Actions that clearly indicate the subject's intent to cause harm or information that the subject may have been involved in a serious crime. For example, a suspect who is waving or displaying a firearm would indicate that the subject poses a serious threat to the officer. Or a computer check may indicate that the suspect's vehicle is stolen.

- **Observations.** The driver, passenger(s), or the stopped vehicle may match a description of a person or vehicle that was involved in a serious crime. For example, the driver may have been reported to have displayed a firearm to other motorists, and the officer may observe the driver doing the same.
- **The suspect has the ability to inflict bodily harm or serious injury on the officer or on another person.** For example, a hostile group of people approaching an officer is capable of inflicting great bodily harm on the officer.

A police officer should always believe that the suspect in question has had better training, such as martial arts, wrestling, and so on. The officer also should assume that the suspect is better armed than the officer and may have multiple firearms, knives, or other weapons.

Stopping the Suspect and the Motor Vehicle

To conduct a safe high-risk or felony motor vehicle stop, the officer should call for backup and select a location that will offer the best advantage to the police officer. For example, to limit the suspect's ability and opportunity to escape, an officer may decide to stop a high-risk vehicle on a bridge or extremely close to a guardrail to prevent the suspect from opening the vehicle's door. The officer also may consider following the suspect's vehicle at a discreet distance until backup arrives. If the officer has made the stop and backup is on the way, the officer should command the occupants to remain in the vehicle. The officer should remain in the cruiser and wait for backup, keeping the suspect(s) in view.

Once the officer indicates to the subject in the vehicle that he should pull over, the suspect may try to evade or elude the officer by attempting to stopping suddenly, especially on a blind corner, and fleeing. If the suspect stops the vehicle suddenly, the police officer should consider speeding up a little in order to pull around the suspect's vehicle and attempt the stop further down the road, preferably with backup. If the officer has a partner and the suspect suddenly stops the vehicle and then tries to run away on foot, each of the two officers should try to apprehend the suspect separately.

Some suspects use the emergency brake or the parking brake to stop the vehicle. Using these brakes does not cause the brake lights to illuminate, thus the police have no indication that the vehicle is stopping. The suspect may use the emergency or parking-brake tactic to try to startle or surprise the officer into stopping in a bad tactical location.

In some cases, the suspect may stop abruptly in order to cause a collision. The suspect may cause a collision in the hope that the officer's airbag will engage and disable or incapacitate officer. Or if the cruiser is in a stopped position, the suspect may drive his vehicle in reverse and accelerate to set-off the cruiser's airbags.

An experienced criminal who has some tactical knowledge may stop his vehicle at a 45-degree angle in front of the police vehicle. The suspect who uses the 45-degree-angle stopping technique will have clear aim at the police officer. The officer should not approach a suspect vehicle in this position without backup under any conditions. If the suspect stops his vehicle in this position, it should be a red flag for the officer. If the suspect stops in front of the police vehicle, the officer should reverse quickly and use the public address (PA) system in the cruiser to order the suspect to straighten his vehicle.

A police officer should *never* park the cruiser in front of a suspect vehicle. When backup officers arrive at the scene, they, too, should never park in front of the suspect vehicle in order to avoid placing themselves in a crossfire situation.

Some suspects may not stop immediately so that they can drive to a prearranged location that is better suited for their escape. Or the suspect may have accomplices at a particular location. If once stopped, the subject drives away, the officer should simply follow the vehicle until backup arrives and the stop can be planned with adequate and additional police personnel.

Initiating Contact with the Suspect

When a stop is made and the backup officers are in place, one officer is designated the primary officer. The primary officer will issue all commands. The primary officer is usually the officer who was first on the scene or the officer who initiated the call or incident.

When backup cruisers arrive in the scene, any vehicles that have been parked behind the other units should turn off all forward lights. Once all of the backup vehicles are in position, the officer should open her driver's side door and crouch behind it. This enables the officer to use the cruiser's door for cover or protection (**FIGURE 14-1**).

The primary officer should use the PA system to give commands to the driver and any passengers in the stopped vehicle. The officer on the PA system should issue brief and specific commands using a loud and clear voice. Commands may include "Do not move suddenly," "Move only after I say," or "Do it now." The initial commands should always be for the operator and passengers to remain in the vehicle and to not make any furtive or overt movements. The operator and passengers should also be instructed to remain in the vehicle until told to do otherwise.

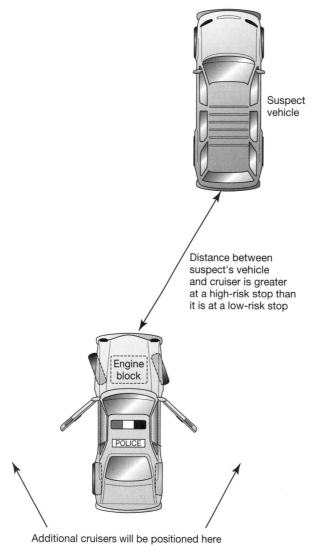

Suspect vehicle

Distance between suspect's vehicle and cruiser is greater at a high-risk stop than it is at a low-risk stop

Engine block

POLICE

Additional cruisers will be positioned here

FIGURE 14-1
Positioning of cruisers for a high-risk stop.

An officer should never approach a vehicle with occupants unless the officer feels that it is safe to do so. The officer should notify or inform the suspects that any movements that are interpreted as suspicious or life threatening may be met with an equal or greater level of force. The officer should then tell the suspects to place their hands either on the dashboard or flat up against the interior roof of the vehicle so that the officer(s) can see the occupants' hands.

If the officer is alone and has requested backup, the officer's primary concern should be to ensure that the occupants are in view and that their hands are visible until backup arrives. Once backup arrives, the officer can then attempt to remove the occupant(s).

If an offender is going to try and flee, he is most likely do so once the vehicle has been stopped. Usually, the attempt will be from the passenger side of the vehicle, away from the officer's cruiser. In addition, passengers may attempt to escape while officers are removing the driver.

Removing a Suspect from the Vehicle

The first suspect to be removed from the vehicle should be the driver. Suspects should be removed from the front of the vehicle and then from the back, from the driver's side and then the middle and/or passenger side.

After the occupants have placed their hands in the officer's view, the driver should be instructed to turn off the vehicle, using his left hand. Once the vehicle has been turned off, the driver should be instructed to remove the keys, still using the left hand, and to either place them on the roof of the vehicle or to toss them out the driver's side window to the pavement. The officer will then tell the driver to open the car door using the outside door handle with his left hand.

The suspect should be instructed to exit the vehicle while still facing forward and away from the officers with his hands in the air with palms open. The suspect should then be instructed to kick the door shut.

Once the driver has exited the car, the officers will instruct the suspect to place his hands high in the air and to side step from the vehicle. If the suspect is wearing a hat, he should be told to take it off with one hand or by using just two fingers. The officer may then have the suspect lace his fingers behind his head.

The next step is for the officer to have the suspect do a complete and slow 360-degree turn. While the suspect is turning, the officer should visually search the suspect, noting the waistband of the subject's pants if his shirt or jacket is raised enough to check for weapons. If a weapon is discovered during this visual search, the officer should tell the suspect and make sure that he understands, in no uncertain terms, that if he reaches for the weapon the officer will shoot.

The suspect should then be instructed to walk backward toward the officer's voice until he is told to stop. When the suspect reaches a safe location behind the suspect vehicle and in front of the police vehicle, the officer should order the suspect to drop to his knees and lie face down, hands outstretched to the side and legs crossed at the ankles. This places the suspect in an unbalanced position and requires the suspect to make an extra move if he attempts to get up. This movement, if made, will alert the officers.

Once the suspect is on the ground, a backup officer should search the suspect and place the handcuffs on the suspect. The backup officer will then assist the suspect to his feet and walk him backward to an awaiting cruiser. Other backup officers maintain cover on the searching officer and watch any occupants still in the vehicle.

Any subsequent occupants will be removed using the same format. All occupants should exit from the driver's side. Once it appears that all occupants have been removed from the vehicle, the officer must remember the "plus one" rule and be prepared that another occupant may be hiding in the vehicle. If no occupants are visible, and there is no response to any commands to exit the vehicle, the officers should approach the vehicle cautiously while being covered by backup officers and peek in the vehicle to clear it of any hidden suspects or other dangers.

Making a Stop When Backup Is Not Available

An officer should never attempt a high-risk stop when alone; however, sometimes backup is not available or able to respond in a timely fashion. If this is the case, and the officer has to make the stop alone, the officer should notify the dispatcher and give the location of the stop, the vehicle's license plate number, the vehicle's description, the number of occupants, descriptions of the occupants, and the reason for the stop.

Special Considerations When Making Motor Vehicle Stops

Tinted Windows

When stopping a vehicle with tinted windows, the officer should turn off the cruiser's headlights and spotlight. The officer should use the driver's inside dome light to illuminate the suspect's vehicle. The officer should instruct the driver to turn on the vehicle's dome lights and tell the driver and any occupants to lower the windows. The interior of the suspect vehicle will be illuminated by the dome lighting, and the occupant's ability to see outside of the vehicle will be limited. Note that flashlights do not penetrate tinted glass and instead alert suspects of the officer's position.

The officer should instruct the driver to exit the vehicle, walk backward to the police vehicle with the necessary information (license, registrations, etc.), stand at the front of the police vehicle, and then pass the information across the hood to the officer, who should be positioned at the front passenger-side corner of the police vehicle.

Vans

Vans are among the most dangerous vehicles that a police officer will confront during a stop. This is because, depending on the type of van, it may be difficult for the officer to see inside the vehicle. Panel vans have solid sides all around, including the back door, thus the officer has no idea what may be inside the vehicle when making her approach. Custom vans have one-way glass on the sides and back or portholes, which may be covered with shades or blinds. As a result, most of the van's exit points are hidden from the officer's view when the officer approaches the driver's side.

Generally speaking, most vans have at least four exit points. Some newer models have five doors. Most vans have two doors on each side in the front and one or two sliding doors in back.

When stopping a van, the officer should park her vehicle farther away from the van than when stopping a car. The officer should then exit the cruiser and walk around to the rear of the police vehicle. The officer should then open the front passenger door of the police vehicle. (The distance between the two vehicles should enable the officer to view both sides of the van so that she can watch both the driver and passenger-side exit points.) The officer should then stand behind the police vehicle's open passenger door and use the PA system to command the driver to exit the van with the keys.

The officer will ask the driver to walk around the front of the van and toward the police vehicle along the van's passenger side. When the driver reaches the rear bumper of the van, the officer should ask the driver to open the van's rear door. If occupants are visible in the van, the officer should have them remain inside the van. If needed, the officer can call for backup.

The officer should also advise the driver that he is responsible for the actions of the passengers. The officer should have the driver stand at the front center of the police vehicle's hood. The driver should then be told to pass his license and registration information across the hood. After doing so, the driver should be instructed to place his hands on the police vehicle's hood in the officer's view. Note that the suspect should place his hands on top of the hood, and on the grille. In hot weather, the hood may be extremely hot, so doing so may not be appropriate. In these cases, the officer can have the driver lock his fingers behind the neck.

If the officer instructs the driver to return to the van, the officer should still remain on the right side of the police vehicle to write the citation or use the computer. The officer should use the right side of the police vehicle to write the citation or to use the computer or to communicate with the station by radio so that his or her firearm is readily accessible.

Tractor Trailers

When a police officer stops a tractor trailer (also called a semi-trailer truck), the officer should stop the tractor trailer on a slight downgrade (the truck stopped downhill). If the tractor trailer is stopped on an upgrade (uphill), it may roll backward into the police vehicle.

The height of the tractor trailer makes it difficult for the officer to view the vehicle's driver and occupants. Also out of sight is the rear compartment of the tractor, or cab unit, which in some long-distance rigs is large enough to be equipped with a bed. Instead of approaching the tractor trailer, the officer may prefer to command the driver and occupants from the vehicle using the cruiser's PA system.

Motorcycles

When stopping a motorcycle, the officer should ask the driver to dismount on the right side, which is the unnatural side. In some cases, and not always intentionally, but by habit, the motorcycle driver may not comply with the dismount as directed. If there are passengers, they should be asked to remain on the motorcycle.

The police officer should ask the driver to place his helmet on the seat of the motorcycle so that the driver cannot throw it at the officer. A helmet can be used as a weapon.

Non-English-Speaking Operators

Sometimes an officer will encounter an operator who does not speak or understand English very well. This may become obvious at any point of the interaction, whether the suspect indicates to the officer by hand signal, or verbally during the initial contact, that their first language is not English. If a non-English-speaking driver exits a vehicle during the stop, the officer should not shout at the driver to get back in the vehicle. If the non-English-speaking operator has already exited the vehicle, the officer should put up his or her hand in "stop" fashion and point to the vehicle to have him or her return to it. People who do not speak English can usually understand common hand signals.

If the driver does not speak English but some of the passengers do, the officer may, as necessary, use them to translate her questions or commands. If the officer becomes aware and is suspicious because the occupants are speaking amongst each other in a different language, the officer should order them to stop speaking immediately. Depending upon the situation, these actions, coupled with some overt acts, may increase the risk level of the stop.

An Argumentative Violator with Children in the Vehicle

In most cases, children are very attentive to the conversation when a police officer speaks with their parents. The conduct and demeanor of the police officer will create an impression on children and other family members that may last for a significant period of time.

If a parent tries to belittle, instigate, or provoke the officer in front of his family, the officer should ask the parent to exit the vehicle so that the parent and the officer can speak privately. Some parents may become argumentative to "save face" in front of their families without realizing the potential ramifications that may come from their disorderly behavior.

When a Violator Exits the Vehicle

In some cases, depending on the part of the country you are in, some violators may exit their vehicles during motor vehicle stops because they are nervous and are trying to cooperate as much as possible or are trying to locate their wallets. In general, older male motorists exit their vehicles so that they can find their wallets. However, in some cases, the violator may exit the vehicle in order to argue with the officer, or even worse, to harm the officer.

In most states, state law does not require violators to stay in their vehicles when stopped. In some states, violators are allowed to exit their vehicles and sit with the officer in the front seat of the police vehicle. For our purposes, and as a safety rule, it is unsafe to allow a violator to exit the vehicle and sit in the cruiser with the officer.

If a violator exits the vehicle, the officer should quickly assess the violator's intentions and threat potential. The officer should be prepared for any situation, while controlling personal fears and emotions. When the officer feels that there is no perceived threat, the officer should employ the appropriate response based on the threat potential and the officer's personal experience and common sense to further instruct the driver or exiting passengers. The officer should exit the police vehicle quickly and meet the violator before he nears the police vehicle. Then the officer should instruct the violator to return to his vehicle. The officer should tell the violator that returning to the vehicle is for his safety as well as that of the officer.

For example, if an elderly male is holding his wallet and obviously searching for his license while walking slowly toward the officer in broad daylight, the officer should not perceive this as a threat and draw her weapon or go into high-risk mode. The officer should treat this as it appears and direct the elderly driver to return to his car. One way the officer can handle this is to ask the man firmly but with courtesy to return to his vehicle. The officer should tell the man that the officer would come to the vehicle to get his license and registration.

When a violator exits the vehicle and immediately begins arguing with the officer, the officer should keep a safe distance from the violator and watch the violator's hands. The officer should not physically touch an argumentative motorist unless making an arrest. The violator who argues may use verbal assault to distract the officer while he prepares to physically assault the officer. The officer should advise the argumentative violator that he will be able to discuss the matter once the violator is reseated in his vehicle and has produced a license and registration.

If the violator refuses to produce his license and registration upon request, the officer may tell the violator that he will be arrested. Refusal to provide license and registration is an arrestable offense in some states. Make sure you check the applicable laws in your jurisdiction. The officer should not use the possibility of arrest as a challenge. The warning of an arrest should be the ultimatum just prior to the placing the violator under arrest if he fails to comply.

Few drivers will exit their vehicles at night. When they do, or if they do so in a threatening manner, the officer should respond by backing the police vehicle to a distance of 100 feet from the suspect's vehicle. The officer should then use the cruiser's PA system to tell the driver or passenger(s) to stop and to explain that if he keeps advancing, the officer may use a chemical spray. If events lead to a greater threat, then the officer should draw a weapon (chemical, baton, or firearm, whichever is appropriate), take cover, and continue to issue commands. The officer should watch constantly the advancing driver or passenger's hands.

It is important to keep in mind that the reason for the stop and the perceived threat will dictate how the officer approaches a vehicle.

Your Assignment 14-1

It is a Friday night at 1:00 A.M. You are on routine patrol in a single-officer cruiser. You receive a radio call from the dispatcher that there have been numerous calls over the last 5 minutes of a carload of kids in a pickup truck knocking over mailboxes. No further description of the vehicle or its occupants is available.

You drive to the area to take reports of the vandalism or malicious destruction. As you approach the neighborhood, you observe a pickup driving toward you with its headlights off. Several youths are in the rear bed of the truck. (Some jurisdictions may have laws about passengers riding in pickup truck beds without proper seating and restraints. For our purposes, although it is unsafe, no law prohibits people from riding in the rear of the pickup truck.)

As the truck passes you, you observe in your mirror a passenger inside the truck pass a baseball bat to the occupants in the rear bed of the truck.

You turn your cruiser around and activate your blue lights. As you pull up behind the truck, you observe the occupants in the rear bed doing a lot of moving and shifting around. As you get behind the truck, the occupants in the rear of the truck begin to make derogatory gestures and begin to yell at you.

You also observe that the driver is trying to control the rear passengers, but to no avail. The vehicle is now stopped, and two of the three rear-bed occupants stand up and continue their inappropriate actions. These two occupants appear to be intoxicated and are now standing in the truck bed. Each is brandishing a baseball bat.

1. When you first made your observations and turned your cruiser around, what actions would you have taken?
2. After observing the behavior of the rear passengers when you first pulled behind the truck, what should you have done?
3. How would you have positioned your cruiser in relation to the suspect vehicle?
4. After observing the occupants' more aggressive behavior, what other actions might you take?
5. Would you have any weapons at the ready? If so, which ones?

You called the dispatcher and requested backup units. The backup units have now arrived at the scene.

6. If the occupants have quieted down, would you now feel that it is safe to approach the truck? Explain why or why not.
7. What steps would you take to remove the driver from the truck?
8. Would you remove the inside passengers first or the ones in the rear of the truck? Explain.
9. How would you remove the remaining passengers? Explain the removal of the one passenger inside the cab of the truck and the three in the rear of the truck.
10. Write a brief narrative report of what you observed and any actions you took.

Your Assignment 14-2

It is Saturday at 11:30 P.M. You are on patrol and have just received a call of an armed robbery that has just occurred at a local liquor store. The suspect vehicle is described as a white older-model Toyota with one occupant, who is the suspect. He is described as a white male with blonde hair and blue eyes. He stands about 5 feet, 11 inches, and was wearing a white T-shirt, jeans, and a blue and white baseball cap.

All units have converged in the area and have placed themselves in strategic locations to observe any vehicles or suspects leaving the area. The robbery occurred approximately 2 minutes ago. You have been assigned to park your cruiser at the intersection of Main Street and Washington Street to observe and be on the lookout for the suspect.

Almost immediately, a red motor vehicle drives by you; the operator matches the description of the suspect. The operator makes eye contact with you and appears to be nervous.

You contact the station with your observations. The station tells you that officers found the suspect's vehicle dumped approximately two blocks from your location. You are told to stop the possible suspect's vehicle that you observed. The station notifies you that backup units are on the way.

As you pull out behind the red motor vehicle, you notice that the driver keeps looking in his rearview mirror and appears to be very cautiously observing all traffic laws. You contact the dispatcher to inform the station that you are going to attempt to stop the vehicle and are informed that the backup units are close by.

You activate your blue lights and siren in order to make the stop. The driver, who has been acting as if he has done nothing wrong, continues driving and suddenly decides to speed up a little. He then makes a right-hand turn to see if you follow him. After taking the turn, he pulls over almost immediately. The possible suspect's vehicle is now pulled over and stopped.

1. Where would you position your cruiser in relation to the stopped vehicle?
2. When backup arrives, what would be your next step? How would you deal with the operator?
3. Explain the procedure for removing the suspect from the vehicle.
4. After the possible suspect has been removed and secured in the cruiser, what would you do next?
5. If he turned out not to be the suspect, what would you do and what would you say to him?

Your Assignment 14-3

It is around noon on a Monday. You are patrolling the downtown business district in a single-person cruiser. You hear a lot of horns beeping and people yelling from around the corner. As you turn the corner, you observe two motorists involved in a verbal argument; one female in a sedan is yelling at the male operator of a white-panel van (solid sides, no windows). He is extremely loud and boisterous and appears to be the instigating element of the confrontation. As you pull up, the male driver, who does not see you, gets back into his van and drives off at a high speed, screeching his tires as he departs.

You tell the other participant and any witnesses to remain there. You call the station for a backup unit to respond to the scene while you go after the now-departed male in the van.

You observe the van a little ahead of you and call dispatch for information, giving the station the van's plate number. You activate your lights and siren in order to gain on him and pull him over. As pull in behind him, still in traffic, you can see that he sees you in his side-view mirror. You also observe that he still appears to be upset.

He pulls over to the curb of the main road in the business district, leaving very little space behind him for your cruiser.

As soon as you stop, he quickly exits his vehicle and, still obviously enraged, walks toward you quickly. You can observe that his hands are empty, and he does not appear to have a weapon on him.

From the station, you have learned that the driver had run a red light and almost struck a pedestrian and did strike another car (the female operator at the scene). He then started yelling at everyone and got back into his van without informing anyone of his identity and drove off when you arrived on the scene.

For the purposes of this exercise, the jurisdiction you are in has a law against leaving the scene of an accident without providing identification. This is a ticketable offense, but not an arrestable one. For the red-light violation, although you did not observe the traffic infraction, you may issue a ticket or citation as long as you feel that you can use the witnesses in court and they agree to testify if the male operator decides to fight the charges.

1. Write a complete narrative report of your observations, from the time of your first observations until you have cleared the assignment and returned back in service.

You can make up names and create your own actions and responses to the operator of the van, making sure you justify your actions in response to his.

Your Assignment 14-4

You pull over a motorist for a minor traffic infraction. As you approach the vehicle, you observe a gun on the front passenger seat. He makes no movement toward it. When he knows that you see the gun, he informs you that he is properly licensed and has just returned from target practice. There are no other people in the car.

1. What would be your first action and command to the operator of the vehicle?
2. Would you retreat back to your cruiser immediately for cover? Why? Why not?
3. Explain how you would verify that the operator is duly licensed for the firearm and was in fact at target practice.
4. Explain how you would either retrieve the gun or separate the operator from reach of the handgun?
5. If he was duly licensed, what action would you take regarding his method of transportation of the weapon?

Chapter Wrap-Up

In-Service Training

A police officer should never reach into a running or moving vehicle. Many officers have been dragged by moving vehicles and seriously injured or killed.

From the Experts

When making a motor vehicle stop, if the operator's vehicle is still running, keep your eye on the taillights for the flash of the vehicle going from park to drive, passing reverse, or the bright red light from the brake pedal, which may indicate the vehicle is still in gear.

Caution

Officers should never be reluctant to call for backup when needed. It is better to be safe than sorry. However, in some jurisdictions that have remote, rural areas or on busy nights, backup may not be readily available. In some cases, it may be safer to back off until you have the proper manpower to do the job necessary.

Reference

Massachusetts Criminal Justice Training Council (MCJTC), 1998. Motor Vehicle Stop Module. South Weymouth, MA.

Domestic Violence

Knowledge Objectives

- Describe the proper procedure for dealing with relationships that may have abusive or violent elements.
- Identify the signals and signs that may alert an officer to a possibly dangerous situation.
- Identify a controlled domestic violence situation that can escalate into a volatile one.
- Identify the effects of domestic abuse on those involved and on other family members.
- Conduct a domestic violence interview safely and effectively.

Skills Objectives

- Demonstrate the ability to respond to verbal and/or physical confrontations presented by an abusive person.
- Demonstrate the ability to control a situation in which two people involved in confrontation with each other may turn and view the officer as the threat.
- Demonstrate powers of observation when dealing with agitated persons in a restricted environment.
- Demonstrate the ability to maintain order and safety when children are present.
- Understand and demonstrate a domestic violence interview technique.
- Recognize suspicious movements or activities by a person involved in a domestic abuse situation that may present a warning sign for aggressive behavior toward you.
- Conduct an aggressive-action call for service safely and effectively.
- Write a clear narrative report that describes your observations, actions, and reactions when responding to a domestic abuse incident.

■ Introduction

In this chapter, you will learn about the potential and actual dangers that officers face daily when dealing with people involved in domestic disputes. These dangers may be real or perceived, but they are nonetheless a realistic part of answering calls for domestic disputes.

■ Domestic Violence and Domestic Abuse Situations

Domestic violence or domestic abuse situations are dangerous and unpredictable. Although many domestic violence incidents are similar, there are no "routine" calls.

When discussing responses to domestic violence or abuse incidents, one of the first things that needs to be discussed is what constitutes a family or significant relationship in the eyes of the law. *Family* or *household members* are people who are or were married to one another; who reside in the same household (including a dormitory); are related by blood or marriage; have a child in common, regardless of whether they have been married or have lived together; or have been in a substantive dating or engagement relationship.

Some courts determine whether a relationship is in fact a substantive dating or engagement relationship by considering the length of the relationship; the type of relationship; the frequency of interaction between the parties in the relationship; and the amount of time since the relationship was terminated, if either party terminated the relationship.

The next thing that must be considered is what constitutes abuse. *Abuse* can be defined as any type of physical harm or attempt to cause physical harm between family or household members.

Abusive actions include punching, kicking, shoving, assaulting, and placing another in fear of imminent serious physical harm. Other instances of abuse would be threats of harm; damage of property; hurting or killing a household pet; or causing another to engage in involuntary sexual relations by force, by threat, or under duress. Note that marital status does not preclude a spouse from being charged with rape.

Domestic violence or abuse calls can escalate from a simple discussion among adults to a volatile and sometimes life-threatening situation. What happens during such calls depends on what issues come into play during the intervention. For example, say that a woman has been struck in the face by her husband during an argument. It is the first time that he has hit her. She is upset and angry and calls the police. The police arrive and talk to the two parties involved and inform the wife that the husband is going to be arrested. Now the reality sets in, and the woman realizes that her husband is going to court and may be placed in jail or restricted from seeing her or her children. He is the working spouse; if he misses work, there goes the paycheck. The woman may have second thoughts. If she does, she may intervene physically to prevent the police from arresting and removing the husband. Or she may refuse to appear in court or testify or she may later call the department and drop the charges.

If children are present, the husband may become combative, and the children may intervene. How this will affect the situation depends on the age of the children. Young children could be crying and screaming because the officer is taking their daddy; the police officer becomes the bad guy. If the children are older, they may try to grab the officer in order to save their father.

Obtaining Information Before Responding to the Call

When preparing to respond to the call for a domestic violence situation, the officer should obtain as much "prior" information as possible. If such information is not automatically provided, the officer should always ask for specific information during the dispatch process. Some radio and 911 systems respond electronically to the dispatcher as soon as the address of the call for service location is entered into the computer. The computer then generates the information the officer needs to know prior to responding to the address.

Such information may include any prior calls to that residence for the same type of call. A number of prior calls would indicate a history of abusive conduct at the residence. The officer may learn whether any restraining orders or orders to keep away have been issued by the courts. The officer may also learn if there are any registered firearms in the house or if the owners (residents) have any licenses to possess firearms. Some department computer systems can also cross reference other systems and identify any outstanding warrants and conduct criminal record checks. This information if readily available and should be provided by the dispatcher before the officer arrives at the scene.

Approaching the Scene

At least two officers should respond to a domestic violence call. If at all possible, a supervisor should be dispatched as well. If the dispatcher receives word from the person who made the call that everything fine and to cancel the call, the officers should *not* be told to disregard. They should respond to all domestic violence calls regardless of whether the caller tries to cancel. All such calls should be investigated.

When the officer arrives at the scene, she should turn off the cruiser's lights and sirens. The officer should stop at least one house away from the disturbance and then listen and look for signs of ongoing violence. The officer should search for open doors and wait for a backup officer to arrive, unless immediate intervention is necessary to prevent serious physical harm.

When the backup officer arrives, the first responding officer should brief the backup officer on the situation. Together, the two officers should decide who will approach the front of the residence, who will speak (contact), and who will provide cover.

Entering the Residence

When attempting to gain entry, the officer should knock on the door and announce the reason for the police presence. The officer should never place a body part in a partially opened door to prevent its closure. Doing so may cause injury to the officer as well as trap the officer in the doorway. The officer should place a flashlight or baton in a partially opened door.

The officer should never take the word of the person at the door, whether husband, wife, or other, that the situation has resolved itself and that everything is fine. If the officer receives this type of response, the officer should *always* investigate the situation further. The officer may ask the victim to step outside of the residence, if necessary.

The officer may use force to gain entry to the residence under the following urgent circumstances: someone in lawful custody (victim) asks the officer to enter; the officer has probable cause to believe a felony has been or is being committed; or the officer has probable cause to believe there is danger of violence and a breach of the peace.

The officer should leave if *both* parties request it unless the officer has probable cause to believe a felony has been committed or feels continued law-enforcement presence is necessary to prevent physical harm.

Inside the Residence

Once inside the residence, the officer should control the movements of the parties by separating them. The primary officer should try to keep in sight of the backup officer at all times. The primary officer and the backup officer should position themselves in separate rooms but still face each other for their own safety. The two parties should stand between the officers with their backs to each other to avoid having the situation to agitate or escalate (FIGURE 15-1).

An officer should never allow a party to leave the room unescorted, even if it's just to get a coat or some other item. If it is necessary for one of the involved persons to leave the room to get or do something, the officer should accompany the person and scan for any firearms or other potential weapons.

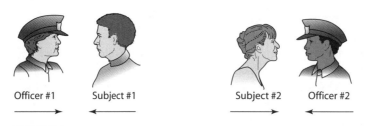

FIGURE 15-1
How to separate the subjects in a domestic violence situation.

If a weapon is found at the scene, the officer should take the weapon into temporary custody. The officer should also search for and take custody of a firearm if one party requests it. If appropriate, the officer should, prior to returning the weapon, make sure that it is legally owned and that the person has the proper licenses to have the weapon.

Observations

The officer should note the appearance of the scene as well as the parties involved. The officer should determine if anything is out of place or if there are signs of abuse or a struggle or some type of disturbance. These observations should take into account furniture, hair, clothing, and any signs of injury to either party. The officer should also note any bruising, swelling around the face or head, red marks on the arms or neck, or complaints of unseen injuries. Such injuries do not have to be recent, because they may be indications of previous incidents, whether reported or not.

Relationships

The officer must determine the relationships of the parties involved and whether there is a history of domestic violence. The officer should determine who has lawful custody of any minors or children involved and if any court-ordered visitation rights, restraining orders, or other documents are being violated. This would be the case if there has been prior abuse with court involvement. The officer should also check for, if not previously informed of, any protective orders that are in effect, including any outstanding arrest warrants on anyone involved in the dispute.

Other Considerations

The officer should make every effort to obtain a statement from the alleged victim. If the alleged victim is out of sight, the officer should make every attempt to speak with her in person before leaving the scene. In some cases, some prodding may be necessary to encourage victims to cooperate or to request help from outside sources. The officer should always express her support and concern for the victim and do so without passing judgment or pointing blame.

Officers should realize that in some cases the victim might not be able to leave immediately to accompany the officer to court. The officer should still process and initiate the court action anyway; hopefully, the officer's statements will persuade the victim to press charges later.

Arrest

When deciding whether to make an arrest in a domestic violence situation, the officer should consider several issues. In some cases, an arrest may be mandated by law if there is probable cause to believe that abuse has occurred or may occur. Note that arresting both parties in a domestic violence dispute is not the preferred response.

Other factors to consider are the legitimacy of the allegations and whether the victim is fearful of retaliation. Victims may often try to lessen the event or minimize or deny the violence. Abusers are extremely manipulative and may portray themselves, often very effectively, as victims. In general, the officer needs to remember that an alleged victim's statement regarding her direct knowledge of the crime is *not* hearsay. The victim's statements give the officer probable cause.

The officer should always interview children alone and should be sensitive to their fears and/or denials that any abuse took place. An officer does not need parental consent to interview a minor who is not a suspect. The officer should be careful to minimize the impact of the domestic violence incident on the child.

Your Assignment 15-1

It is a Thursday night at 10:00 P.M. You and your partner have been assigned to a loud noise disturbance at an apartment complex, possibly involving a husband and wife. The call was reported to the station by a neighbor who lives next door to the residence in question.

As you arrive on the scene, you can hear a verbal argument going on from the courtyard of the apartment complex. The argument does not seem to be escalating or dwindling. As you approach the door to the apartment, you can hear more distinctly that the female voice is crying and the male is still yelling.

When you knock on the door and announce who you are, you hear footsteps walking toward the door and assume that the resident is looking through the peephole. You next hear the male say, "Don't say anything, it's the police."

The door then opens with the husband standing in the doorway, limiting your view of the interior of the apartment. He asks if there is a problem and inquires as to why you are there.

You tell the man that you responding to a call of loud arguing coming from the apartment. You further state that you heard the arguing as well and also heard a female crying. The husband states that he and his wife had an argument and that everything is now fine.

You inform the husband that you would like to speak with his wife in order to check her welfare and make sure that everything is fine. The husband then yells to his wife, "Hon, tell them everything is okay." The wife responds from the other side of the room from somewhere that you cannot see her that she is fine.

You insist that you must speak with her face-to-face, and the husband, although reluctant, opens the door to allow you inside. As you enter the apartment, you see the wife sitting across the room on the couch. As you approach her, you can see she has been crying and notice a red mark on the side of her face.

1. Where should your partner be during the initial entry into the house? Explain.
2. Describe how you and your partner should be positioned during the interview process.
3. When interviewing the wife and the husband, what should you look for? What observations should you be making?
4. The husband has decided that he would like to leave for the evening, and he starts to go into his bedroom to pack a few things. Should you allow him to proceed alone? Should you allow him to leave? Should you arrest him? Explain your answers.

Your Assignment 15-2

It is a Tuesday afternoon, and you and your partner have received a call to respond to a residence for an unknown problem. The call came from a woman who sounded very upset.

During your approach to the residence, the station dispatcher informs you that there have been no previous calls there, there are no weapons registered for the residents, and there are no outstanding warrants.

When you arrive at the residence, you observe two women sitting outside on the porch; one is visibly upset, the other is offering consolation. You speak with the two women and find that they are sisters. The upset sister, Susan, states that her live-in boyfriend has been drinking all day and has been yelling at her constantly. Susan decided to leave with their 3-year-old son, and the boyfriend said that she couldn't take him and threw her out of the house, pushing her out the door. Susan went to her sister's house, which is a short distance away. This is when she called the station and provided them with the address and said that she would meet the police there and explain what happened.

Susan states that her boyfriend is alone in the house with their son. When the sister went to the door to get the boy, the boyfriend would not allow her into the house and closed the door on her.

Susan explains that there are no weapons in the house and that her boyfriend would never hurt the child. She states that you can see through the front window that the boyfriend is sitting on the couch and that the child is in the bedroom. You look through the window and see that the boyfriend is on the couch and that the child playing quietly in the back bedroom.

You call for an additional cruiser for a backup unit and stand by until it arrives. A few minutes pass, and the backup unit arrives. You fill the officer in on the events up to this point and ask him to remain outside with the women while you and your partner go to the door to speak with the boyfriend.

You go to the door and knock. The boyfriend opens the door and returns to the couch. He does not appear to be in an agitated state, and you allow him to remain seated as you and your partner approach him.

You ask him about the child. He states that the child is fine and in the bedroom playing. You ask if your partner may see that the child is okay. The boyfriend states that he can, and your partner gets the child and moves to take the child outside to the awaiting backup officer. The boyfriend asks where you are taking his child; you inform him you are just taking the child outside until you can resolve the issue.

He begins to verbally protest, but quickly decides against any intervention, allowing the child to leave.

The boyfriend has been drinking and appears to be drunk, but is not showing any signs or indications of any aggression toward you or the other officers. Your partner returns and is now at your side. The house is empty except for the three of you.

1. What would you ask the boyfriend?
2. What information would you obtain from the sister and Susan?
3. Would you give the child to Susan, return the child to the house, or turn the child over to a social service agency?
4. What action would you take with the boyfriend?

Your Assignment 15-3

You have just received a phone call from a neighboring police department that a woman from their community has received a threatening phone call from her ex-husband. There is an active restraining order out on the husband forbidding any contact whatsoever. The noncontact order covers any form of communication in person, by phone, by computer, by letter, or by any third party. In this state, any violation of the restraining order is an arrestable offence, and the officer is mandated to take the violator into custody to be held until the next scheduled court session.

The neighboring department has faxed over a valid copy of the restraining order for your verification, as required by the law.

You have all of the pertinent information regarding the husband, such as the address of the husband's brother's house where he is staying temporarily, which is in your community, and a description of his vehicle. You and your partner have been assigned to make the arrest.

As you and your partner pull up to the brother's house, you observe two cars, one of which is the suspect's vehicle. You knock on the door and a male opens the door.

1. What is the first thing you should do?
2. For the purposes of this exercise, the violation of the restraining order is just cause for arrest. However, under certain circumstances, it may be necessary to obtain a third-party warrant that enables the police to enter a home owned by a third party to arrest an individual who is not a resident at that location. Which avenue for the arrest would you take and why?
3. If the suspect is visible in the house from your location outside the house, what would you do?
4. If the suspect is outside the house on your arrival, what would you do?
5. If the brother answers the door and states that the suspect is not there, what would you do?

Your Assignment 15-4

It is a Monday evening around 7:00 P.M. You have been dispatched for a loud disturbance coming from a neighborhood house.

When you arrive at the residence, a neighbor meets you outside and explains that the husband and wife have been arguing for most of the evening. She also informs you that there is a 7-year-old child in the house, who is the wife's daughter from a previous marriage.

The husband answers the door when you knock. It is obvious that he has been in an altercation, because his shirt is torn and there are scratches on his arm and a red mark on his left cheek. As you enter the house, the wife and her daughter are sitting on the couch. It is apparent that the daughter is upset and crying and that the wife is in an agitated state.

Your partner is talking with the wife while you speak with the husband. The husband states that his wife is very upset with him because he has been out of work for two months and today he went to play golf with his friends. She is upset because money has been tight and he shouldn't have spent money to play golf.

You ask him about the scratches and torn shirt. He tells you that when he got home from the golf outing, his wife was so mad that she tried to grab his golf clubs from him. She struggled with him. He held on to the clubs; she was kicking, fighting, and scratching him.

She slapped him in the face, at which point he dropped the golf clubs and went to the cellar. She continued to yell at him up until the time you arrived at the scene. He stated that he saw the cruiser from the window and that's when he came upstairs to open the door.

Your partner relates that the wife was very upset because he spent money to play golf at a very prestigious golf course, which they can't easily afford. She said she confronted him when he got home and was going to trash his golf clubs and that a struggle ensued while she was trying to get the clubs. She also states that the scratches occurred during the struggle, and that he did not strike her at all. She denies slapping him in the face, or at least doesn't remember doing so.

1. How will you determine what actually happened and who is telling the truth? How can you verify any of the facts?
2. Would you make an arrest in this case? If so, who would you arrest?
3. What would tell the daughter if she asks what is happening to her mother or stepfather?
4. In this case, if you arrested the mother, what will you do with the daughter?

5. If you did not make an arrest in this incident, what would you do to ensure that a similar incident doesn't occur in the future? How would you prevent any other violence from occurring?

6. Write a complete narrative report of the incident from the time of your first observations to clearing the assignment and returning to service. You may make up names as well as any responses or actions as long as they fit with the facts presented. Make sure you justify any actions that you take.

Chapter Wrap-Up

In-Service Training

When speaking with the involved parties in a domestic violence situation, you should always have sufficient officers on the scene so that there is at least one officer to cover each person.

From the Experts

When speaking with the involved parties in a domestic violence situation, always keep your partner in view. He should also do the same for you.

Caution

Never allow a person involved in a domestic violence situation to leave the room and get something or go elsewhere in the house without being accompanied by a police officer. The person may be trying to get a weapon or affect an escape.

Suspicious Persons, Motor Vehicles, and Activities

Knowledge Objectives

- Identify what constitutes a suspicious person, suspicious motor vehicle, or suspicious activity.
- Understand the risk involved when an officer faces a potentially dangerous situation.
- Identify the circumstances presented by an incident and predict the incident's outcome based on the responses and actions of the persons involved.
- Know how to determine when people are being truthful in their responses and descriptions.
- Know how to deal with persons whose actions have drawn the attention of others in an unknown environment.

Skills Objectives

- Demonstrate the ability to respond to a verbal and/or physical confrontation presented by a person in an unknown situation.
- Demonstrate the ability to control an unknown situation when information about the situation is not available.
- Demonstrate powers of observation when dealing with suspicious persons whether on foot, in a motor vehicle, or in a building or other location.
- Demonstrate the ability to maintain order and safety.
- Understand and demonstrate one-on-one interview techniques.
- Recognize suspicious movements and activities by a suspect that may indicate the potential for an aggressive response.
- Write a clear narrative report that depicts your observations, actions, and reactions.

◼ Introduction

In this chapter, you will read an overview of what a police officer faces in the day-to-day performances of her duties. Many of the calls that an officer responds to are in response to a suspicious person, motor vehicle, or activity. These calls may be initiated by the public in general or by observations made by the officer during patrol.

◼ Situation Assessment

At this point in the text, you can take what you have learned and use it to make decisions about what actions you may take in a particular situation. One area where you can apply the information you have learned is incidents involving suspicious persons, motor vehicles, or activities.

Determining When an Incident Involves Suspicious Behavior

Calls based on suspicious persons may involve a person who is on foot in an area where he should not be or whose presence has attracted the attention of others. An example of a suspicious person may be a man watching children in a schoolyard during recess. In this day and age, parents as well as school officials would be justifiably concerned by such behavior. However, the situation could be innocent; maybe the man is just watching the children play. Or, the situation could be more serious in nature, involving a person who is not interested in the welfare of the children but rather his own devious thoughts and needs.

Such calls may also involve a person in a motor vehicle in an unusual location or actions by a person in a vehicle that have aroused the attention of others. Again, the situation could in fact be quite innocent. For example, say that a person calls about a suspicious man who is sitting in a motor vehicle in a quiet neighborhood and watching a house. The man in question may be a private investigator or a plainclothes officer on an undercover assignment. Or the man may be a salesperson who has an appointment and is waiting for the proper time or for the person that he is to meet to arrive home.

The officer may also respond to calls regarding suspicious activity. Such calls may be in response to a person calling about a group of kids hanging around in a mall parking lot. Again, the activity may be quite innocent; the group of kids may just be waiting for a ride home after an evening of shopping.

There are an unlimited number of types of suspicious calls. Some situations may be innocent and have no criminal intent; however, others may be of a criminal nature where the intent and purpose of the suspicious activity is unlawful.

Handling Calls for Suspicious Persons

The goal of this chapter is to identify some of the types of suspicious persons, vehicles, and activities that a police officer may have to deal with in hopes that it will enable you to resolve any situation in a safe manner.

When dealing with a suspicious person, motor vehicle, or activity, the approach is always the same in that the officer *should be prepared for the unexpected.* Previous chapters examined how to handle suspects in public, in buildings, and in motor vehicles. The techniques you learned in those chapters still apply in ensuring the safe and successful completion of the task in hand.

When you observe a person who is in a location where he should not be, make sure that you keep your eye on the person as you make your approach, especially if the person sees you coming. Be alert to the person's actions: Is the person hiding something? Does the person look nervous, as though he does not belong there? What type of area is it? Is the person at the back door of a business or near an accessible window? Are there others in the area that you might not be able to see?

A suspicious person may be as innocent as someone stopping behind a building after hours in order to relieve himself, which in most cases is illegal. Or he may be attempting to break into the business, and his intentions are not so innocent.

The officer investigating such a call for a suspicious person must look at all the facts that are presented, as well as those that aren't. Is the suspect there for a legitimate reason? Does he belong here?

If a man is behind a building or in some unusual or suspicious location and states that he is there to relieve himself, is the ground wet? Is he near a wall or is he near a door or some other point of entry? Does he have anything with him, such as a duffle bag, gym bag, or some other type of container that could hold burglarious tools or that could be used to carry away stolen merchandise? When the officer confronted the man, was the man nervous? Were his answers evasive? Answers to such questions can help the officer determine whether the man's presence in this location is justified or warranted. For the most part, there are few legitimate reasons for a person to be behind a business or residence after hours.

Officers may also receive calls to investigate suspicious persons in residential areas. Many such calls are for suspected prowlers or peeping toms.

A *prowler* is a person who is lurking around a residence usually, but not necessarily, at night. The person's intent could range from an impending assault to just looking in the windows. Calls for prowlers may turn out to be innocent in nature. For example, a suspected prowler may turn out to be just a kid cutting through a yard on her way home or to another destination.

Peeping toms, or voyeurs, are just that, they scout out neighborhoods in the evening hours looking for windows with the shades up where they can look in and watch the residents inside. The peeper may just want to watch people, watch them undress, or in some cases, watch them in intimate situations.

As you can imagine, there is no template for handling all situations involving suspicious persons or activities. In order to resolve such calls, an officer must be alert, aware, and observant.

Your Assignment 16-1

It is Friday night at 1:00 A.M. You and your partner are on routine patrol in the business district of the downtown area in your community. You are conducting your normal patrol, driving in the cruiser at 15 to 25 miles per hour so you can observe the area businesses. While driving down an alley, you see an individual at the rear of one of the business blocks. He is behind a stationery store.

You tell your partner to bring the cruiser around to the other side of the alley; you leave the cruiser and walk toward the individual. As you approach him, you can make out that he is standing with his back to you, facing the business's rear door next to the dumpster. Your partner has parked the cruiser on the opposite end of the alley and is approaching the suspect from the other side.

1. What precautions should you and your partner take as you approach the individual? Explain why you would take these precautions.

2. If the individual states that he is just relieving himself, what should you look for to determine if he is telling the truth?

3. If you and your partner are satisfied with his response, what else might you do before sending him on his way?

4. If the suspect states that he was just cutting through the alley, and you are not satisfied with his answer, what other questions would you ask and what other actions would you take? Explain.

5. What observations could you make that would either corroborate his story or implicate him in some other activity?

Your Assignment 16-2

It is 10:00 P.M. on a Friday, the night before the big high-school football game. You have been assigned to respond to the wooded area of your community by the lake. The dispatcher informs you that they have received a call of some unknown activity and loud noises in the woods. The area is a well-known hangout for kids and the site of many keg parties. The area has been the focus of many unsuccessful attempts by the department to put an end to underage drinking and the lighting of bonfires. The department has spent many thousands of dollars on overtime and has reassigned individuals in order to make these activities a thing of the past.

Thinking this may be a good chance to quell this activity once and for all, you have asked for additional backup units to assist you in breaking up any parties you might find. The other units have arrived, and you have a good portion of the area covered, but there are some areas that the kids could flee through without being apprehended.

The backup units have secured what you and they feel are the most likely routes of escape and have located where the vehicles of those involved are parked.

As you enter the wooded area, you hear a large group of kids yelling and partying. You also observe the glimmer of a bonfire. As you get closer, you hear one of the kids yell, "Cops!" The group then disperses in all directions. Most of the kids run deeper into the woods, away from the waiting backup officers. You have alerted the backup officers by radio that the kids are running.

As you enter the clearing, you observe three kids still standing there. One is on crutches; you recognize him as an injured high-school football player. You also observe several coolers, empty beer cans, and three kegs of beer sitting in barrels of ice.

During the next few moments, the backup officers inform you that they have several of the kids in custody. A majority of the youths are still in the woods somewhere. Two officers are standing by the vehicles in the parking area.

1. In a narrative report, explain what actions you would take. Base your decisions on the information provided in the situation summary. For the purposes of the report, you may either identify the subjects with fictitious names or numbers such as "youth 1," "youth 2," etc. Make sure you justify what you did or did not do.

Your Assignment 16-3

It is approximately 3:00 P.M. on a Wednesday afternoon. You and your partner have received a call of a person parked in a motor vehicle for several hours. This has several neighbors in this upper-class neighborhood concerned. The caller has provided you with the vehicle information: the make, model, and color of the vehicle as well as the license plate number.

On your way to the location, the dispatcher informs you that there is nothing unusual about the car registration, the vehicle is not stolen, and there are no warrants outstanding on the registered owner of the vehicle.

You approach the area and observe the vehicle. There appears to be a single occupant sitting on the driver's side of the vehicle. You pull in behind the vehicle and approach the occupant.

The operator states that he is an insurance investigator and that he is watching a resident in the neighborhood. He is investigating a case of suspected fraud.

1. How would you approach the vehicle in question, considering that it is daylight?
2. How would you verify who the occupant is and why he is there?
3. If his story checks out, would you allow him to remain or would you ask him to leave, considering that the neighbors have complained?

4. If a neighbor approaches you and asks what is going on and states that she was the one who called the police, what would you tell her?

5. What would you do if the occupant were unable to prove who he was or what he was doing there and the dispatcher tells you that he is from a neighboring community?

Your Assignment 16-4

It is a Monday evening around 10:00 P.M. You and your partner are on routine patrol in the business district in your jurisdiction. Most of the businesses are retailers. All of the stores close between 9:00 and 9:30 P.M.

As you are driving up the street you observe an individual standing in a doorway to a business. He is looking up and down the street. He glances in your direction, and when he sees the cruiser, he steps back further into the darkened doorway, as if to avoid being seen or detected.

This suspicious activity draws your attention. You and your partner pull the cruiser up to the individual in the doorway. You immediately recognize him as an individual you have arrested in the past for burglary (breaking into a business and stealing the cash box). You remember him being convicted by the court and sentenced to serve time in the county jail.

He recognizes you, too, and offers a cordial nonconfrontational greeting. You ask him what he is doing, and he states that he is waiting for a ride from a friend. You and your partner approach the man and begin to question him.

1. Describe the steps you would take when interviewing the person. List the questions you would ask and what information you would like to obtain.

2. What would he need to say for you to believe him? How could you verify the information?

3. What actions would make you suspicious of his reason for being there?

4. In this case, do you have the rights to make a threshold inquiry or to conduct a stop-and-frisk? Why or why not?

5. If he is found to have a legitimate reason for being there, what might you say to him?

Your Assignment 16-5

You have been assigned by your supervisor to solve a problem that has plagued the residents in your patrol area. It seems that over the past several weeks between the hours of 7:00 and 10:00 P.M., someone has been terrorizing the residents by looking into the windows of two homes.

Both of the houses in question have young daughters, and the peeper has been seen there on several occasions. You work the 4:00 P.M. to midnight shift, and it is up to you to apprehend the suspect.

1. Explain what you would do and what information you would obtain from the victims in order to best attempt to apprehend the suspect. In other words, write out your plan of action.

Chapter Wrap-Up

In-Service Training

Suspicious persons, motor vehicles, and activities are incidents that may be dispatched as unknown events. When the officers arrive at the location, they often find themselves dealing with individuals. The officers should always use the training they have received when handling these situations.

From the Experts

When responding to a call for any suspicious activity, have the dispatcher obtain as much information from the caller as possible. The more information you have, the better prepared you will be.

Caution

When in a darkened and/or isolated location and dealing with an unknown situation, don't become comfortable or complacent with the obvious. Always assume that there is one more suspect, one more weapon, or that the suspect may respond in an aggressive manner. Do not put your guard down until the call or incident has ended successfully.

Alarm Responses

Knowledge Objectives

- Describe how the police should respond to an alarm at a bank.
- Describe how the police should respond to an alarm at a business.
- Describe how the police should respond to an alarm at a residence.
- Determine what signs or clues an officer should look for before clearing a false alarm call.
- Understand the risks an officer faces when responding to an alarm call.

Skills Objectives

- Demonstrate the precautions that should be taken during alarm responses.
- Demonstrate the ability to control a possible hostage situation.
- Demonstrate awareness and alertness when responding to alarms.
- Demonstrate the proper response to an alarm call based on whether a business is open or closed or whether it is daytime or nighttime.
- Write a clear narrative report that depicts your observations, actions, and reactions.

■ Introduction

In this chapter, you will learn about alarm responses. Calls for alarms may be generated by audible sounds; telephone calls to the dispatcher; or, in some cases, the police may be notified by a third-party alarm company. Alarms are found in banks, businesses, residences, and warehouses, as well as vehicles. Alarms may be triggered accidentally, by weather, or by an individual in need of assistance. Alarms may also be triggered during business as well as nonbusiness hours.

■ Alarms

This chapter examines responses to three main types of alarms: bank alarms, business alarms, and residential alarms. However, before describing the specific types of alarms, you will learn about false alarms.

False Alarms

In most cases, false alarms are caused accidentally by employees or residents. An alarm can be triggered accidentally in a number of ways. For example, some alarms are set off when they are not deactivated in time. Most alarms have a timed system. With such systems, once a person has entered the structure, he or she has must turn the alarm off within a predetermined amount of time or the alarm will fire. For example, if a person sets a home alarm and then leaves, when the person returns, the alarm is active. Unless the person goes to the alarm box and turns the alarm off within the preset time frame, the alarm will sound.

A person may become delayed in getting to the alarm box because of a distraction, such as a ringing phone. Or, perhaps one family member left the house and another one was returning and didn't know the alarm was set. Or perhaps the person forgot the deactivation code.

Storms are another cause of false alarms. During severe weather, thunder and lightning can trigger an alarm to go off.

Notification of a Triggered Alarm

The police are notified of triggered alarms in a several different ways.

Alarm Is Connected to the Police Department Telephone Line

Alarms may be connected directly to the police station by the telephone line. When the alarm is triggered, a signal is sent through the phone lines to the police station. When the police receive the signal, dispatch will send a cruiser to respond to the alarm.

Third-Party Alarm Monitoring Companies

Alarm signals may also be sent by a third-party alarm-monitoring company. When an alarm is set off, the alarm company will notify the police, and in some cases, depending on the contract, the alarm company may send a private security officer to respond as well.

Alarm-monitoring companies vary with regard to service and reliability. They also vary in response time, depending on the contract with the alarm company. Time can be essential when an alarm is triggered. The response time for the most part will probably be approximately 2 to 5 minutes after the police have been notified that the alarm has gone off.

Alarm-monitoring companies often serve specific territories. The alarm company may have a security officer who covers several cities, towns, or counties. If this is the case, the response time is determined by staffing and territorial limitations, and it may take several hours for a response. It should also be noted that some larger security companies have more resources and less territory to cover, and thus have faster response times.

Noise Alarms

Some alarms emit an audible signal but are not hooked up to telephone lines. When the alarm is triggered, an audible alarm in the form of a siren, horn, or other loud, attention-getting device is sounded. These alarms rely on others to hear the alarm and notify the police. This is the most inexpensive type of alarm because a dedicated phone line is not needed and there is not a private security response.

Responding to an Alarm Call

When an alarm is received, regardless of how the police have been notified, the normal course of conducting this type of call for service is performed in several phases. When responding to an alarm call, the officer should position the cruiser so that it cannot be seen from the building. If responding to a business area, the officer may want to park the cruiser a few doors down from the targeted business. This will provide some safety to the officer, because she does not know if the alarm is a false one or real. If it is a real alarm, and the suspects are inside and have weapons, the officer wants to avoid becoming an easy target by parking in front of the building.

After the cruiser has been positioned, the officer should do a perimeter check of the premises. This entails looking for obvious signs of entry, such as open doors and whether they have been smashed, pried open, or accessed by some other means. The officer also should check out the windows. The officer also should physically check the doors and other ways of getting in to make sure the doors have not been opened and then left closed to look undisturbed. An alert officer also will check for other signs of entering, such as items moved or piled up under windows or for access to the roof.

The officer also should look for any cut wires. Occasionally, perpetrators will stake out a business and cut the wires to set off the alarm. They may even place or tape the wires back in place to make it look like they have not been tampered with. They do this to check the response time of the police and to see if the officers find the cut wires. These observations, and others, can be made from a distance.

The suspects may do this on several nights to see if the response is the same each time or to see if the police or owner become complacent and evidentially disregard the alarm. In other words, they are setting up the business for a break-in or burglary.

The subjects also may watch for severe weather and then make an attempt to enter the building. During severe weather, when numerous alarms are going off, the police will likely do a quick building check and report that the building looks secure in response to the alarm. The police dispatcher will then notify the owner that the building is secure and that the alarm was probably weather related. In the meantime, the perpetrators are inside the building.

On stormy nights, the police department can be inundated with calls for false alarms. Such nights are perfect opportunities to commit crimes. The criminals know this. The responding police officer(s) should be diligent in responding to every alarm and not short-change the service to the community.

Bank Alarms

When there is a report of a bank alarm, the officer must consider a number of different variables. Did the alarm call come when the bank was opening or closing? If so, it might indicate an accidental false alarm.

However, it is important to determine whether the alarm was accidentally set off or if it is in fact a real alarm incident. If the alarm is set off during bank hours or as the bank was opening or closing and there are hostages inside, the police response may place those inside the bank in danger or injury or death. If the police respond in an aggressive manner, any suspects inside who may be actually robbing the bank may panic at the police arrival and react in an unwanted way.

The police officer should be careful not to place herself in danger when approaching the building. If a bank has a glass front, depending on the lighting inside and outside the bank, the officer may not be able to see what is going on inside. The officer may unwittingly walk into a hostile situation.

To avoid such dangerous situations, some police departments have established signals and systems with the banks in their communities. For example, if an alarm from a bank is received at the police station, an officer may call the bank and ask the manager to provide a code word that would indicate whether it is a false alarm or an actual alert.

Business Alarms

When an alarm call is received from a business, the officer should consider the type of business the alarm is being received from. The type of business may be a preliminary indication if there is a threat of a possible robbery or some other incident.

If an alarm comes in from a warehouse during business hours, in all likelihood the alarm was set off accidentally by an employee. However, remember that all alarms need to be checked out.

In some cases, an alarm may be triggered and the building will appear to be secure from the outside. This should not be taken as a sign of a false alarm. The suspect may have defeated an alarm at the business next door and entered the targeted business through a wall, ceiling, common cellar, or attic crawl space.

In some circumstances, a business will not have an alarm system and the suspect will enter that business to access the targeted one. The suspects will then smash through the wall between the two businesses and set off a motion-detector alarm in the targeted business. When the police respond to the alarmed business, the outside of the building will be secure and show no signs of entry. The officers may do quick visual inspection of the business next door, the one that was actually broken into, and fail to see any signs of a break-in because the suspects may have been discreet in their entry. Because no alarm sounded from that business, the police did not give it a lot of attention. The police do not always know which businesses have alarm systems.

When checking a building where an alarm has sounded, the officer should always check the walls, ceilings, vents, and any other means of entry. The officer should also check if the building that houses the business has a common cellar or attic space, which means that all of the businesses can be accessed through a minimally secured door cellar door.

When an officer is in doubt as to whether a break-in has actually occurred, the officer should have the dispatcher contact the owner or a representative of the business and ask her to respond and allow the officer to access the building for a thorough check. In some cases, the business owners or representatives may refuse to come down and open up the building, in those cases, all the officer can do is conduct as thorough a check as possible. The dispatcher should record the name of the person who refused to come to the scene, just in case the false alarm turns out to be otherwise.

An officer should never consider any alarm call as being routine. The complacency of a routine call may lull an officer into a false sense of security and cause the officer to let her guard down. Such an attitude may result in the officer getting hurt if she comes upon an actual breaking-and-entering incident.

During business hours, all approaches to alarm calls should be made cautiously and with alertness. The police officer should park the cruiser away from the front of the business and observe if there is any indication of foul play.

Residential Alarms

In most cases when an alarm is received from a residence, the alarm was activated by a family member or resident who forgot to shut the alarm off or didn't enter in the correct code to deactivate. The officer should not become complacent and treat these as just another false alarm call. He should respond as if it was an actual alarm, as it very well may be. Approaching the residence cautiously. Once he has secured the outside of the residence and has adequate backup, he should then approach the house and check the doors and windows. Once all exterior entrances are secured and he is satisfied, should he then approach the door and attempt to notify the resident.

If he does make contact with the resident he must make a positive identification that the person who he is speaking to, is in fact a resident and does live there. Simply being greeted at the door by someone does not assure the officer that the person is lawfully there in the house.

If there is no answer, then the officer should notify the station or dispatcher that the house is secure if that is the case. The dispatcher may be tasked with notifying the owner or alarm company, whichever one the information is provided at the station. If the house is not secure and there is reason to believe that there is a break in, then the officer should conduct a search of the residence, and after finishing, have the dispatcher contact the owner or alarm company to respond.

Your Assignment 17-1

It is 2:00 A.M. You and your partner have just been assigned to respond to an alarm at a shoe store in a local shopping plaza. The building is a strip mall and the shoe store is in the center of the complex.

1. What would you and your partner do first? Explain.
2. Explain what you would look for and where.
3. If the shoe store is found to be secure, what would you have the dispatcher do?
4. What else might you do before you leave the area?

Your Assignment 17-2

It is a Tuesday evening around 11:00 P.M. You and your partner have been assigned to check out a residential alarm call. The dispatcher informs you that shortly after the alarm came in, someone claiming to be a resident of the house called the station and stated that the alarm was accidental. The caller also told the dispatcher that everything was all set and that there was no need to send a cruiser to the scene.

You arrive at the residence. As you approach the house, you are met outside by a teenage boy, who is halfway down the walkway. He informs you that he is the one who called and that the alarm was accidental. He states that he is all set and thanks you and your partner for checking up on him.

1. Would you check the outside of the house? If so, why?
2. How would you verify the identification of the teenage boy?
3. Would you insist that he let you inside the house to check it out?
4. If you decide to go inside the house, how would you justify your reasons?
5. If you and your partner were to check the outside of the house, what would you do with the teenager? Explain your search method.

Your Assignment 17-3

It is a Monday night around 11:15 P.M. You and your partner have been assigned to check on an alarm at a local video store. As you pull into the parking lot, a car is attempting to exit it. The operator of the car sees you and stops his vehicle.

You and your partner observe the operator get out and approach your cruiser on foot. He states that he is the manager and was just closing up the store. Your partner approaches the man's vehicle while you speak with the operator.

Suddenly your partner yells over to you that there is a moneybag on the front seat and on top of the moneybag is a handgun. The man raises his hands and says that he is legally licensed to carry a firearm and is on his way to make a night deposit of the store's nightly receipts.

1. In a narrative report, explain what you and your partner would do in this case.

Your Assignment 17-4

It is 2:00 A.M. on a Sunday morning. You and your partner have been assigned to respond to an alarm call at an electronics warehouse. This warehouse is the main storage facility for a large chain of electronics stores.

As you and your partner arrive, you observe that there is an open window on the side of the building. The window is approximately 5 feet from the ground, and you cannot determine whether the window was forced open or if it was just left unlocked. No K-9 units are available.

1. In a narrative report, describe what you would do in this case. Be specific and identify any additional support you may need. backup units are available. If you decide to do a search, write the narrative up to that point. Do not describe the search of the building.
2. If you summon additional assistance, what you would do until it arrived?
3. Where would you position the additional units?
4. What would you have the dispatcher do?

Your Assignment 17-5

Using Your Assignment 17-4, explain how you would search the building. If you feel that a search is not necessary, explain why.

If you decide to search, note that the warehouse is a large open warehouse with two small rooms off to one side: one is a restroom and the other is an office.

Chapter Wrap-Up

In-Service Training

Do not become complacent. Although you may think that many calls for service are similar, they are not. There is always something that makes each situation unique. Complacency may result in a false sense of security.

From the Experts

When responding to an alarm, never enter a room through a window when you do not know the drop to the floor below.

Caution

When responding to an alarm call during business hours, be cautious of all persons you confront. In some cases, the suspects may disguise themselves as hostages or as customers in hopes of getting the extra edge they need in order to make an escape.

Pulling It All Together

In this final chapter, you will pull together everything that that you have learned in this text and apply it to a number of different situations. The following scenarios may be acted out in the classroom, recreated in elaborate and realistic scenarios outside of the classroom, written up as narratives, or discussed in a group format, with the entire class providing input.

In each of the scenarios presented, you will receive information about a particular incident. If you will be writing a narrative report based on the situation, you can make up any information to fill in any holes in the scenario (e.g., names, motor vehicle information, etc.). In addition, if writing a narrative, you must detail the steps you would take and justify them. This includes any notifications to the dispatcher and any communication between you and your partner or the backup officer.

All scenarios portray an officer in either a one-officer cruiser or a two-officer cruiser. If you are in a single-officer cruiser and a backup officer is needed, be sure to state that in the narrative report or in the group discussion.

Your Assignment 18-1

It is 10:00 P.M. You are responding to a report of a speeding motor vehicle. Upon your arrival to the area, you observe the speeding vehicle and pull it over. The operator refuses to give you his license. In this situation, refusing to provide a license to an officer is an arrestable offense. After making several failed attempts to get the operator to show you his license, you decide to arrest the operator. After you arrest him, he produces a valid drivers license. What will you do?

Your Assignment 18-2

It is midnight and you are on patrol. On a main street, you stop a known drug dealer for a broken taillight. As you approach the vehicle, you observe in plain view a hash pipe in the ashtray and a large quantity of what appears to be drugs under the seat.

Your Assignment 18-3

It is 11:00 P.M. You have just stopped a motor vehicle after a 5-minute pursuit for speeding and a red-light violation. You make the stop on a dead-end street in a wooded area. There are four people in the vehicle. As soon as you stop the vehicle, all four doors of the vehicle open and the four suspects take off and run in different directions.

Your Assignment 18-4

It is 7:30 A.M. You have just stopped a vehicle for a stop-sign violation on a main street. As you approach the vehicle, you observe the operator, a young woman approximately 18 years of age, roll up her windows. You then hear her lock all of the vehicle's doors. You ask her to roll her window down and pass you her license and registration. She ignores you and stares straight ahead. You tell her that she is subject to arrest if she does not produce her license and registration. In this situation, refusing to provide a license to an officer is an arrestable offense. She places her license and registration against the inside of the glass of the driver's door window so that you can see it, but she still does not open her door or make contact with you.

Your Assignment 18-5

It is 3:00 A.M., and you are on patrol. After a brief pursuit at speeds of up to 60 mph, you have just stopped a speeding motor vehicle that has run two red lights and one stop sign. The vehicle has no passengers, only the operator. In this situation, refusal to stop for a police officer's signal is an arrestable offense.

Your Assignment 18-6

It is 11:00 P.M. You have just stopped a vehicle on a side street for a red-light violation. There appears to be five minors in the vehicle. As you approach the vehicle, the four passengers, who appear to be drunk, exit it and walk away from the scene. The driver is sober and does not appear to have been drinking.

Your Assignment 18-7

It is 11:00 P.M. You have just stopped a vehicle on a side street for a stop sign violation. There appears to be five adults in the vehicle. As you approach the vehicle, the four passengers, who appear to be drunk, exit and walk away from the scene. You tell them to return to the vehicle. All of the passengers return, but they refuse to show you any identification. The driver has not been drinking.

Your Assignment 18-8

It is midnight, and you have just stopped a vehicle for speeding. The operator is alone. As soon as you stop the vehicle, the dispatcher informs you that the vehicle was reported stolen about an hour ago. As you get out of your patrol car, the driver exits the vehicle and runs.

Your Assignment 18-9

It is 1:00 A.M. You have just stopped a vehicle on a side street because you suspect that the operator is driving under the influence of alcohol. As you approach the vehicle, the operator exits it and states that he is an officer from a neighboring town. He is obviously drunk and should not drive. He flashes his badge and I.D. and asks you to give him a break.

Your Assignment 18-10

It is 11:00 A.M. You have just stopped a speeding motor vehicle on a side street. There was no pursuit. You approach the operator and ask him for his license and registration. The driver subtly passes you a $20 bill when he hands you his license.

Your Assignment 18-11

It is 8:00 P.M. You have just stopped one of two speeding motor vehicles that had been playing tag. The second vehicle flees the scene. The operator of the first vehicle exits his car immediately upon being stopped. He then walks to the rear of the vehicle and places his foot on the rear bumper of his vehicle. When doing so, his jacket opens to reveal a 0.38 caliber revolver in his waistband. The dispatcher informs you that he is legally and duly licensed to carry a firearm. He does not make any moves or gestures toward his weapon.

Your Assignment 18-12

It is 10:00 P.M. You are responding to a radio call of two suspicious males in a vehicle in the parking lot of a fast-food restaurant. As you approach the vehicle, you observe the two occupants passing a marijuana cigarette (joint) back and forth. When one of the occupants sees you approaching, he eats the joint; the other occupant reaches under the seat and conceals a bag of marijuana.

Your Assignment 18-13

It is 11:00 P.M. You have just stopped a vehicle for a stop-sign violation. As you approach the vehicle, you observe that the vehicle has all the indications of being stolen: a license plate is attached with string over another license plate and there is a screwdriver in the ignition. The driver tells you that he has just retrieved the vehicle from the tow lot after another police department recovered it as stolen, but he has no paperwork. The recovering police department cannot be called. What will you do if the vehicle is still reported as stolen? What will you do if the driver is telling you the truth?

Your Assignment 18-14

It is 11:00 A.M. You have stopped a vehicle on a main street for a stop-sign violation. The operator is very cooperative, but nervous.

Your Assignment 18-15

It is 1:00 A.M. You have observed two males sitting in the front seat of a vehicle for 5 minutes on a minor side street. You recall that there have been many breaking and enterings in the area. You approach the vehicle, and the two occupants appear to be nervous upon seeing you. The occupants become belligerent and difficult when you confront them. They explain that they have rights and that they have done nothing wrong. When asked, they present all of the proper identification. As you are speaking with then, you *think* you smell the odor of lit marijuana in the vehicle.

Your Assignment 18-16

It is 1:00 A.M. You have just stopped a motor vehicle on a side street for speeding. Once the vehicle stops, the operator flees and the passenger remains in the vehicle. The vehicle is stolen. The passenger appears to be confused and scared. He tells you that he was hitch-hiking, that he does not know who the operator is, and that he did not know that the vehicle was stolen.

Your Assignment 18-17

It is 8:00 A.M. You have just received a report of a suspicious motor vehicle. A male has been sitting in a vehicle in front of a residence for the past 10 minutes. As you approach the vehicle, you observe a firearm in plain view. The driver tells you that he is waiting for a friend to exit the house so the two of them can target shoot at the local range. He has all necessary paperwork for the firearm.

Your Assignment 18-18

It is 9:00 A.M. You have just stopped a motor vehicle on a busy street for a red-light violation. The driver is very cooperative and tells you that he is extremely late for a very important appointment. He asks you to give him a break so that he can continue on his way.

Your Assignment 18-19

It is 10:00 P.M. You have just stopped a vehicle on a main street for a speeding and a red-light violation. The operator of the vehicle is the police chief's son. There is one passenger in the vehicle. The operator is being difficult and boasting about his father's authority.

Your Assignment 18-20

It is 2:00 A.M. You are on foot patrol, and you are walking down an alley behind a block of small businesses. You observe a male standing at the rear of a building. The male is on parole for breaking and entering and assault and battery by means of a dangerous weapon. Your radio is not working. The male is cooperative and states that he is there to urinate.

Your Assignment 18-21

It is 2:00 P.M. You have been instructed to investigate a report of a man threatening suicide in a secluded residential area. The man may or may not have a weapon. Upon your arrival at the scene, his family informs you that he is in the back yard and that the man is a hunter and an avid target shooter. When you arrive in the back yard, you observe the man holding a firearm. He sees you and tells you, "I'll put down my gun if you put down yours." As he speaks, he starts to walk toward you, occasionally pointing the firearm in your direction, but not directly at you. He is not behaving in a threatening manner.

Your Assignment 18-22

It is 11:00 A.M. You are on patrol and parked on a residential street. You are approached by a woman, who states that her purse was stolen about half an hour ago at the mall. The woman states she followed the suspect home and that she saw the thief place the purse in the trunk of his vehicle. The woman is from the next town over and appears to be a solid, reliable citizen. She explains that she placed her purse in the cart while she was shopping. She was alone in the aisle with the suspect, and she stopped to examine some merchandise. At that time, the suspect walked past her and bumped her cart. The suspect quickly walked out of the store. At that point, she noticed her purse was missing. She states that only the suspect was near her cart. She then ran from the store and saw the suspect open his car trunk and throw her purse inside. The suspect then locked his trunk and drove away, and she followed him here. She tells you that she wants her purse and she wants the suspect arrested. She tells you that she has many pieces of identification in her purse and about $750 in cash. She is very upset and slightly unreasonable.

You go to the residence she followed the suspect to and you ask the suspect a few questions. During your questioning, the suspect states that he was never in the store or in the area. He also states that he has never seen the victim before and that he knows his rights. He then tells you that he is leaving for an appointment and is already late. He then tries to enter his vehicle. The suspect tells you to let him go or he will sue you and "own your house" and so on. He refuses to produce any identification or a vehicle registration. In this situation, refusal to provide a license to a police officer is an arrestable offense. Note, however, that the suspect has not driven the vehicle in your presence.

Your Assignment 18-23

It is 11:00 P.M. You are responding to a group of four to six teenagers who have gathered in front of a pizza parlor, which they do nightly. You know that business owners and residents complain regularly about the noise and disruption they cause. As you approach the group, you observe that they are clustered in a small, closed group with their backs to you. One teenager (you cannot determine which one) drops a bag of marijuana on the ground. All of the teens walk away and deny ownership of the bag.

Your Assignment 18-24

It is 2:00 P.M. You are assigned to meet a person in a parking lot who was allegedly threatened by someone during an argument over a parking space. The person who was allegedly threatened points to a person (the suspect) who is nearby in the parking lot. The person tells you that he and the suspect argued over a parking space. He also tells you that during the argument the suspect produced a knife and threatened to kill him. The person describes the knife and shows you where the incident occurred. He also tells you that the suspect may have thrown the knife away. As you approach the suspect, you observe a knife on the ground between the two individuals. The suspect denies making any threats and states that there was an argument over the parking space, but that he left when the person who called the police pulled a knife on him.

Your Assignment 18-25

It is 8:00 P.M. You are assigned to investigate a report of an individual acting suspiciously around some motor vehicles in a parking lot. Upon your arrival, you observe a male who matches the description given sitting in a motor vehicle. He tells you it is a friend of a friend's car, that he does not know the name of the owner, and that he is just waiting for them to come out of the movie theater.

Your Assignment 18-26

It is 2:00 A.M. You have received a report of a break-in in progress at a warehouse. A suspicious person was seen in the area and may have entered the building. The outside of the building appears to be secure, with no open doors or signs of any break-in.

Your Assignment 18-27

It is 2:00 P.M. You have received a radio call that there is a loud disturbance at the residence at 86 Main Street. As you approach the residence, you hear a man and a woman yelling. The husband and wife tell you that each was yelling at the other. The wife is meek and timid; the husband is loud and aggressive. You learn during the interview that the husband hit the wife and that the wife wants the husband to leave. If the allegation is substantiated, you are legally required to make an arrest.

Your Assignment 18-28

It is 12:00 P.M. You are responding to a call that an angry local merchant wants to see the police regarding parking in front of his store. On your arrival, the local merchant is very upset because the police are ticketing all of his customers and ruining his business. He is loud and boisterous.

Your Assignment 18-29

It is 1:00 P.M. At the beginning of your shift while at the station roll call, you receive anonymous information that Mike Smith has been selling narcotics near City Hall, which is on your beat. You have arrested Smith three times for dealing drugs from his residence. An hour after receiving the information at roll call, you see Smith near City Hall holding a bag and looking very nervous. You approach him, but you have not observed a drug sale. Smith sees you approach, and he answers most of your questions, but he is evasive about allowing you to look in his bag.

Your Assignment 18-30

It is 8:00 P.M. You have responded to a call of a fight in progress at a local residence. When you arrive, one of the suspects claims to have been the victim of an assault. The alleged assailant is at the scene. The victim, who has minor injuries and complains of numerous pains, is very excited and claims that the assailant struck him in the stomach and back without reason. The assailant admits that he committed the assault, but he refuses to cooperate with you. After verbally abusing you, he walks away. He gets about 10 feet, and then he returns to tell you that he has thought it over and will assault the victim again and you as well if you continue to bother him. In this jurisdiction, you cannot arrest him for a simple assault and battery (i.e., hitting another) unless the assault is witnessed by the officer. Threats are arrestable if they occur in the officer's presence.

Your Assignment 18-31

It is 12:00 A.M. You are in your patrol car when you receive a report from dispatch that a male, described in detail by the dispatcher, has dropped a firearm to the floor of a local bar several times. You enter the bar and observe the male. The male, who is legally and duly licensed to carry a firearm, makes no gestures and does not give you any reason to fear for your safety. The gun is visible and is in the male's coat pocket. He makes no moves toward it. He does not want to turn the firearm over voluntarily.

Your Assignment 18-32

It is 9:00 P.M. You are on foot patrol in the city park. You observe a young male (under 21, the legal drinking age) give a second person, an older male (an adult), some cash. You then observe the exchange of the cash for a 12-pack of beer.

Your Assignment 18-33

It is 9:30 P.M. You are responding to a call at 123 Peach Street that a female is afraid of her boyfriend. According to the report, the boyfriend drank all day, struck the female, and then fell asleep on the couch. The dispatcher states that there are no warrants or weapons reported for the residence. When you arrive, the male is sleeping. When awakened, he is irate and verbally abusive toward the female, but not physically abusive or threatening. Initially, he denies hitting the female, but later states, "It was just a light slap," during the interview. If the allegation is substantiated, you are legally obligated to make an arrest.

Your Assignment 18-34

It is 1:00 P.M. You receive a report of a domestic violence call at 123 Maple Drive that was initiated by and responded to by a plainclothes officer. Upon arriving at the scene, you note that the two parties are sitting on the couch and are calm but scared; both are handcuffed. The plainclothes officer seems to be in control of the scene. The couple is nonthreatening and complying fully with the plainclothes officer, but the plainclothes officer is yelling and verbally abusive toward the couple. In addition, the plainclothes officer is beginning to become physical with both parties. He is poking and prodding them as he yells at them.

Your Assignment 18-35

It is 10:00 P.M. You receive a report of gunshots behind the residence at 85 Dogwood Lane. As you arrive, you are greeted by a neighbor who states that he observed the resident of 85 Dogwood Lane possibly firing a gun into the air. The neighbor heard the noise and stayed in his house until you arrived. The neighbor also states that the suspect is now in the backyard of the 85 Dogwood Lane. You walk behind the house and observe the resident sitting in the backyard. He appears to have had a few drinks, but he is not drunk. He states that he was lighting fireworks, and he shows you a package of firecrackers, which are illegal in this state.

Your Assignment 18-36

It is 2:00 A.M. It is a very cold, rainy night at 333 Melody Lane, which is in a remote residential area. You are responding to a call from a resident who has found an unknown person in his basement. You arrive at the residence and observe the uninvited guest, who appears to be homeless. He states that he has hitchhiked from New York. He also tells you that he only broke into the caller's basement to sleep and to get warm.

Your Assignment 18-37

It is 12:00 A.M. You have just received a report of a vehicle parked on the side of the road. According to the caller, the driver appears to be slumped over the wheel. When you arrive and approach the vehicle, you observe that the driver is slumped over the wheel. He is unresponsive to your attempts to speak with him.

Your Assignment 18-38

It is 2:00 P.M. You have received an anonymous report of a suspicious male looking into vehicles in a parking lot. You arrive on the scene and see a male in the parking lot. You observe that he is carrying something. The man sees you and begins to walk away as you approach him. You tell him to stop, which he does. You find a bag of tools in the parking lot, but you observe no evidence of tampering with or entering of any of the vehicles in the lot. When you ask the suspect who he is and why he is there, he states that he was just cutting through the parking lot and denies any knowledge of the bag of tools.

Your Assignment 18-39

It is 9:00 P.M. You are responding to an officer-in-trouble call in the hallway of a multifamily dwelling. The officer is a 32-year veteran plainclothes officer who is about to arrest an individual. The reason for the arrest is unknown. When you arrive, the suspect is handcuffed on the floor and is in the fetal position. The veteran officer is standing over the handcuffed suspect and striking him continuously across the back and legs with a nightstick while yelling, "This'll teach you to spit at my cruiser."

Your Assignment 18-40

It is 9:00 P.M. You are responding to a call of a male down on the ground for an unknown reason at a multifamily house in a residential neighborhood. When you arrive at the scene, the man appears to be sleeping. A bystander informs you that the man is homeless and has been in the area for several days. He also tells you that he has bothered no one. When you awaken the sleeping man, he appears proud and unwilling to accept the help of a shelter. In addition, he is coughing and may need medical attention.

Your Assignment 18-41

It is 10:00 P.M. You are responding to a call of a large, out-of-control party at an apartment house in a residential area. As you approach the apartment house, which shows litter indicating drinking and drug use, a 17-year-old male meets you. He tells you that his parents, who are out of town for the weekend, gave him permission to invite a friend over to stay with him. He then tells you that he and his friend invited other friends for a party, and the party grew out of control. The 17-year-old tells you that he would like you to help him clear his house. When you enter the house, you are drawn to a scream in another room. When you and the 17-year-old enter the room, you see a youth with a bloodied towel over his hand, indicating a severe laceration. He states he just put his hand through a window.

Your Assignment 18-42

It is 11:30 A.M. You have just been assigned to stop in and see the owner of Joe's Dining Palace. Joe, the owner, has been having trouble with his alarm system, and you respond almost daily to false alarms. Today, there was no alarm. Joe, the owner of the restaurant, greets you in a friendly and apologetic tone. Joe states that the alarm company just left and gave him adequate time on his alarm to open and secure the restaurant without setting it off. He wants to thank you for your patience during the past. He then hands each you and your partner a gift certificate for $60.00 toward dinner at the restaurant. Joe insists that you take it, and will not take no for an answer, even to the point of putting it in your possession.

Your Assignment 18-43

You are responding to a report of a suspicious package left at the rear of a building located in an industrial park. Upon arrival, you see a backpack lying on the ground unattended. The caller, who is the business owner, approaches you and tells you that he just saw some guy drive behind the building and then stop and get out. The owner thought he was just urinating, so he thought nothing of it. He later returned and saw the backpack and decided to call the police. The business is an electronics distribution center.

Your Assignment 18-44

It is 11:30 A.M. on a school day. You have just been assigned to check out some youths who are drinking or just hanging around in a secluded, wooded area. The youths are 14 to 16 years old. As you approach, you see the youths, and there is no evidence of any alcohol or drugs. The kids are sober and have not been drinking.

Your Assignment 18-45

You are responding to a report of a suspicious package left at the rear of a building in an industrial park. Upon arrival, you see a backpack lying unattended on the ground and a male fleeing the area. You yell at him to stop, and he does, but he refuses to come any closer. The backpack is full of beer, the subject denies that it is his.

Your Assignment 18-46

It is 1:30 A.M. You have just completed a building search/check of a jewelry store with the owner and your partner as a result of an alarm call. After completing the building check, you and your partner have a conversation. The business owner is not present. Your partner shows you a piece of jewelry from his pocket. Your partner states, "So what do you think of my new piece of jewelry?" A moment later your supervisor, the sergeant, approaches and asks how the search went.

Your Assignment 18-47

It is 2:00 A.M. on a sub-zero night in the middle of February. You have just stopped an operator for driving in an erratic manner. The operator was swerving, weaving, and applying the brakes repeatedly. When you stop the vehicle, it is obvious that the operator is intoxicated (i.e., slurring words, bloodshot and glassy eyes, etc.). The woman tells you that she only had two beers and is on the way to the store to buy some milk for her baby, who is in the rear seat. The baby is dressed in only a diaper and T-shirt and is not belted into the car seat. The woman states that it is her child, that she has sole custody, and that there is no other parent. She states that she has not gotten around to buying the baby winter clothes yet.

Your Assignment 18-48

You are responding to a report of a suspicious package left at the rear of a building in an industrial park. Upon arrival, you see a backpack lying on the ground unattended. The caller, who is the business owner, approaches you and tells you that he just saw some guy drive behind the building and then stop and get out. The owner thought he was just urinating, so he thought nothing of it. He later returned and saw the backpack and decided to call the police. The business is a manufacturer of missile guidance systems for the U.S. military.

Your Assignment 18-49

You are responding to a report of an unknown problem at a popular political candidate's campaign headquarters. When you arrive, you find that people are down in the building. As you enter the building, you see that some of the workers in the building are lying down unconscious, others are coughing or choking, and some are attempting to leave.

Your Assignment 18-50

You are responding to a report of a suspicious person at the reservoir who is carrying two thermos-like containers. Upon arrival, you observe a man carrying two containers. The man states that he is employed by the water company and that he is testing the water.

Abandoned property. Garbage or trash that has been left in public view for the purpose of having strangers collect and dispose of it. They forfeit the protection they would normally possess with private property.

Administrative search. Warrantless searches or inspections the police may engage in as part of their administrative functions under certain circumstances.

Arraignment. The first stage of a formal charging of an individual with a crime or offense, this is usually the first appearance of the accused before the court. The accused enters a plea of guilty or not guilty.

Assault. A verbal assault does not constitute an unlawful touching, or a battery. An assault and battery occurs when there is an unlawful touching.

Bail. Collateral that is usually submitted as an assurance for the defendant's appearance before the court at the next proceeding. Bail can be in cash or in a surety.

Battery. An unlawful touching.

Beat. An area a police officer is assigned to patrol on foot or by some other mode of transportation. This is his primary area of responsibility, where he is usually required to remain during his shift, unless otherwise assigned.

Body cavity search. An intrusive search. A search that includes some degree of touching and probing of the anus and vagina. It allows the searcher to examine a person's body cavities in order to search for contraband or fruits of the crime.

Bulletin. Specific issues such as a training school announcement, or a step-by-step procedure for a police function, or safety tips, or reminders.

Calls for Service (CFS). The calls that an officer responds to in the course of his tour of duty. These calls may be generated by citizens, victims, witnesses, or others.

Concealment. When an object can prevent the officer from being seen, but cannot protect an officer from a suspect's bullets. Bushes, trashcans, darkness (shadows), and picket or stockade fences offer concealment.

Consent search. A search of an individual's property by the police with the individual's consent. In many cases, it is a recognized exception to the search warrant requirement. It may be the quickest and easiest way for the police to gain lawful access to the premises, whether a residence or business, in the investigation of crime.

Contraband. Anything that is illegal to possess.

Cover. Some sort of protection that an officer can use to protect himself or herself from gunfire. The cover object should be something solid, such as a tree, building, cement wall, or motor vehicle.

Cover officer. An officer who protects the primary, or lead, officer, keeping alert to any dangers or threats that may arise from an officer's unguarded side.

Crossfire. A situation where two or more officers are positioned so that other officers, bystanders, or others will be in the direct line of fire in the event that the officers have to fire their guns.

Deadly force. A level of force that is likely to result in the death of, or serious physical injury to, another person. An officer may use deadly force in self-defense or in the defense of another.

Disposition. The outcome of a court proceeding. The disposition could be guilty, not guilty, not guilty by reason of insanity, or continued without a finding, and so on.

Exigent circumstances. A police officer is authorized to conduct a search without a warrant when faced with an emergency situation whereby a delay would endanger his or the public's safety or might result in the escape of the offender or the destruction of evidence.

Fatal funnel. Any location where an officer is vulnerable to an attack from an unknown source.

Felony. Serious crimes that are punishable in the state or federal prison system. These crimes usually involve a physical injury or are of a serious nature.

Formalized training. Training classes that have been designed specifically to deal with the issue that is being changed.

General Order. The most authoritative directives that are permanent; they usually mandate a procedure or policy change, and can also amend or supercede a previous order.

Gifts. Items given purely out of thankfulness, with no intent of redeeming any favors as a result of them.

Gratuities. Something of value given to an officer that may be interpreted as requiring a favor in return.

Hold for trial. When a judge orders a defendant to be held in custody until the trial. The decision of whether to hold the suspect is based on the suspect's past record, whether the suspect is a flight risk, as well as the severity of the crime and whether there is a likelihood of the suspect committing a similar crime while awaiting trial.

In-service training. Usually an annual training session that all police officers are required to attend, or strongly encouraged to attend. These sessions can include legal updates in Criminal Law, Motor Vehicle Law, and Constitutional Law. This annual training may also include Firearms qualifications, re-certification for police batons, chemical sprays, defensive tactics, CPR, First Responder, and so on.

Interrogation. When you question a person you believe is involved in the crime you are investigating.

Interview. A voluntary conversation that is usually performed at the start of an investigation to help an officer determine what has transpired. The purpose of the interview is to determine if a crime has, in fact, occurred, and if so, who may have committed the crime.

Legalistic style. A style of policing where the police department is required to enforce the laws the same way for everyone. This style requires standardized enforcement.

Memorandum (or memo). An informal "note" to all or selected personnel as an informational reminder. These are used to inform personnel of policy infractions, available equipment, out of service cruisers, etc.

Minimum amount of force. The least amount of force that is proper, reasonable, and necessary to achieve a lawful objective.

Misdemeanor. A crime that is punishable by imprisonment in a local or county jail, not in a prison run by state or federal authorities. A misdemeanor may be distinguished by the value of the property stolen.

Motions. The process by which the defense attorney can request evidence, statements, and other information that the attorney feels may have been obtained illegally and should be eliminated from the court proceedings. Motions take place prior to the trial.

Nondeadly force. The use of force that is not likely to, or intended to, cause serious physical harm or death. Such force includes the use of approved defensive/physical tactics, approved chemical substances, canines, and the authorized baton.

Open fields. A field that may be searched without a warrant even if the terrain in question is not easily accessible to the public and even if the owner has posted "No Trespassing" signs and has a locked gate [Oliver v. U.S. 466 U.S. 170 (1984)].

Personal recognizance. A person being charged who is released but signs a document promising to be in court at the appointed time. This is done when the court has no reason to hold the accused until the trial date.

Personnel Order. Orders used for personnel changes in the department, such as a reassignment, promotion, or suspension.

Philosophy of less-lethal force. The level of force that meets the objectives with less potential for causing death or serious physical injury than the use of deadly force.

Plain view. If an officer has lawfully stopped a motor vehicle and is in the process of questioning the operator of the vehicle and the officer notices an incriminating item in or on the vehicle in plain view, including anything observed with the use of a flashlight, then the officer has probable cause to search the vehicle and seize the items observed without a warrant.

Point of entry. The location where it is believed that the suspect may have illegally entered the premises.

Point of exit. The location where it is believed that the suspect may have exited the premises.

Preliminary report. The first report that is written upon receiving a call for, or observing an incident that initiates, the law enforcement function.

Pretrial conference. Where the attorneys, both defense and prosecution, meet with the judge to outline the court case before them. If there are any plea bargains or "deals" to be negotiated, this is where they will be presented.

Probable cause. A phrase that describes the facts observed, information obtained from others, and personal knowledge and experience that is sufficient to lead a reasonable and prudent person to believe that seizable evidence of a crime exists, and that it will be found in a specific location, or on a specific person.

Quality of life. Concerns in a neighborhood that may not necessarily be a crime, such as children loitering or skateboarding, shops or businesses operating loudly late at night or early in the morning, dumpsters being emptied in the early morning.

Quick peek. A technique that enables an officer to "look before leaping." With this technique, the officer looks quickly around the corner or through the crack of an opened door with one eye.

Racial profiling. Any police–initiated action that relies on the race, ethnicity, or national origin of the individual under suspicion, rather than the behavior of that individual or intelligence that leads to a specific individual coming under suspicion.

Reasonable belief. What or how an ordinary and prudent person would act or think in a similar way under similar circumstances.

Reasonableness. An action within reason that is justified or suitable for the confrontation.

Roll call. A briefing prior to the start of a shift where supervisors take attendance, inspect uniforms and equipment, inform the oncoming shift of any outstanding incidents that may have occurred, inform the shift of suspects to be looking out for, or relate any law or procedural changes, etc.

Roll call training. Training conducted by the department and most likely instructed by department training personnel that deal with issues that are procedural within the department, or to discuss specific issues that deal with that agency. This is usually done at roll call.

Run the walls. A search technique whereby the officer places his or her firearm in the "ready" position and moves around the perimeter of the room with his or her back against the wall.

Search incident to an arrest. A police officer is allowed to conduct a warrantless search of an arrested person if the following conditions exist: the arrest is lawful and the search is reasonably related to the circumstances of the arrest; the search is conducted only for the purpose of seizing fruits, instrumentalities, contraband, and other evidence of the crime for which the arrest was made; to prevent the destruction or concealment of evidence; to remove any weapons that the arrested person might use to resist arrest or to affect his escape. A traditional exception to the warrant requirement of the Fourth Amendment [*Chimel v. California*, 395 U.S. 752, 89 S. Ct. 2034 (1969)].

Serious bodily injury. A physical injury that creates a greater risk of death, can cause serious permanent disfigurement, or can result in long-term loss or impairment of any body part or organ.

Service style. The main priority of this type of policing is *service*. The police will make arrests and use the courts only when necessary. Their focus is on keeping their community safe from outsiders who enter or pass through its protected boundaries.

Signature. A specific, unique act that can link an individual to other crimes.

Slice the pie. A technique of rounding the corners and softening rooms.

Special Order. Orders that are recreated to reach a specific outcome and may temporarily affect a change in a current policy. These orders usually expire once their objectives are met.

Specialized training. Training, similar to formalized training, where specific certifications may be obtained, such as fingerprinting, crime scene processing, evidence collection, accident investigation, or photography.

Staging. When a suspect tries to make the crime scene appear as if something else has occurred or tries to make it so that the evidence will lead the investigators away from him or her.

Stop-and-frisk search (pat search). A search based on the person, time, location or other circumstances. These searches are not intrusive and may be conducted on people of the opposite sex if there is reason to believe that there may be a weapon or contraband.

Strip searches. The U.S. Supreme Court has described examinations of a persons genital and anal areas without any sort of touching to be "a practice which instinctively gives . . . the most pause" [Bell v. Wolfish, 441 U.S. 520 (1979)]. A Massachusetts court has defined strip searches as "an inspection of a naked individual without any scrutiny of his or her body cavities" [Pursuant to Commonwealth v. Thomas (1999)].

Subject. An individual who is a part of an investigation.

Subpoena. A notice to a person that they must come forward as a witness either for the prosecution or for the defense.

Summons. A notice that requires a person to come forward to face the court for possible impending charges.

Surety. A token of the total bail amount, or collateral.

Suspect. An individual who is believed to be responsible for the commission of a crime and is the primary focus of the investigation.

Threshold inquiry. A police officer, in appropriate circumstances and in an appropriate manner, may temporarily stop and briefly detain a person for the purpose of inquiring into possible criminal behavior even though the officer does not have probable cause to make a lawful arrest at that time.

TRIAD officer. A member of the community, in most cases an employee of the police department, who has received training from the AARP in the reduction of victimization and vulnerability of senior citizens.

Victim. An individual who has been hurt either physically, mentally, or emotionally as a result of the action of another.

Watchman style. A style of policing where the police maintain order and keep things in line with the status quo. Police will respond to and be on the lookout for "serious" crimes and may not pay attention to calls for service that relate to minor offenses. With this style of policing, the police will attempt to resolve as much as possible informally and will not refer cases to the next level or social services, such as juvenile services or family services, unless a serious crime has been committed.

Witness. An individual who, by virtue of their presence or awareness of a situation, is looked to for information that will lead to the rightful facts in determining the events of an incident.

Written Directives. A directive or an order that is initiated by the department to convey a specific goal, order, mandate, or to gain information.

strip searches, 81, 91
stun devices, 30
subject, 46, 50
subpoena, 63, 69
summons, 63, 69
supplemental report, 54–58, 61
surety, 64, 69
suspect, 46, 50
suspicious behavior, determination of, 160
suspicious persons, 18, 160–161

T

"Tazer" devices, 30
Tennessee v. Garner, 5, 6
Terry v. Ohio, 87
theft, 17
third-eye firearm position, 109
threshold inquiry, 86–87, 91
tinted windows, and motor vehicle
    stops, 142
"totality of the circumstances"
    requirement, 88–89
tractor trailers, and motor vehicle
    stops, 143
training, of police officers, 6–7, 12–13
TRIAD officer, 54, 58
trial, 65–66
triggered alarm notification, 166–167
trunk, and motor vehicle stop, 119
two-officer approach, in motor vehicle
    stop, 119

U

United States v. Bowdach, 84
unknown problem calls, 18
U.S. Constitution. *See* Fourth Amendment

V

vans, and motor vehicle stops, 142–143
verbal communication, 24
vests, ballistic, 30
victim, 46, 50

W

walk-and-turn, heel-to-toe test, 130–131
warrant, searches with, 94, 102–103
warrant, searches without, 94–96, 104
watchman style, of policing, 35–36, 40–41
watercraft patrol, 10–11
weapons, 25–26, 109
weather, and false alarms, 104
Wilson, James Q., 35
witness, 46, 50
wraparound technique, for entering rooms, 110
written directives, 6–7, 13

X

"X" technique, for entering rooms, 110

CREDITS

Chapter 1

FIGURE 1-1 Courtesy of Library of Congress, Prints and Photographs Division [LC-USW36-743]; FIGURE 1-2 © Dennis MacDonald/PhotoEdit; FIGURE 1-3 © Corbis; FIGURE 1-4 © A.T. Willett/Alamy Images; FIGURE 1-5 © Tom Strickland/Bloomberg News/Landov; FIGURE 1-6 © Corbis; FIGURE 1-7 © Justin Case/Alamy Images

Chapter 3

FIGURE 3-1 © Comstock Images/Alamy Images; FIGURE 3-2 Courtesy of DeSantis Holster and Leather Goods Company; FIGURE 3-3 Courtesy of Galls, an ARAMARK company. Refer to *www.galls.com*; FIGURE 3-4 © Corbis; FIGURE 3-5 Courtesy of Motorola; FIGURE 3-6 Courtesy of Streamlight, Inc.; FIGURE 3-7 Courtesy of Safetec of America, Inc; FIGURE 3-8 Courtesy of Mace Security International, Inc.

Chapter 4

FIGURE 4-1 © Photodisc/Getty Images

Chapter 5

FIGURE 5-1 © Rachel Epstein/PhotoEdit

Chapter 9

FIGURE 9-1 © Brand X Pictures/Creatas

Chapter 10

FIGURE 10-1 © A. Ramey/PhotoEdit

Chapter 11

FIGURE 11-1 © Corbis